IN SEARCH OF

Credit: Antony Donaldson

CHRISTOPHER ROBBINS is the author of *Assassin*, a non-fiction book on political assas-sination, two non-fiction books on the Vietnam War, *Air America* and *The Ravens*, and the biography of the war hero, Nazi hunter and language teacher, Michel Thomas, *The Test of Courage*. His most recent book, *The Empress of Ireland*, is a memoir of his friend-ship with the Irish film director, Brian Desmond Hurst. *Empress* received wide critical acclaim, was chosen as the Film Book of the Year by the Cork Film Festival, awarded the Saga Prize for Wit in 2005 and picked as a Book of the Year by the *The Times*, *Guardian*, *Daily Telegraph*, *Sunday Telegraph*, *Daily Express*, *Observer* and *Sunday Times*.

IN·SEARCH·OF
·
KAZAKHSTAN

THE LAND THAT DISAPPEARED

CHRISTOPHER ROBBINS

PROFILE BOOKS

Text illustrations and map by Bob Gale
Cover design by Jonny Hannah

This paperback edition published in 2008

First published in Great Britain in 2007 by
Profile Books Ltd
3A Exmouth House
Pine Street
Exmouth Market
London EC1R 0JH
www.profilebooks.com

1 3 5 7 9 10 8 6 4 2

Designed by Geoff Green Book Design, Cambridge

Typeset in Quadraat by MacGuru Ltd
info@macguru.org.uk

Printed and bound in Great Britain by
CPI Bookmarque, Croydon, CR0 4TD

A CIP catalogue record for this book is available from the British Library.

ISBN 978 1 86197 109 8

This book is printed on FSC certified paper

Mixed Sources
Product group from well-managed
forests and other controlled sources
www.fsc.org Cert no. TT-COC-002227
© 1996 Forest Stewardship Council
FSC

CONTENTS

For my Kazakh friends

PROLOGUE

A very ordinary man was seated beside me on the flight from London to Moscow, and when I look back and try to remember him I realize he was spectacular in his ordinariness. He had a round, podgy face with timid eyes, and balanced upon his almost bald pate was the sad construct of an artfully coiled comb-over. He wore a thin anorak of dull brown synthetic material, polyester trousers a shade lighter in colour, and a cream, short-sleeved, nylon shirt with a row of ballpoint pens in the breast pocket.

The words of mumbled greeting as we sat down placed him as an American from the South. At first I took him to be an engineer on his way to Russia to ply his trade in some rust bucket Soviet-era factory in need of Western know-how, but as the plastic dinner trays were placed before us and we made small talk it became apparent that my travelling companion was a man with a story.

He had already flown that day from Atlanta, Georgia, but his home, he told me, was Little Rock, Arkansas. 'I guess everybody knows that's where Bill Clinton comes from,' he said with a laugh. 'Little Rock's not a bad place – if your luck holds and the creek don't rise.' His luck, it soon became clear, had not held. The creek had risen. His wife had fallen ill, remained ill for a long while, and then died. The medical bills wiped him out. But it was the solitude of his grief, not the debts, which brought him to breaking-point. 'Lord, I was lonesome.'

Abruptly, the gentle but unworldly redneck stopped talking, as if instinctively sensing that revealing such intimacies broke one of air travel's unwritten rules. He only continued when I encouraged him to take up the story. The world as he knew it had disappeared, he said, along with his wife and his savings. Life lost its point. 'Drank a good bit. Then one day driving past the Greyhound bus station I saw this homeless guy with a supermarket trolley piled high with everything he owned. And it struck me that's where I was headed and it shook me. I didn't want to end up homeless with my stuff in some shopping cart.'

So he worked and worked and worked, not as the engineer I had imagined, but as a lowly factory hand. Double shifts. Graveyard shifts. Weekend shifts. 'All the hours the good Lord created. Must have done that for five years. And I paid off those medical bills and even began to put a bit aside. I wasn't spending nothing. So my life got back in order – but you know what saved me?'

I braced myself. Out of boredom and as a distraction from tasteless food, I had been happy to hear the stranger's tale, but now it seemed I was going to pay the price. I was about to be told how he had been saved. I dreaded what would come next – the Lord, Alcoholics Anonymous, Islam, line-dancing ...

'The Internet,' my companion announced unexpectedly. 'That's what saved me!'

'The Internet?' I said, somewhat relieved.

'Yup! The Net. My Lord, I must have spent ten hours a night at my computer. Night after night. Sun would come up and I'd find myself on the Net.'

My temporary relief evaporated. I was now going to be over-whelmed by the boundless, late-night enthusiasms of the cyber bore: stamps, firearms, genealogy, train numbers, butterflies, pornography. What did it matter? I sat tight and prepared for the worst.

'The lonesome feeling didn't leave me, no matter how hard or long I worked. So I decided to find a wife. On the Net. And I'm on my way to meet her.'

A rush of genuine compassion overcame me and I studied my companion more closely. A nice man, no doubt, but hardly the stuff of the American dream. Neither rich, nor handsome, nor even young, he was surely destined to dash the capitalist fantasies of any Internet fiancée. I wondered how much he had saved and how long it would take some hubby-hunting Russian honey to relieve him of it. This naïve Arkansas romantic was a lonesome pigeon ready to be plucked.

'And you found a wife in Moscow?'

'Nope! I'm just changing planes there. I'm bound for Kazakhstan!'

'*Kazakhstan!* Good Lord!'

'Yeah, can you believe it?' He shook his head as if he couldn't believe it himself. 'I sure wasn't expecting to find love in Kazakhstan but the Net knows no frontiers. I didn't look for a young girl but a woman my own age who had lived a bit and had her own share of unhappiness.' He took out his wallet and handed me a small colour photograph. 'Eighteen months ago I found Ludmilla – a Russian widow, lives in Almaty. We've been writing and phoning ever since. I reckon I know her better than anyone in the world and we've never met! Ludmilla's not too sure about America and wants me to live there in Kazakhstan. We'll give it a little time to see how things go and then, God willing, we'll get married.'

Ludmilla looked a nice sort, somewhat careworn by her portion of unhappiness; no beauty, but she had a wide, honest face and a mass of untidy red hair, and I could see her on my companion's arm easily enough. 'I hope you'll both be very happy.'

'Thank you,' he said, putting the photo back in his wallet. 'Know anything about Kazakhstan?'

'Not much, no.' Next to nothing, would have been a more honest answer: Genghis Khan and the Mongol hordes, the Silk Road, miles and miles of empty steppe.

'A big place,' my companion said, confident of his subject. 'You could put Texas or France in it five times over – or the whole of Western Europe. When I looked for it on the map on the Net, I found a mess of Stans down there in that part of the world. Not just the ones you've heard of, like Pakistan and Afghanistan, but a whole bunch of others – Uzbekistan, Kyrgyzstan, Tajikistan, Turkmenistan.' He recited the list automatically, names learned by rote from the Net, countries without reality for either of us. His mood suddenly changed as excitement became subdued by doubt. 'They've had trouble in some of them – kidnappings and killings. Riots and uprisings. Muslim fundamentalist stuff. But Ludmilla says that Kazakhstan isn't like that. All sorts rub along together.'

On the remainder of the flight my friend repeated the little Russian he had learned, counting uncertainly up to ten and naming the days of the week and months of the year. He told of the difficulties experienced in applying for an extended visa, and of his many trips to Washington to obtain one – journeys that seemed to be the only ones he had ever made outside the state of Arkansas. Then he fell silent and looked worried.

I tried to imagine what his future life in Kazakhstan could possibly be like. Tried to imagine what Kazakhstan might be like and drew a similar blank. It seemed strange to know so little about somewhere so large. I prodded my companion for a little information.

'Those ol' boys out there go riding over the prairie in the snow on little fat ponies hunting foxes with eagles,' he said with renewed vigour. 'Golden eagles! Perched on their arms. Birds with a wingspan big as a man. That country's got gold and every other metal, and more oil than the Arabs. And they're building a shiny new capital out in the middle of the prairie, pretty as a picture.'

'Sounds like you're on an adventure,' I said.

'That's God's truth.' The idea seemed to frighten him as boyish enthusiasm once again became clouded by doubt.

We were silent for most of the rest of the journey. As we neared Moscow he expressed concern about negotiating his way through the airport for the transfer to a connecting flight, and hoped an airline agent would be on hand to point him in the right direction. 'That Russian alphabet – you can't make out nothing!' The role of romantic adventurer on the brink of the unknown sat awkwardly upon his rounded shoulders, but the courage he showed gave him a dash of the heroic. I wished him good luck and meant it.

As my friend from Arkansas pulled down a bulging new scarlet rucksack from the overhead compartment, he turned and made a throwaway remark that seemed insignificant at the time. The last words he addressed to me were, 'Apples are from Kazakhstan.'

CHAPTER ONE

APPLES ARE FROM KAZAKHSTAN

The line about the apples stayed with me. Every time I went into a greengrocer and saw piles of Bramley, Pink Lady and Cox's apples, I thought of the Arkansas romantic and Kazakhstan. The idea that the country was the birthplace of the apple had somehow captured my imagination, although I had no idea if it were true. Apples, of course, are to be found on every fruit stall in every country in the world, but it had never occurred to me that they must once have originated from a specific location.

I passed on my discovery to my local greengrocer in Hampstead as I bought six of the English variety. 'Did you know apples are from Kazakhstan?'

'Where?'

'Kazakhstan.'

'Yeah?' He sounded sceptical. "These are from Somerset. Those over there are from Chile and New Zealand.'

Over dinner one evening I told a friend about the origin of the apple, and of my encounter with the Arkansas Romeo, flying into the unknown to find his Internet Juliet and gamble his lonely heart on cyber-love. I declared authoritatively that Kazakhstan was larger than Western Europe (I had not yet got around to looking it up in the atlas, so took this on trust), and remarked that it was strange nobody seemed to know anything about the place. My friend seemed unmoved by the love story and uninterested in the birthplace of the apple, but he did mention that by coincidence he had a date to play snooker with a banker from Hong Kong who had a Kazakh business partner. The men were all going to play together at the RAC Club the following week. 'Why don't you join us and make a four?'

'I'm not very good at snooker.'

'Neither am I,' my friend said. 'And presumably this Kazakh's never played in his life.'

The rabbits duly assembled in the best-appointed snooker room in London, a quiet, serious place inhabited by men who have misspent their youth honing their skills at the game. Our group expertise was such that we had to get a member's son to come and show us the correct position for the coloured balls. Umbetov, the Kazakh businessman, proved to be fluent in English and well travelled, but a newcomer to snooker. In the circumstances it seemed unsporting on the part of the Hong Kong banker to suggest playing for fifty pounds a head, but to be expected of the breed.

What the Kazakh had not revealed was that he was a dab hand at Russian billiards, a demanding game played on a table of similar size with fifteen numbered white balls and a single red. The balls are larger than snooker balls and barely fit the small, triangular, hard-edged pockets of the Russian table. A skilled player can automatically transfer his technique to snooker, and Umbetov took to the game like a regular on *Pot Black*. He also proved to be a ferociously competitive man with a deep-seated desire to win. Balls were slammed into pockets in one difficult shot after another. The tactics of the game were also quickly assimilated and the Hong Kong banker snookered twice. Umbetov took fifty quid off each of us. 'In America you are what is known as a "pool hustler".' I explained the term and he smiled at the compliment.

Over drinks I asked about the apples. 'Yes, apples come from Kazakhstan. Tulips too. I'm surprised you find it so interesting. Most people want to know about oil – the Caspian possibly has as much as a quarter of the planet's remaining reserves. But the real wealth of the country is its minerals – coal, copper, uranium, platinum ... gold.'

I asked why the world seemed to know so little about so big a place. 'In the nineteenth century the Russian tsars closed the country to foreigners as they expanded their empire eastwards. And then the Soviets sealed it tight for another seventy years.' He shrugged. 'It disappeared.'

'That's quite a trick.' It was something to make a country the size of Western Europe disappear and to keep it hidden from the West, out of sight and mind, for more than a hundred years. I had to admit that I didn't know *exactly* how this vast land mass fitted into the world map. And I was certainly not alone in my ignorance. Even people who might have been expected to know something about the place – journalists, world travellers, people who thought they knew a thing or two – became vague and muddled when asked. Was that the country where the president boiled his enemies alive? No, that was the reputation of the Uzbek president south of the border. Was it the place where the president had golden statues made of himself and placed on revolving platforms to lead the sun? No again, that was next door in Turkmenistan. It was an anarchic, narco-state, wasn't it, embroiled in permanent civil war? No, that was the fate of poor, blighted Tajikistan. Somebody told me they had recently attended a fascinating lecture on the country – but then sent me an email to say, sorry, it had been Azerbaijan. Businessmen at least knew that Kazakhstan had a lot of gold and oil – but then stopped short.

I started to read about the country, and occasionally I came across people who had been there: a woman who had gone to the northern steppe to see the tens of thousands of pink flamingos that migrate to the salt lakes in the summer; a couple who had spent an idyllic ten days walking in unspoilt, empty mountains when the wild tulips bloom; an oiler who worked on a rig in the Caspian and who had been stitched up by the police for an exit visa; a couple who had adopted a Kazakh baby; a lawyer who lived in the capital for two years in the 1990s working on privatization deals.

But mostly, people only knew about Borat, the comic creation of comedian Sacha Baron Cohen, who pretends to be a Kazakh 'media personality'. The joke depends on an audience's absolute ignorance of Kazakhstan and its culture. I made the somewhat PC point to a female fan that no comedian would dare to traduce the identity of Jews, African-Americans or Welshmen in such a crude way. 'Well, of course not,' she said puzzled, 'that's why he invented a country!'

Modern Kazakhstan occupies a region of Central Asia that is not only a lacuna in the knowledge of most of the West, but has also been shrouded in mystery from the beginning of time. To the ancients it was an unexplored and inaccessible world more myth than reality, a place perhaps of dragons and monsters. Herodotus wrote of impenetrable deserts and impassable mountains wreathed in eternal mists, and of a tribe of fearsome female warriors known as Amazons. This was the land of the Scythians and Sarmatians, ancient races that were to vanish from the face of the earth. Alexander the Great had crossed the great Central Asian river, the Oxus, but he never penetrated into Kazakhstan; Marco Polo saw the country's towering mountain peaks on his travels, but he never crossed them.

I began to envy the naïve Arkansas adventurer. He was not just travelling to an unknown country, he was making a voyage of discovery to a lost world, with its oil and gold, nomad horsemen and golden eagles, and shiny new city in the middle of the steppe. A vague idea formed in my mind to follow in this most unlikely explorer's footsteps. I would go in search of Kazakhstan.

I bought a cheap notebook with a hideous turquoise cover that began to blister in an odd way almost immediately. (The ritualistic purchase is always the first step for me on the long journey of writing a book, and I wrote 'Apples Are from Kazakhstan' on the front page as a working title – later abandoned after the publisher said brutally, 'That's a bloody silly title – nobody will buy a book called that!') Inside the notebook I began to accumulate jottings gleaned from here and there: a jumble of facts and figures, names of hotels, phone numbers of possible contacts, statistics, slivers of history and contemporary politics, and hundreds of questions – scraps that might eventually lead to a book. One day. Perhaps.

After a while I put the notebook away on a shelf.

•

More than two years passed. Unexpectedly, vague curiosity developed into real interest during that time, and continued to grow, until I became determined to visit the birthplace of the apple. The decision to go to Kazakhstan was about all the planning I undertook before, blistered turquoise notebook in hand, I set out on my quest.

The direct flight from London takes eight hours – four hours to cross Europe, and another four to cross the country itself. The plane made a stop in the early hours of the morning at Yekaterinburg, inside Russia, the city where Nicholas II, the country's last Tsar, had been taken down into a cellar and murdered together with his family. Most of the passengers on the plane slept as newcomers filed aboard and took their seats. We were then in the air again, heading south into Kazakhstan and across the steppe.

The scale of the country began to register, even flying over it in a jet. The great sea of grass beneath, vaster than the American prairie or the Argentine pampas, is the essence of everything Kazakh. Far from the sea, with little rainfall because it is hemmed in by mountain ranges, steppe is defined as terrain between forest and desert, too dry to sustain traditional agriculture. Man has moved across it on horseback for thousands of years, herding his sheep, cattle and goats before him. A Kazakh relates to the steppe like a fish to the sea, and all his culture harks back to it.

It was dawn as we approached Almaty, the old capital of the country, pushed up against the mighty Tien Shan mountains that rise in the south like a steep, black wall. The outskirts of the city we flew over were an odd mixture of ramshackle wooden cottages from Soviet times, and clusters of brand-new, post-modern, American-style housing. The airport itself was oddly shaped, a mixture of the modern and the homely – and I learned later that it was designed by a Japanese architect to resemble a traditional Kazakh hat.

The terminal was disappointingly up-to-date. Not a nomad to be seen. The customs and immigration officials have kept their Russian uniforms but lost the intimidating Cold War scowl of suspicion that once met every outsider. There were a large number of young women among them, with big dark eyes and shy smiles. However, all the uniformed officials continue to sport the universal headgear of authority inherited from the Soviets. These giant *opéra bouffe* hats of red and brown are ludicrously out of scale and have a cartoon quality, like ten-gallon bus conductors' caps. Those worn by immigration officials are topped off in green felt.

The first thing I saw on leaving the airport was a large red-and-white tented restaurant with the Coca-Cola sign emblazoned upon it. It was Western and capitalist, all right, but it had a pleasingly shabby air about it, more Mexican than American. The smell in the air, though, was pure Soviet – the distinctive reek of crudely refined petrol that wafts throughout the Commonwealth of Independent States as a memory of the old Iron Curtain empire. Even today, sixteen years after independence, Almaty has the atmosphere of a Russian city. A young man stripped to the waist stood outside a wooden cottage washing himself from a cold tap running into a bucket, splashing water on his face, arms and hands, and down the back of his neck. It was a timeless image that might have come from a nineteenth-century Russian novel.

My hotel, the Otrar, was a creaking concrete construction in the centre of town that in Soviet times had been the pride of Intourist. Except, of course, no foreign tourists came to Kazakhstan then, only officials from within the USSR. The place has moved on, but traces of the old ways linger. There is tight security at the entrance, and unfriendly and obstructionist staff on reception. One young woman spoke good English, an accomplishment that made her bossy and quick to anger. She sighed audibly when I was a little slow in producing my passport. A demand was made for extra money, as I had arrived early and wanted immediate occupancy of my room. I protested gently: 'You wouldn't want me sleeping over there on the sofa, would you?'

'Not allowed,' the harridan snapped.

I asked for a room with a view of the park and mountains opposite the hotel. She seemed not to hear as she stamped papers, took a credit card imprint and went about some elaborate system of multiple registration that involved a lot of biro work in triplicate on an assortment of clipboards. I raised my voice a little and repeated my request for a room with a view. 'Yes, yes, yes,' she said, jabbing a key at me with a look of fury. 'Room with view. Park. Mountains. Finished. Go!'

•

The first thing on my agenda was the country's wild apple orchards. I accept that it is an unorthodox way to set about telling the story of a country and its people, and it immediately became clear that the locals considered my mission eccentric. There were many more beautiful things to see in Kazakhstan than apple trees, people insisted. The wild flowers of spring, for instance, when the mountains are covered with tulips (Kazakhstan is home to thirty of the world's eighty species), and the steppe is carpeted with blood-red poppies, yellow and blue irises, and delicate wands of desert candles two metres tall. 'Our apples look like your apples,' a mystified Kazakh said.

Food historians, biologists and geneticists have argued interminably over the birthplace of the apple. One long-accepted theory held that the ancient Romans introduced sweet apples to northern Europe. Miffed Northerners, on the other hand, declared that the apple had originated in the Baltic and travelled south, citing Nordic myths long predating the Romans in which apples were part of the staple diet of the old Scandinavian gods and their human followers. The discovery of fossilized apples in ancient Swiss and Celtic settlements further confused the picture. Less Eurocentric scientists named the Caucasus as the place of origin – or possibly the slopes of the mountain ranges of Kazakhstan.

The argument was finally settled by the great Russian geneticist Nikolai Vavilov. Crossing the mountains on horseback from the south, accompanied by a mule train loaded with equipment, he visited the Kazakh capital in the late 1920s. 'All around the city one could see a vast expanse of wild apples covering the foothills which formed forests,' he later wrote. 'In contrast to very small wild apples in the Caucasian mountains, the Kazakh wild apples have very big fruit, and they don't vary from cultivated varieties. On the first of September, the time that the apples were almost ripe, one could see with one's own eyes that this beautiful site was the origin of the cultivated apple.'

In his day Nikolai Vavilov was the Soviet Union's most famous scientist, and he identified the birthplace of more plants than anyone else in history. He travelled over five continents investigating a theory he had developed early in his career that defied traditional wisdom: he believed that farming had arisen not in fertile valleys, like those of the Nile or the Euphrates, but in mountain areas where water was plentiful and man could more easily defend himself. And so it was mostly mountain ranges – the Andes, the Rockies, the Caucasus and the Tien Shan – where he chose to seek out the original forms of modern plants, fruits and grasses.

The whole of Almaty struck Vavilov as one great orchard, surrounded by forests of wild apples in which every tree was of a different variety. After the Russian Revolution, the city formerly known as Verny had been renamed Alma-ata, meaning 'Father of Apples', and it was renamed once again after independence as Almaty – Kazakh for 'appleness' (fittingly, the Kazakh word for man is *adam*).

Even today, modern Almaty is a city of apples. Away from the centre's main boulevards there are trees in every garden, some carefully pruned and tended, others gnarled and neglected. They lean crookedly against rickety fences, are left standing lonely in abandoned lots, and take up unlikely position beside bus stops and on street corners. And among the foothills of the Tien Shan, bordering Kyrgyzstan and China, the original Kazakh apple can still be found – *Malus sieversii*, ancestor of practically all the apples eaten in the world today. Further north, in the virgin vastness of the Dzungarian Alps, wild apples flourish over thousands of acres, untended and so far unthreatened by man.

And so on a fine September day, three-quarters of a century after Vavilov rode out with his mules and packhorses, I followed in the great man's footsteps. I had asked a Ukrainian-born botanist, Anna Ivashenko, to take me into the foothills of the Tien Shan, or Heavenly Mountains, to seek out the original wild apple. Something of an egalitarian when it came to plant species, Anna did not seem to find my interest as peculiar as everybody else. 'Most people want to see wild tulips in bloom,' Anna said. 'In spring I take groups from all over the world into the national park near Shymkent. Nobody has ever asked to see apples, although,' she added quickly, 'apples are interesting too.'

Anna was now retired, but she had spent most of her working life on horseback in the unspoilt Shymkent National Park, often camping out for weeks at a time, her two young children at her side on ponies. The water there was so pure, Anna said, that people from Leningrad would ask her to bring it to them, prizing it over wine.

Our driver for the apple expedition, Ivan, was a middle-aged ethnic Russian with a nostalgic attachment to old Soviet Kazakhstan. Over the course of several trips together, he made it clear that old communists were a conservative breed, and that the shifting tectonic plates of history and politics were hardest on the middle-aged. He had driven a petrol tanker in the good old days of central planning when life was hard but ordered, and had felt secure, with a respected place in society. 'Now nobody wants me,' he said, and he shrugged in bitter acceptance.

Ivan drove us out of the city into the foothills. He had expressed bewilderment bordering on contempt that anyone would go so far to look at apples, and he shot me sly, sidelong glances that suggested I had a screw loose. On the journey Anna talked tulips. 'The tulips that are popular in the world today come from Central Asia. They were first taken by traders to Persia and Turkey, and then four hundred years ago the Russians took them from Tashkent to Holland. And the world went mad for tulips. In Amsterdam in the eighteenth century single bulbs went for enormous sums. There are five thousand types of tulip today and three classes of wild ones. In the springtime, in southern Kazakhstan, there are a couple of weeks when you can find fourteen types of wild tulip growing.'

'Tulips!' Ivan said. 'Now, that's something to see!'

'There's a particular type of white tulip about a hundred and sixty miles outside Almaty,' Anna continued, 'where the air is so dry the flower has evolved folds in one of its leaves to trap moisture.'

The road had now become little more than a rocky track. Anna raked the mountainside with a professional gaze. After a while she told Ivan to pull over – she had spotted wild apple trees – and we all scrambled down a hillside where a torrent roared through a ravine. Wild apples were everywhere. Anna picked a couple for me, and a tiny wild pear the size of a crab apple that was remarkably sweet. I was surprised to find wild apples so close to the city. We had been driving for little more than an hour. Although we were in wild country the spot still bore witness to one of the plagues of the developing world – rubbish. Kazakhs litter with abandon. 'I could kill them,' Anna said.

Ivan frowned. He said that there was no littering in the old days. The Soviets took a dim view of litter louts and so did he. 'There was no rubbish lying around then. If an inspector came out and saw litter, the person in charge of the area would be finished.' The national parks were better run too, he said, whereas now some of them had unmanned checkpoints and were closed, or were manned by soldiers who demanded money to let you in. In the old days it was all free. Not the sort of thing the Soviets would have tolerated. Oh, no. Anna said nothing, but she did not disagree.

We drove on. The landscape was magnificent, unspoilt and unpeopled, ablaze with autumn colours. Anna directed us to a spot where the road ran out – the rest would have to be done on foot, she announced. Once out of the car she busied herself with her rucksack, preparing like a soldier for battle. She was already wearing a camouflage combat jacket and sensible trousers, and carrying a telescopic mountain walking-stick. Now, from out of the beaten-up rucksack, she took binoculars, stout hiking boots, gardening gloves and a pretty Uzbek scarf covered in a design of red roses that she tied over her hair.

I stood and watched, sadly unprepared. Ivan leaned against the car and closed his eyes to the sun. He would not be joining us in our exertions, he said, but would stay where he was. '*Apple trees!*' he said dismissively. 'I've seen apple trees.'

'Many foreign scientists come here to study these apples,' Anna said, coming to my defence. 'All the best eating apples we have throughout the world originated from here.'

Anna and I set off. In minutes she was striding up the mountain far ahead of me, utterly absorbed in the world around her with the uncomplicated pleasure of a dog on a walk. I spent the rest of the day trying to catch up. Anna shook fruit from trees, picked wild flowers – she held in her left hand a slowly expanding bouquet – and crushed leaves for me to smell. She rooted around the undergrowth like a wild boar: in the space of a hundred metres she found wild mint, blue chicory flowers, a wild carrot, tarragon, ginseng that looked like a blue tulip, thistles of deep imperial purple, oregano, wild raspberries, half a dozen species of chives, and a root from which she said chewing gum was made.

After a while wild apricot trees appeared, dotted among the apple trees. The fruit was sweet and delicious. Apricot trees begin at 1,500 metres, Anna said, while apples stop at 1,700. I asked casually what sort of wild life lived up here. 'Lots of different sorts of deer,' Anna said. 'And bears, of course.'

'Bears?'

'Yes – I often come across them.'

'Big bears?' I asked, nonchalantly studying a leaf Anna had thrust at me.

'Depends. Bears like apples and create havoc with the trees. In the autumn and spring they leave you alone and go up to the glaciers. The thing to do if you come across one is not to show fear. They have very bad eyesight, but they can smell you. Our bears are plant-eaters and if you shout at them they run away.'

We returned to find Ivan leaning against the car, enjoying the mountain air between cigarettes. On the journey back into town we passed hundreds of acres of orchards full of ripe Almaty Aport apples. Folklore has it that the Aport variety found its way back to the Tien Shan in 1865 when a Russian soldier, Egor Vasilievish Redko, arrived in a cart with half a dozen saplings on board. The saplings were planted and thrived, and soon the Aport became famous.

In Tsarist times the Aport was valued above all other varieties, and was correspondingly pricey – thirty apples cost more than a chicken. When the apple was exhibited at the Mannheim

International Exhibition in Germany, in 1907, a judge enthused: 'The giant Aport apple exhibited by the Verny Orchard School is creating a furore ... the size, taste and colour of the Central Asian fruit is amazing.' Horticulturalists rushed to plant the trees in Great Britain and the USA, but their efforts proved a failure. For some reason the capricious Aport was only truly happy around Almaty, in the foothills of the Tien Shan.

The Aport could grow as large as a baby's head, and it was famous for its flavour and scent throughout the Soviet Union. Kazakhs travelling to Moscow took bulging string bags of apples to give as presents, and traditionally piled the fruit in bowls throughout the house as a natural air-freshener. In Soviet times, 20,000 tons were sent every year to Moscow in wooden crates, each apple individually wrapped in paper and packed in sawdust. All the large State orchards had designated 'Kremlin plots' where the best trees received special care. The trees were carefully watered and fertilized, the fruit covered in gauze, and each apple hand-picked by gloved hands. At State banquets, bowls of Aport apples were as ubiquitous as caviar.

But the collapse of the State collective system after independence in 1991 limited the Aport to an ever-diminishing domestic market. When we stopped by the side of the road, we were surrounded by mountainsides of neglected orchards, heavy with unpicked fruit. The apples were thick on the ground and as we walked the heavy smell of scrumpy cider rose from them. Many of the trees were diseased and untended, and yet even on the higher slopes the grass between each one had been cut and stacked into neat little ricks that looked like old-fashioned loaves of Hovis. It seemed hard, hard work for very little return, as all the apples were left to rot. 'Nobody eats them any more,' Anna said sadly. 'And the best Calvados in the Soviet Union was also made here out of wild apples, but they stopped that too.'

Ivan shook his head and sighed.

Although the Aport can still be found in great pyramids in the city's Green Market, they seem taken for granted and are mostly bought only by older people. In a supermarket in Almaty I found Chinese, German and Dutch apples – cellophane-wrapped and offered in pairs on white plastic trays – but none of the local variety. Imported apples from Europe are novel and more glamorous, an example of the global economy gone mad. The Aport apple is uncool. 'They have gone out of fashion,' Anna said with a helpless shrug.

So far out of fashion that the mayor's office in Almaty launched an advertising campaign in 2005 in an attempt to restore the apple's image. In recent years locals have noticed a marked decline in quality. 'The Aport has left our tables,' one Almaty resident said. 'At first we lamented the fruit of ten years earlier, then fifteen ... and finally we just stopped complaining. We no longer notice that it takes four or five apples to make a kilogram, when before it only took two or three. The smaller apples are less tasty, and we grieve the loss of the wonderful aroma of apples drifting over the city's bazaars. People leaving Almaty no longer take with them the mandatory nylon net full of our famous apples.'

On the drive back to Almaty we spoke about life in Kazakhstan since the collapse of the Soviet Union, and I asked if Anna, as a Ukrainian, was as discomfited by independence as Ivan, the Russian. 'I feel Ukrainian, but my life is here. So I am Kazakh. It is okay for everyone here. There is no real tension between the ethnic groups, although there could be. If the first Kazakh president had been an ultra-nationalist or an anti-Russian or a fundamentalist, the country would have exploded. The transition has been carefully managed.'

Ivan grudgingly agreed, though he was clearly irked by the loss of status for Russians, now merely fellow citizens instead of being first among equals. 'In the old days,' he said, 'you could travel all over without passport or visas. Just your ID papers. Now just to go to Uzbekistan or Kyrgyzstan across the border you need a passport. You even need a passport to go to Moscow!'

'That was then, this is now,' Anna said, finally losing patience. '*In the old days* there was always fear. Even a scientist ran risks. It was safe to be a botanist or an ornithologist – but genetics was a political minefield, and the man who confirmed Kazakhstan as the country of origin of the apple was blown up by it.'

'Vavilov?'

'Yes, poor Vavilov.'

◆

So many Kazakh stories, I would learn, are sad stories. The fate of Academician Nikolai Vavilov has all the ingredients of a tragic novel. Once famous throughout the world, today he is scarcely remembered even by scientists within his own discipline. Like so many gifted men in the Stalin years, Nikolai Vavilov fell out of favour with the all-powerful State. A brilliant career was destroyed, and the great scientist disappeared. The official Soviet version of events states: 'Academician Vavilov's scientific activity was interrupted in 1940.' The story behind this bland understatement fills ten bulging secret police files.

For more than a decade after the Revolution, Vavilov had been one of the Soviet Union's favourite sons. As a scientist he was an all-rounder – botanist, geneticist, agronomist and geographer. Something of a genius, in fact. The trust and respect invested in him by the government was demonstrated by the freedom he was given to travel abroad at a time when the Soviet Union had become a giant prison.

Vavilov was allowed to visit more than fifty countries in pursuit of his research: he crashed in an aeroplane in the Sahara where he lived off dried locusts, he was caught in landslides in the Caucasus, and he confronted bandits in Ethiopia. He was the first European to lead a caravan across remote mountain provinces in Afghanistan, where he indulged in a little amateur espionage and photographed a British border fortress. He travelled all over Central and South America, the United States and Canada, visited Japan, Korea and China, and explored every corner of the Soviet Union.

The Soviet press covered his activities with banner headlines, treating him as a celebrity. He was awarded the Lenin Prize – the highest decoration for science – and became the youngest full member of the Soviet Academy of Science. He founded the Institute of Genetics, which rapidly became recognized internationally as one of the most important centres of research in the field. His work was universally respected and his 'scholar's charm' made him popular with foreign colleagues.

Modest, with an open, boyish face, Vavilov was the archetypal absent-minded professor, who worked eighteen-hour days. Throughout his life he tended to avoid political issues and adhered to the sacred concept that science was separate from politics, ruled by objective facts revealed through research and advanced by demonstrable argument based on data tested in controlled experiments. This was a naïve notion in the world evolving around him, entirely unsuited to the backroom brutalities of academic politics under Stalin.

The great scientist's nemesis entered his life disguised as a protégé. Trofim Denisovich Lysenko – later regarded as the Rasputin of Soviet science – was eleven years younger than his mentor. He was an agronomist who had earned his degree through a correspondence course, but like the older man he was a workaholic and fanatically interested in plants.

At first Vavilov admired the younger man's energy and was eager to encourage a hard worker with an original mind who showed enormous promise. He believed that an observant agronomist in the field – however limited in formal education – could make a valuable contribution to science. Although some of Lysenko's claims seemed downright peculiar, his mentor supported research into them and was prepared to examine the results. It was beyond Vavilov's comprehension to suspect any scientist of falsifying data, but for Lysenko, natural talent was employed as a tool in the service of unprincipled personal advancement, unhindered by intellectual probity.

In time, Lysenko's career would be shaped and propelled forward by an evil genius in the form of a scientific spin doctor who matched his ambition and lack of scruple. Isai Prezent knew nothing of biology, but he had completed a course in social science, and he was adept at injecting Marxist-Leninist jargon into scientific argument. Together, the two men hatched and promoted unproven scientific theories that astounded Vavilov: 'Is it some kind of religion?'

Lysenko responded to criticism by launching political attacks on those who opposed him. He dismissed genetics outright as 'harmful nonsense'; pure theoretical research was declared a waste of time; international literature on the subject was 'foreign stuff' – unnecessary and politically unsound intellectual clutter. Serious scientists were appalled by Lysenko's hokum, but science proved no match for politics. Lysenko's ideas had attracted the interest of Stalin, who was in the process of formulating a five-year plan to enforce collectivization of all farms.

Nowhere suffered more from the policy than Kazakhstan with its population of nomads. Although only 10 per cent of the population were wholly nomadic, at least 60 per cent were semi-nomadic and migrated with their herds in the summer. Most nomads had permanent winter homes with wooden outbuildings, as well as a fixed summer habitat. It was now decreed that they were to give up their traditional pastures and way of life, and live on large, state-owned 'collective' farms known as kolkhozes.

The Communist Party under Stalin not only misunderstood the nature of nomadism, it also wanted to destroy those aspects that it did understand. There were strong ideological reasons for this. Although in reality nomad society was more 'communistic' than any Soviet model, the Kazakhs were traditionalists who adhered to a strict clan-based, hierarchical system. It was considered shameful for a Kazakh not to know seven generations of ancestors. Grandmothers – *apais* – traditionally passed down the family history to their grandchildren through stories.

The bonds between families were sacrosanct, the young looked up to and admired their elders, and children were taught to respect parents and honour women. Within the family, the oldest son took responsibility for the well-being of his younger brothers, while the youngest son remained in the house where he was born to care for his parents, even after marriage and starting his own family. The Communist Party realized that in order to impose political control, it needed to destroy such traditions.

The policy was to 'eradicate the economic and cultural anachronisms of the nationalities', and nothing could be more anachronistic to the Soviet way of thinking than the nomadism of the Kazakh world where concepts such as 'class struggle' and 'the dictatorship of the proletariat' were meaningless. The Soviets saw the traditional Kazakh nomadic way of life as random wandering about the steppe, when in reality it had always been carefully structured. The nomads' large herds of cattle required vast areas of steppe upon which to graze, but these areas were also highly regulated by traditional laws. The various clans knew exactly who held rights over what land, and where the borders began and ended. It was forbidden for one clan to cross into land belonging to another.

The Soviets viewed the nomadic agricultural system as nothing more than the relic of a bygone age. They wanted to replace it with intense grain cultivation and turn the Kazakh steppe into a gigantic silo for the whole of Siberia and the Soviet Far East. Experts like Vavilov, who pointed out that much of the semi-arable land suitable for animal husbandry was useless for growing crops, were ignored. Traditional nomadic land was duly confiscated and transformed into kolkhozes intended to produce millions of tons of grain. But the poor soil of the steppe proved unsuitable for the project, which was why the natives were nomadic in the first place. All objections were met either with meaningless slogans – 'Better too much salt than too little' – or ominous ideological phrases – 'The broom of the revolution must sweep up the Kazakh village.'

The success of the plan launched at the end of 1929 required the forcible resettlement of more than half a million nomads over five years. From the outset the process was chaotic. The new collectives mostly existed on paper. In reality they lacked housing, farm buildings, tools, sufficient livestock and, in a number of cases, even arable land. Some nomads found themselves forced on to collectives that had no livestock or working capital. There were insufficient agronomists or agricultural experts to run the collectives, and most lacked any plan whatsoever. Many were set up in desert or semi-desert locations without adequate water, and although it was now forbidden to drive a herd to pasture, fodder for the static herd was often not provided. Many farmers tried to get round the rules by taking their animals to pasture in remote ravines and woods, but when winter arrived they were forced to slaughter them and to live off the frozen carcasses until spring.

The reaction of the Kazakhs was predictable, and resistance was ferocious. In the first three years of collectivization, 80,000 Kazakhs took part in 400 uprisings, while roving bands attacked the farms and took away or killed livestock. Rather than hand over their animals, many nomads slaughtered them. It is estimated that half the country's livestock was killed in the weeks following the launch of the policy. Within three years the number of cattle in the country dropped from 7 million to less than a million, while the number of sheep fell from 19 million to less than 2 million. Communist Party activists charged with carrying out collectivization often met with armed resistance, and some were killed.

The Soviet authorities blundered on, employing Red Army troops and squads of NKVD to shoot those who actively resisted the process. Throughout the Soviet Union millions of kulaks – the more successful class of peasant who owned some livestock – were exiled or murdered. The cost in human life in Kazakhstan was more than a million – a quarter of the population, either killed by troops or starved to death. By the time collectivization was completed in 1935 the nomadic way of life had been destroyed and whole communities eradicated. Ideology had overruled economics, and a way of life that had existed for a millennium was destroyed almost without trace.

The policy was a catastrophe, but it was against this background that Lysenko's theories for a quick and easy agricultural fix found favour with Stalin. Lysenko was allowed to transfer agricultural research from scientists in institutes and place it in the hands of farmers on collectives. Again, the results were a disaster, but no blame attached to him personally, for this might suggest that Stalin himself was wrong-headed.

In his public speeches, Lysenko always praised Stalin as 'The Great Gardener'. And like Stalin, he thought big: one cross-pollination experiment on collectives called for 800,000 pairs of tweezers. It failed, like most of his experiments, but the scale was impressive. At a congress for collective farm workers at the Kremlin in Moscow, attended by Stalin, Lysenko played his trump card against detractors: 'It is not only on collective farms that you come across kulaks out to wreck our system,' he told delegates. 'They are no less active and no less dangerous in the scientific world ... The class enemy always remains an enemy, whether he's a scientist or not.'

At this point in Lysenko's diatribe there was an interruption from the floor: 'Bravo, Comrade Lysenko, bravo!' It was Stalin himself who spoke. The hall immediately broke out in sycophantic applause, and Lysenko's dotty scientific theories became Soviet policy. And in the relentless political logic of the time, the reliability of every scientist who opposed him was instantly called into question.

Lysenko had become unstoppable while the reputation of Nikolai Vavilov plummeted. At scientific conferences he was treated with open contempt by Lysenko, while Stalin demonstrated his disapproval by ostentatiously leaving the room every time Vavilov began to speak. The Academy of Agriculture degenerated from an organization run by first-rate scientists into one controlled by ignorant and uncouth bureaucrats, and when collectivization failed, wave after wave of biologists, agronomists and veterinarians were arrested and paid the price for Lysenko's and the Great Gardener's blunders.

Perhaps a more astute political operator than Vavilov might have been able to avoid Lysenko's machinations, though it seems unlikely. The years of collectivization took a terrible psychological toll on Vavilov, and a sense of doom descended upon him, together with a presentiment of early death. In his final days of freedom he seemed reconciled to the inevitable, and in his last speech at the Institute he told students, staff and colleagues: 'We shall mount the fire and we shall burn, but we shall not give up our convictions.'

Suddenly, out of the blue, and much to Vavilov's surprise, he was given permission in 1940 to go on a field trip to the Western Ukraine – the first allowed in six years. In retrospect it seems clear this was a ruse to separate him from friends and colleagues. After a typical day collecting plant and seed specimens, he returned to his hotel to be met by agents of the internal security organs. They flew him back to Moscow where he was taken to the Lubyanka, headquarters of the secret police.

For the next twelve days Vavilov was called out in the night and questioned until daybreak. The brutal young interrogator always greeted the eminent scientist in the same way: 'Who are you?'

'I am Academician Vavilov.'

'You're a load of shit,' the interrogator spat. And the questioning would then begin.

At first Vavilov attempted to defend himself. He denied the preposterous accusations that he was an active participant in a subversive anti-Soviet organization and a spy for foreign intelligence services, but after a marathon session on the twelfth day of his captivity, when he was interrogated for thirteen hours straight without being allowed to sit, he cracked. Humiliation, physical threats and exhaustion had broken the professor. He made his first confession: 'I admit that I was guilty from 1930 of being a participant of the anti-Soviet organization of right-wingers that existed in the People's Commissariat for Agriculture.' In subsequent confessions he admitted that as head of the Academy he had set up useless departments aimed at harming agriculture, deliberately wasted state funds on worthless projects, created a shortage of seeds and disrupted the rotation of crops. In one ludicrous charge, he was accused of 'damaging the landing grounds in the Leningrad military region by sowing the airports with weeds'.

He was placed in solitary confinement for six months, during which time accomplices were arrested, including one dangerous subversive who was the country's leading authority on the pea, the runner bean and the lentil. A second round of interrogations began and the charge of espionage was built up. The invasion of the Soviet Union by Nazi Germany in June 1941 put pressure on prosecutors to bring cases quickly before the courts, and contradictory charges were hastily brought against Vavilov. He was accused of being both a monarchist and a Trotskyist and of supporting the Provisional Government which had brought down the monarchists.

Vavilov's trial was held before a closed session of the Military Collegium of the Supreme Court of the USSR. It lasted only a few minutes. No lawyers were present and no witnesses were called. The chairman took a prepared written statement from his briefcase, declared the defendant guilty and pronounced sentence: 'To be shot – all personal property to be confiscated.'

The condemned man returned to his cell to await execution. But the war was going badly for the USSR, and a decision was made to review the sentences of important scientists condemned to death to see if they could contribute to the war effort. When German Panzers were within seventy kilometres of Moscow, the order was given to transport the entire prison population out of the capital.

Vavilov was sent to Saratov, on the Volga, a journey that took two weeks. After a further three months in solitary confinement in a damp, underground cell, his health became so poor he was given permission to attend the prison hospital. While waiting in the freezing yard he came across a 16-year-old schoolgirl who had been imprisoned for 'trying to organize an attempt on the life of Comrade Stalin'. The girl was terrified she was about to be shot. Her fear was made greater when she was forced to join a group of men standing with their hands behind their backs, their faces turned to the wall. She found herself beside Vavilov. She later described him as having a sunken but intelligent face, and remembered his calm, soothing voice: 'Why are you crying?'

The girl replied that she did not know where she was being taken, was very frightened and in pain, and wanted to go home. 'Listen to me carefully,' the scientist said. 'Since you will almost certainly survive this, try to remember my name. I am Vavilov, Nikolai Ivanovich, an academician. Now don't cry and don't be afraid, we are being taken to the hospital. They have decided to treat even me before they shoot me. I am being held alone in a death cell. Don't forget my name.'

One day in midsummer Vavilov received the news that his death sentence had been commuted to twenty years' corrective labour. Although he knew he could not possibly survive such a term, he hoped to be sent back to Kazakhstan, to serve out his time in the famous agricultural prison camp at Dolinka. It was a forlorn hope. Weakened by scurvy, he finally succumbed to an epidemic of dysentery that swept through the prison.

Nikolai Vavilov, the man who had established Kazakhstan as the birthplace of the apple, died of starvation in the prison hospital of Saratov on 26 January 1943.

CHAPTER 2

MY NEIGHBOUR, TROTSKY

I took to Almaty, the apple city, from the beginning. The site, inhabited by humans since at least the sixth century, became a secondary staging-post on the Silk Road during the eighth and ninth centuries, and the city itself was founded in 1854 as a fortress named Verny ('Loyal' in Russian). It was manned by Cossacks and was one of the furthest points on the map of the expanding Tsarist empire. Today the ruins of the old fortress walls can be glimpsed, crumbling and neglected, in what has become a seedy part of town mostly inhabited by Meskhetian Turks from Georgia, deported to Kazakhstan by Stalin.

The Russians slowly turned a barren and dusty military outpost into parkland. In 1872, the military governor of Verny, Gerasim Kolpakovsky – a tree-hugger and Green ahead of his time – asked the governor-general of the Seven Rivers region for the sum of 2,194 roubles and 60 kopeks to create parks and plant avenues of elms, poplars and mulberries. The work was continued on a grand scale by the horticulturalist Ernest Baum, who planted the great forest on the outskirts of the city known as Baum Grove and which became notorious as a hiding place for robbers, escaped convicts and political victims. (Locals say it's still not a good place to walk.) Baum also issued an order obliging every resident to plant no less than twenty ornamental and fruit trees, provided by the city free of charge, and he took on anyone who tried to cut down old trees, especially Tien Shan firs. The result is a garden city of squares and parks, and avenues lined with mature trees.

The Hotel Otrar was perfectly placed in the centre of town, but it had a number of eccentricities and mysteries. The phones were one. Guests who wanted to make local calls were advised: 'Dial O, after continuous honk to dial necessary number.' The continuous honk, alas, was not always forthcoming. Another oddity was a cubby hole in the lobby where guests changed money. This was a serving hatch with a list of exchange rates for various currencies posted to its left above an electric bell. On the other side of the hatch was an elaborate system of full-length and half-length curtains that screened the moneychanger from her customers, so that a transaction was like consulting a gypsy in a fortune-teller's booth. After the bell had been rung and money pushed through the cubby hole, there was a rustling of curtains as a pair of hands and a bosom appeared beneath the half-length curtain. The cash was swiftly taken up, after which the hands and bosom retracted momentarily while the whirl and clatter of an old-fashioned adding machine could be heard. The bosom then reappeared and hands pushed notes in the local currency, *tenge*, back through the cubby hole. A different bosom changed money in the morning to that in the afternoon, and yet another at the weekend, all of which added a mildly erotic frisson to a routine procedure.

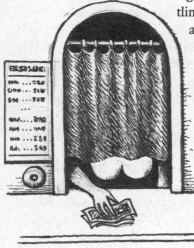

The rooms in the Otrar were small but comfortable, with an Art Deco design that made them seem like cabins in a luxury liner.

I had been given the view I'd demanded – mountains, park and Russian Orthodox cathedral – but directly across from my room was the office of the floor manageress. When not in situ she placed the phone outside her office at the end of a long cord so she could hear it ring from a distance. I heard it close up. It rang sporadically throughout the night, and almost non-stop in the early morning as people began to order breakfast.

After an exhausting night I decided to risk a bruising from the harridan at reception and ask for a room change. A young Japanese student was at the desk before me, receiving a ticking-off for not being understood. He had no Russian and very little English, and he was paying a high price for his ignorance. He smiled helplessly, holding up a single finger before his nose to express his wish to extend his stay for another night: 'Wun maw ni.'

'Do you have voucher?' the harridan demanded.

'Wun maw ni!'

'DO YOU HAVE VOUCHER?'

The student looked desperate and lowered his voice, so that it became a cringing plea for mercy as well as accommodation: 'Wun maw ni!'

'He wants to stay another night,' I said.

'Are you with this man?' It was an accusation.

'No. Just trying to be helpful. He doesn't seem to understand English.'

'He must have voucher.'

'Wun maw ni.'

'Oh, why can't you understand?' the harridan said, coming to the end of a very short fuse. 'VOUCHER! VOUCHER! VOUCHER!'

'I think that's the bit he doesn't understand,' I said. 'Voucher.'

'He must have voucher.'

The harridan's inappropriate fury had irritated me and I became reckless. 'I've extended my stay and I don't have a voucher.'

'You don't have voucher!' The outrage was lofty, as if I had violated some fundamental taboo of life. The tone further alarmed the Japanese student, who edged away from me, fearful I might forever scupper his plans for wun maw ni in the Otrar. The receptionist picked up the printed guest list that lay on the counter. She stared at me hard: 'Name?'

I backed away from the desk and headed for the door. 'I'll come back later,' I said over my shoulder.

◆

My plan for the day was to visit the Red Canyon, through which the Charyn river flows. Said to be one of the most spectacular sights in Kazakhstan, it lies close to the Chinese border, a four-hour drive from Almaty. My companions on the trip were a retired Kazakh professor of philosophy, who had never visited the canyon before, and his 30-year-old son. Ivan had agreed to drive us – somewhat reluctantly, I thought, suggesting a continuing loss of faith in my choice of expeditions.

The philosopher was a man in his early sixties with grey hair, sharp, intelligent eyes, and a languid serenity that is not always the lot of practitioners of his discipline. The passion he held for his country was expressed quietly in almost everything he said, but in an attractive, relaxed manner based on deep cultural knowledge, rather than in flag-waving, tub-thumping rhetoric.

The road out of town was lined with lofty elms, trees not seen in Europe for a generation, and every village we passed through had stalls where women sat beside buckets of pomegranates, mountains of watermelons and water-filled pails of live fish. Ivan pulled over from time to time to inquire about prices, and his response was always a theatrical display of enraged amazement. After berating the sellers for outlandish overcharging, he would drive off in self-satisfied fury. I quietly asked the philosopher's son why the women seemed so reluctant to bargain. 'Because the prices really are most reasonable,' he replied.

Trucks coming out of China passed us
on their way into Almaty, so overloaded they
looked comical. Great ungainly mountains of
cargo three times higher than the trucks themselves, and twice as wide, were precariously
held in place with rope and prayer, defying grav-
ity and good sense. We passed one truck that had
been tipped over by its burden and lay neatly on
its side like a discarded toy. Another had been

stopped by the police. Overloading is so common and so dangerous that Chinese trucks are periodically banned from entering the
country.

The villages we passed seemed poor but clean, and the houses
were the pretty white-and-blue wooden cottages to be found
all over the country. Many had racks of tobacco leaves drying in
the sun in the front garden, a smallholding operation funded by
Philip Morris, the American tobacco giant. We drove through one
village that seemed exceptionally orderly, and Ivan explained it had
once been entirely inhabited by Volga Germans, one of the many
nationalities deported to Kazakhstan by Stalin. After independence, when the economy took a nosedive, most accepted an invitation to settle in Germany – a decision since regretted by many.

As we drove along, I asked the philosopher about his early life.
The son of illiterate peasants, he was born and brought up in a
small aul – a Kazakh settlement – in a remote region of the steppe.
There were only three children in his class at kindergarten, and
only seven at primary school. 'Because there were so few students
the teachers really paid attention to each pupil, so when we all
moved on to the Kazakh language school in a nearby mining town
we all had good grades.

'My father was very proud that I did well at school. You have
to understand that all the old men in the village of his generation – all of them illiterate peasants – spent their money on their
children's education. That was the point of their lives. One of the
things you have to credit the Soviet system with is education. It

was very good, and if you were bright it helped you go all the way, even to Moscow University. And even the small towns had good libraries. I began to read the Russian classics, and grew to love and be greatly influenced by Chekhov.'

'I like Jack London myself,' Ivan said. 'The American. Very good.'

Almost everyone from the old Soviet Union is well read by Western standards. Not only are they steeped in the Russian classical canon – Pushkin, Tolstoy, Dostoyevsky and so on – but they have also read French and English literature and, almost to a man, Jack London. The philosopher told me he had once spent two months' salary on a set of Conan Doyle. The cut-off age for this pleasing literacy seems to be about forty – younger than that and everyone is as ill-read as his Western counterpart.

I asked the philosopher how much the Kazakhs had resented being a Russian colony. He told me it was only when he went to school in the mining town that he learned that Kazakhs were a minority in their own country and looked down upon by ethnic Russians. 'I had my first encounter there with Russian kids who would call us names. It was a childish form of discrimination. Not terrible or anything, but it was there. And if you were Kazakh you became aware that you were regarded as a second-class citizen.'

Russian peasants had swarmed on to Kazakh territory in the nineteenth century, and in the last decade so many arrived that there was not enough farmland to go around in the north. The Russian governor therefore ordered a mass migration of armed settlers to the south. In all, 50 million hectares of Kazakh land was expropriated, and Russians now made up a third of the population. More and more continued to arrive: by 1905, 300,000 were living on the steppe; by 1910 the figure had risen to 700,000, and by 1916 it had doubled to 1.5 million. At the time of the Revolution, Russians made up 42 per cent of the population, and in due course they would become the majority.

The professor went on to Almaty University to study ethics and the history of philosophy. 'At that time Almaty was a very clean city, with a population of half a million. And in those days if you had permission it was very cheap to fly. There was no real airport then – you slept on newspapers under the trees and waited for your plane. Study at university was difficult for me because Russian was a foreign language. I must say the Russian students appreciated that we were from the provinces and were trying hard to learn in Russian, and they had a good attitude towards us, yet we were sad that it was impossible to take further education in our own language.

'Before the First World War the Russians didn't really interfere with the traditional Kazakh way of life. They had built their forts and were expanding their empire, but the nomads were left to live in their own way. But then Kazakhs were recruited to fight in the war in Europe and they rebelled. There were serious riots in 1916. It was then that the Russians began to persecute Kazakhs.'

The European bloodbath of the First World War was remote and unimaginable to the nomads of the steppe. The years preceding it had been hard enough, with land seizures by Russia, a drop in prices for livestock, and a shortage of almost everything. An added provocation was that Kazakhs were obliged to support Russia in a war in which the enemy included Turkey; as a Turkic people themselves, who were also Muslim, this meant fighting for the infidel against those they felt to be their own.

At first, the Kazakhs had been exempted from the draft, but they were required to work on the homesteads of Russian peasants sent to the front. During the war the nomads were expected to provide meat, hides and their best horses free of charge to the imperial Russian cavalry. In the first two years more than a quarter of a million head of livestock were taken and taxes increased. Growing resentment exploded into open rebellion, and acts of violence against ethnic Russians, particularly officials, became commonplace.

In 1916 the Tsar issued an ukase demanding the conscription of Kazakhs into labour brigades, which led to organized, armed resistance involving tens of thousands, when every section of

Kazakh society united in violent protest against Russian authority. The Russian response was predictably harsh. A special expeditionary force, including detachments of Cossacks, was dispatched to quell the rebellion. The troops moved from *aul* to *aul*, arresting draft dodgers and ruthlessly killing rebels. It was common for whole villages condemned as hostile to be burned to the ground.

By the time the revolt had been crushed, the Kazakhs had paid a high price. It is impossible to know exactly how many died, but the Kazakh population was halved and their livestock similarly reduced. More than 500,000 Kazakhs fled to China, but many died on the way. In the aftermath Kazakhs were expelled from their land, group fines were levied, exclusive Russian zones created, and captured rebels executed. In the circumstances, and given that the Kazakhs were even more harshly treated under the Soviets, I was surprised that they were not seething with hatred.

'No, it's not like that here,' the philosopher said. 'The Kazakhs have no lasting resentment towards Russians. People know that the way things were was because of the system. Ethnic Russians weren't spared either. We Kazakhs have always been clear that it was not the Russians who were to blame for our plight – it was the State.

'Under the Soviets many Russians were sent here forcibly to work as slave labour in the Gulag. They were victims, not oppressors. And we Kazakhs knew that the same applied to all the other nationalities deported here – Chechens, Turks, Germans, Koreans. It was very hard for them – they had nothing and they faced terrible privation. Perhaps that's why the Kazakhs became the most tolerant people in the Soviet Union.'

Ivan had been silent throughout this conversation, and I wondered if this was the first time he had heard so directly what native Kazakhs felt about their former Russian masters. Later he would say, 'Those Kazakhs blame us for everything these days. But we did a lot for them. A *lot*!' In the car his irritation only came to the surface once, when the philosopher remarked that before the First World War few Kazakhs smoked or drank. 'So now the Russians made the Kazakhs smoke and drink! So that's the Russians' fault! I thought the Kazakhs liked to smoke and drink.' And in a non sequitur presumably added for my benefit, 'Everybody talks about how Russians drink, but you should see how the Germans drink! I've been to Germany – believe me, those Germans drink *a lot!*'

The philosopher and his son seemed bemused by the outburst and made no comment. Ivan's own cultural arrogance demonstrated itself by a suggestion that the national opera, *Abai*, based on the work of the great Kazakh poet was a bore. 'It's true, opera is not a natural form for us,' the philosopher said mildly. 'But there is a wealth of folk music that is truly wonderful. It might sound alien to the Western ear but it is very beautiful.'

The conversation shifted to the healthful properties of koumiss, the fermented mare's milk that was a staple of the Kazakh nomads. The philosopher said that Tolstoy recommended it to all his friends as a cure for depression, and drank eight litres a day. (Ivan later poured scorn on this. 'You think koumiss cures depression? You believe Tolstoy drank eight litres a day?')

After we had driven for a couple of hours villages and trees became sparse, and the country opened out into grassland. Occasionally we came across hundreds of horses scattered widely across the landscape, with a single Kazakh herder slumped in the saddle as if asleep. Whenever we passed a burial ground the philosopher would raise his hands and then pull them towards him in the traditional Kazakh act of respect for ancestors, a gesture more nomadic than Islamic. His son failed to do so, and I asked him why. 'I do it in my head,' he said. 'It's a generational thing.'

Father and son enjoyed an easy relationship. The respect that the young traditionally show their elders in Kazakhstan seems to lead to less tension and greater understanding between generations than in their Western counterparts. The son accepted his father's mild criticism of the younger generation's abandonment of Kazakh tradition in favour of mobile phones, designer clothes and cars, while the father was clearly proud of his son's achievement and ambition. But just as the father had spoken little Russian when young, the son spoke practically no Kazakh. 'Everything was taught in Russian at school,' he said. 'There were only two Kazakh lessons a week. We learned more English than Kazakh.' Father and son agreed that traditional Kazakh culture was in danger of vanishing. Modernity coupled with globalization – plus a fatal dose of prosperity – threatens to eradicate what remains of Kazakh identity. For the son it was regrettable; for the father a tragedy. 'It is the greatest disaster for the Kazakhs – the loss of their traditions, their language and their strong moral values,' he said. 'Soon there will be nothing Kazakh left.'

Close to the Chinese border, parts of the road suddenly became exceptionally wide for stretches of 500 metres. Ivan explained that during the Soviet period, when there was tension between the USSR and China, the road doubled as a military landing-strip. Bull's-eyes on the tarmac intended to guide in helicopters could be clearly made out.

A buffer zone between the borders of the two countries still exists, mostly because 8 million fellow Muslims, the Uighurs, who live in the neighbouring Chinese province of Xinjiang, are agitating for autonomy. But the Chinese have thwarted their political ambitions by dint of their overwhelming numbers. There were only 300,000 Chinese in the province in 1949, at the advent of communist power, but today they outnumber the Uighurs, and tens of thousands of new immigrants arrive each week. In the face of being deliberately swamped as a matter of policy by another people and culture, the Uighurs have grown to hate and fear the Chinese. What is happening in Xinjiang is an object lesson in long-term Chinese objectives that makes Kazakhs profoundly uneasy.

The steppe suddenly fell away sharply to a valley forming a lush strip of green along the Charyn river created by a thick grove of rare Sogdian ash trees, survivors from the last Ice Age. As we descended, two Chinese lorries with heroic loads were being given a helping tow up the incline by what looked like old Soviet military vehicles. We reached a checkpoint at the entrance to the buffer zone, our papers were closely scrutinized, and we were allowed through.

We decided to seek out a village for some lunch before cutting across country to the Red Canyon. Women were taking freshly baked flat bread off the wall of a brick oven, but they were reluctant to sell it, for it was meant to last them the week. Instead they directed us to a little town further towards China. There we found a restaurant full of workers, and ordered laghman – a Central Asian speciality of thick noodles served with lamb, peppers, tomatoes and onions in a spicy soup. We were also given good bread, milky tea and cold beer. Lunch cost a dollar a head.

'I was delighted with independence,' the philosopher said as we ate. 'Kazakhs were always mild dissidents because we wanted independence, but we didn't believe it was ever going to happen. In fact, we thought it impossible because we had become a minority in our own country – but we yearned for it.'

At first, independence brought disillusion in its wake. 'Everything collapsed. People stopped receiving their salaries. In the countryside there were simply no supplies. In the big cities there was no heating, no petrol ... a shortage of everything, worse than under the Soviets. People were nostalgic for Brezhnev and stagnation.' The economy has since boomed, life is relatively comfortable, and the future of Kazakhstan is bright, but the flowering of Kazakh culture has not yet happened. 'And there has been a disastrous decline in the education system. It began in the 1970s when 40 per cent of students started failing their exams. That was considered too many by Moscow so an order came from the top to make the students look good. The quality of the teaching dropped off.'

'Sounds like England,' I said.

Ivan, who had maintained a grumpy silence when the philosopher spoke of independence, suddenly found his voice: 'And you can't go to Moscow University any more now, can you?'

'No, but you can go to Harvard or Oxford,' the young Kazakh retorted. He himself had gone to university in Montana. The government pays all tuition fees and gives money for accommodation to 3,500 exceptional students each year, with the stipulation that they return to Kazakhstan to work for three years once they have graduated.

To reach the canyon we had to drive back through the check-point, then cut across the steppe along a dirt road for about forty-five kilometres. It was a bone-rattling, dusty drive in a featureless landscape. Then, in the distance, there arose out of nowhere the curious image of a blue Lada parked next to a blue sentry box with a single soldier standing beside it.

We drove towards the bored soldier, who looked into our car and pointed vaguely to the right, indicating our destination. All I could see was more steppe. I began to fear that the Red Canyon was going to be a disappointment. It was either a very long way away or a good deal smaller than advertised. As we bumped along a track I prepared myself for an interminable journey across unchanging terrain. Suddenly, to our right, the steppe was pulled away from beneath us like a carpet to reveal two massive red sandstone canyons that fell away for hundreds of metres. It was a breathtaking sight, made doubly impressive by the abrupt way in which it came into view. It seemed impossible that such an enormous natural feature could remain so completely hidden. We drove carefully along the ridge as far as we could, parked the car, and continued on foot. One of the canyons had a dry bed, while the other contained the ribbon of a river. A mile or so away, far below, there was an island green as an oasis. We walked and climbed along ledges and promontories for hours, dwarfed and alone, awed into silence. Even Ivan was affected: 'Yes,' he said thoughtfully, as he lit a cigarette, 'this is beautiful.'

The most pleasing aspect of the gorge for me was the evident pleasure the philosopher and his son took in it. Here was a unique and spectacular feature of their native land that neither the tsars, nor the Soviets, nor even globalization could ruin. It was as if we had a scaled-down Grand Canyon all to ourselves, with its fantastic, wind-sculpted red towers and arches. One of the deepest of the northern Tien Shan, the canyon runs for 150 kilometres and contains a number of astonishing rock formations with names like Ghosts' Gorge, the Devil's Gorge and the Valley of Castles. The philosopher risked life and limb to take photographs.

One of the rewards for the traveller to Kazakhstan's wild places is to find them almost always empty of people. We continued to explore for a couple of hours without sight of another person, not a soul. But as we were preparing to leave, a jeep appeared in the distance carrying four soldiers. It pulled to a stop and one of the occupants jumped out and began to urinate. 'Typical military,' the philosopher's son said. 'They come to this beautiful remote place and the first thing they do is piss on it.'

On the long drive back to Almaty the philosopher and I talked about Lenin. It was clear he maintained a residual respect for the man whose statue was once in every town square in the USSR, and felt that Lenin's sudden, universal demotion from god to monster was partly opportunistic. It was Lenin who first drew the boundaries of Kazakhstan on the map after the Revolution of 1917, the philosopher told me, and Lenin who first criticized Russian attitudes towards Kazakhs and declared that every nation within the Soviet Union had the right to its own identity. 'I ask you to name a greater political thinker and activist, not just in modern history, but in all history,' the philosopher asked. 'I mean in terms of his influence on world events.'

He had a point, though I held back from saying that the creation of a ruthless terror state – while of enormous historical significance – struck me as a profoundly negative achievement. But I liked the philosopher and enjoyed his company too much to start an argument. Besides, he had spent a lifetime filtering and interpreting philosophy through a spectrum of Marxist-Leninism, although he laughed when I asked if he had been a Communist Party member. 'It would certainly have been good for my career. And there was a time when I thought of getting involved in politics. But it was never decided whether I was a genuine member of the proletariat, because of my peasant background, or a member of the intelligentsia. So no, I never joined the Party.' In reality, the philosopher was one of those whom the Soviets mistrusted most

– a romantic. Throughout his life, he confided, he'd kept a copy of Turgenev's *First Love* on his study desk.

•

It had been a long day. I arrived back at the hotel at nine in the evening, planning an early night, but before turning in, I thought I might have a drink. A notice in the lobby promoted the hotel bar as a sophisticated, international watering-hole, and urged me to seek it out on the third floor. As I stepped out of the lift I found a deserted room and a shuttered bar. A hotel security man came round the corner and eyed me with suspicion. 'I was hoping to get a drink,' I said.

'This way.' Obediently, I followed the security man back into the lift. We descended to the basement, a gloomy area I had previously assumed was reserved for members of staff. I was led along a dark corridor and began to wish I had gone straight to bed. We passed a brightly lit room that claimed to be a hairdressing salon. Two bored women sat smoking with their feet up on stools. There were no customers.

At the end of the corridor we came to a locked door. Turning to me with a slimy grin and conspiratorial wink that should have had me running back to the lift, the security man took out a bunch of keys and unlocked the door. As I stepped through into the unknown, he purred, 'Booful wimmin ... booful gurls.' I turned to see him leering hideously, and before I could respond he stepped back through the door. And locked it.

I found myself in a cavernous and almost deserted discotheque. To one side a couple of dangerous-looking bouncers guarded an alcove where a gangster type was drinking champagne with a couple of gaudy hookers. When the gangster type saw me glance in his direction he gave me a threatening look. I turned away and took a seat at the bar.

There was only one other customer. A sad-sack foreign slob was locked in a slow dance with an unattractive prostitute. He was round and overweight, dressed in what seemed to be gardening clothes; she wore high white boots, jeans flecked with silver, and a pink sequinned tank top. I felt myself sinking into depression, and wished I was curled up in bed with Dostoyevsky's relatively cheery *House of the Dead* – a work begun in Kazakhstan and my current light reading.

The barmaid was pleasant enough in the resigned manner of the long-suffering, and I decided to have one quick drink. I asked for my favourite vodka. The barmaid shook her head, and continued to shake it as I recited every brand I knew. 'Okay,' I said, 'surprise me.' Sighing, the barmaid heaved an industrial-sized bottle of vodka into sight, the only brand on offer. It was not even cold, so she poured a measure into a glass over ice. It glugged over the cubes like hair oil. Industrial in size and industrial in nature, I took a sip of the vilest vodka I've ever tasted. 'It's disgusting,' I spluttered.

The barmaid nodded and looked sympathetic. It was clear I was not the first to gag over the stuff. 'You want orange juice in it?'

'It might help.' But nothing could disguise the vodka's distinctive taste of rancid engine oil. I decided to call it a day. The barmaid gave me the tab. I paid up, went to the door and asked a bouncer to unlock it. He shrugged. 'I don't have the key.'

'Look, I want to leave. Open the door!'

Suddenly, the various unpleasant aspects of the disco came together in an ominous and sinister whole. I glanced in the direction of the dangerous character in the alcove. He glared at me. I looked away – to be confronted by the fat foreigner passionately kissing the ugly hooker. The two bouncers muttered to one another and laughed, and one took out a mobile phone and made a call. 'Take it easy,' the bouncer said. 'Hotel security is coming. Have a drink.'

Eventually, the hotel security man unlocked the door from the other side. Angry, but pleased to be let out, I asked: 'What sort of bar locks people in?'

'Too early for booful wimmin,' the security man apologized. 'Come back later – two, three. Many, many booful wimmin.'

'No thanks, I'm off to bed.'

An hour later I was lying happily on the bed in my room with Dostoyevsky's House of the Dead, when the phone rang. A voice said, 'Mistuh Roben?'

'Yes.'

'You want massage?'

'No thank you.'

'Okay. What you want?'

'Nothing thanks.' I put the phone down and returned to my book.

Five minutes later there was a knock on the door and I went to answer it. Standing in the corridor was a squat, overweight Kazakh woman in her mid-fifties. She was wearing a grey, shapeless tracksuit and big felt boots. She smiled to reveal a mouth full of bulky gold teeth. 'Mistuh Roben?'

'Yes?'

'Me massage girl.'

'I don't want a massage. I told you on the phone.'

'Okay. What you want?'

'I told you – I don't want anything.'

'Half hour – fifty dollars. Make you happy.'

'No. Look, I'm really rather busy,' I said, beginning to close the door. 'Excuse me.'

'Okay,' the woman said, flashing me a golden smile.

I went back into the room and stood looking out of the window across the park towards the mountains. I contemplated the strange encounter. As an experience it was a first. A hooker had called me by name in my room. And then confidently presented herself at the door. Presumably the security man had consulted the hotel register and passed my name on to some 'massage girl' who paid him off. It was funny, yet unsettling.

And did I really appear to be so desperate and sad a figure that I would seriously entertain a romp with a tubby, middle-aged woman with a mouthful of gold teeth dressed in a tracksuit and felt boots? Did foreigners locked in the basement disco, swacked on foul industrial vodka, take this homely creature to their beds for a half hour of happiness at fifty bucks a pop?

As these thoughts passed through my mind, I saw the woman leave the hotel and cross the street to a beaten-up white Lada. I watched her climb into the car and drive off and felt a little sorry for her.

•

The following day, after another night broken by the sound of the floor manageress's telephone, I went down to the lobby to try to change my room. The harridan had gone home and one of her less officious colleagues was happy to oblige. As I took my new key, I said playfully, 'I don't need voucher?'

'Voucher?'

I walked across the road to Panfilov Park. In it stands the Russian Orthodox cathedral, a rococo confection of yellow-and-white stuccoed wood. Built in 1904, it is one of the few buildings to have survived the earthquake that destroyed most of the town in 1911, perhaps because it was so expertly pegged by master carpenters – there is not a nail in it. Closed by the communists after the Revolution, it was used first as an officers' club, then as a museum, until after independence it was restored in all its glory as a place of worship.

Inside the cathedral each of a score of icons attracted its cluster of devotees who lit cheap candles that sizzled and hissed like sausages in a pan. Mass was well attended. A small army of clergy – there must have been twenty bearded priests in vestments of crimson and gold – emerged from mysterious doors, swinging censers full of incense, while a hidden choir sang from the beautiful repertoire of Russian religious music.

Sitting on a wall outside was a line of three beggars, two men and a woman. Over the course of the following year, whenever

I wandered through the park, I would see them – in the heat of
summer or in deep snow. Passers-by occasionally dropped small
coins into their hands, or gave them buns and bread. At each
donation they would all bow their heads in humble thanks. Once,
in winter, as men with wide shovels worked to clear the park of a
recent fall of snow, I was touched to see the beggars sharing their

bread with the pigeons. I was less touched when I figured out the scam.

The first male beggar scattered crumbs in the snow near his feet. As the pigeons moved closer to peck at them, the second male beggar snatched the nearest bird in a lightning action so fast it was almost invisible. He furtively handed the captured pigeon to the woman beside him who pulled it under a coat and, with a quick flick of the wrist, wrung its neck. The body was then placed in a plastic bag bulging with tiny cadavers. The operation was swift, efficient and well-practised, and the beggars gloated and leered horribly at each successful kill.

Apart from the cathedral, the other great feature of the park – from which it takes its name – is a monumental bronze memorial dedicated to the memory of soldiers of the Panfilov Division who took part in an action in 1941 credited with helping to save Moscow from being overrun by the Germans. While antiquated Kazakh artillery pounded the Nazis, wounded soldiers armed only with bottles of petrol rolled under tanks. In this way a brigade of 28 soldiers and sappers managed to destroy 47 tanks. Only three men survived.

The memorial to this display of courage is in the Socialist Realist style and portrays the men as giant angry gods, brandishing grenades and bayonets. They seem monstrous and inhuman, an impossible, propagandist breed of Soviet supermen who glower down upon an alley of black polished marble at the end of which burns an eternal flame. The monument is greatly revered by the Kazakhs who have their wedding pictures taken in front of it.

I took tea with Ulua Panfilova, the half-Kazakh, half-Russian, elegantly dressed granddaughter of General Ivan Vasilyevich Panfilov. She showed me a book of newspaper cuttings and photos, leafing through them with an abstracted air of sleepy sadness. I remarked that her grandfather must have been a particularly valuable soldier to have once served as an officer in the Tsar's army and then to have survived Stalin's purge in the 1930s. 'Yes,' she said. 'My other grandfather was shot by Stalin.'

General Panfilov had seen action in the First World War, and had been sent to Kazakhstan to form a division at the beginning of what the Soviets called the Great Patriotic War. More than a million Kazakhs served in the Red Army. The Panfilov Division was multi-ethnic, but mostly made up of Kazakhs, and it was known as the Wild Division because it was from the east. The men were poorly armed, scarcely trained and taught to fight with tractors rather than tanks. They were also prepared to expect the worst. The Kazakh second lieutenant, Baurjan Momysh-Uly, who led the battalion that destroyed so many German tanks, had decided before the battle that if his men were overrun he would kill all his wounded so that they would not fall into the hands of the enemy, and then kill himself.

Ulua showed me a photograph of her grandfather taken by an official photographer two hours before a shell hit his head-quarters and killed him. He had been commander of the division for three and a half months. 'My mother, who was 18 at the time, was at the front in an evacuation company that brought back the injured from the battlefields. She learned of her father's death from a wounded soldier who had lost a leg. He was crying and my mother tried to calm him, saying they had good surgeons and he would be all right. "I'm not crying because of my leg, I'm crying because my father is dead." And then he made it clear he meant his general was dead – and, of course, the general was my mother's father.'

I looked at pictures of Ulua's mother, the general's eldest daughter, a sturdy, indomitable Russian of the old school. 'She was injured four times in the war,' Ulua said. 'Two of the injuries were very severe. Her face was burned, she was made deaf and dumb, and she had to have a leg amputated. She has been very strong and endured everything, but a sad and very upsetting thing happened later – in 1995 my mother began to suffer post-traumatic stress syndrome and has had terrible psychological problems. Fifty years after the end of the war!'

I walked back through Panfilov Park and stopped to take an-

other look at the memorial. It now seemed a mockery of the men involved. The monsters in bronze dwarfed the slight forms of the Kazakhs having their photos taken. It struck me that the courage displayed by the poorly armed and scruffy band of Kazakhs who helped save Moscow was altogether more ragged and human. The brute heroics portrayed by the figures in the memorial suggest the mechanical fearlessness of cartoon superherocs rather than the strength of character of soldiers running on empty – men who are scared, hungry and exhausted but who fight to the end. The Kazakhs possessed the day-to-day, around-the-clock, two-in-the-morning bravery that really does make heroes out of ordinary men. Perhaps the true memorial should be a statue of a gaunt soldier in a threadbare overcoat with a Molotov cocktail in his hand. But then, I don't suppose many people would want to have their photos taken beside him.

•

My new room still had a view of thc park and was at the other end of the hotel, far away from the floor manageress and her telephone. I looked forward to a night of uninterrupted rest and fell into a deep sleep the moment I was in bed.

At first the sound was like a dull, faraway drumming that didn't fully wake me but took me into a semi-conscious state akin to mild fever. The distant throbbing would start and then stop with no pattern so that my subconscious could never quite ignore it. Finally, I was fully awake. I looked at the clock. It was 4.30 a.m.

The sound filtering up through five storeys of concrete and carpet was the muffled beat of bass and drums. I had moved into a room directly over the bunker discotheque. I tried to go back to sleep. But just as I was about to nod off, the rhythm would change, and I was awakened again. This continued until six, when the disco closed.

That morning, sunken-eyed and very tired, I presented myself at the reception desk to complain. The harridan was back on duty. To my surprise she did not attempt to argue. There was a tired, defensive tone to her voice: 'It is discotheque. Yes.'

'It's insane to have an unsound-proofed disco in the basement of the hotel. I'm sure I'm not the only person to complain.'

'Everybody complains,' she said in weary resignation. The problem, she explained, was that the hotel did not own the head-banging establishment in the basement, so had no control over it. This accounted for the strange routine of being led along basement corridors and locked inside.

I couldn't face moving rooms again, so stuck it out for another night. It was torture. Even earplugs didn't help. Wun maw ni of this, I thought, and I'll be waving mad.

I decided to check out. I had extended my stay by paying in advance, so asked for a refund. 'Refund not possible,' the harridan said, regaining her edge. I asked why it was possible to pay for a room in advance on a credit card, but not to have a refund on it. 'Moment please.' She retired to the manager's office for a ten-minute consultation, then returned. 'Moment please.'

After a while I gave her a hard, questioning look. 'How long is this going to take?'

'Moment please.' She disappeared again. I waited. And waited. Finally, she returned. 'Refund on credit card not possible, but ...' She handed me a printed slip of paper. It was a voucher. For two maw nis at the Otrar.

◆

I rented a studio apartment just a few hundred metres away from the hotel along Gogol Street, a stone's throw from Leon Trotsky's first lodgings in exile. My landlady was one of nature's hard-wired entrepreneurs, a breed that seventy years of brutal communist oppression had failed to smother. Dressed for combat in a padded camouflage jacket with many pouches and pockets, she was forever on the move. She barked orders and threats into a walkie-talkie that crackled perpetually in her right hand, while strapped to her left arm were two mobile phones. Her person was her office, and she moved perpetually from property to property – God help cleaners caught smoking when they should have been on their hands and knees scrubbing floors.

The landlady had managed to buy half a dozen apartments of various sizes for a song in the early days of independence and privatization. They had since gone up in value ten times, while she rented them out for short-term lets. The rate was the equivalent of forty-five dollars a night in cash, up front – and yes, she said, of course she took dollars. I worked out that the business turned over between five and eight thousand a month on an initial investment of a hundred grand.

The apartments were all in the centre of the town and had once been inhabited by the nomenklatura, the Communist Party élite. The block I was in had plaques on the wall of a photographer and political activist dimly famous long ago for services to the Party. Nomenklatura or not, the building's condition was one that only Soviet architecture could manage to achieve – unfinished, yet in an advanced state of decay.

The entrance to my apartment lay in an alley at the back where an outdoor stairway led to a walkway over the roofs of a row of garages covered in tarmacadam. The concrete of the block itself was stained and discoloured. The outdoor banisters were crumbling, there was a lot of buckled and rusted corrugated iron, and the tarmacadam, lightly covered in moss, was erupting. It needed great dexterity to punch a three-number code simultaneously into an outside door – a feat made doubly challenging in the dark. And close to impossible after vodka.

The apartment itself had a double front door: the outer one was like something on a bank vault; the inner one was heavily padded against the cold. The lock system also dated from Soviet times and operated on different mechanical and logical principles to those of Chubb and Yale. The keyhole revolved and had to be lined up to turn the lock. And then there were the individual idiosyncrasies created by age and extremes of temperature, which in the case of my apartment necessitated leaning gently on the door and coaxing the key very slightly to the left until there was a click. The sound of the bell was surprising and rather wonderful – a curious chirping of strangled birdsong.

The grim exteriors of Soviet buildings often contain pleasingly compact and cosy human nests. Inside, the apartment was immaculate. A narrow corridor, with a bathroom to the left and spacious bedsitting-room to the right, led to the kitchen. The sitting-room had peach net curtains, wood-patterned lino on the floor, and a large sofa with two enormous matching armchairs covered in mud-coloured synthetic material. There was an appealing Dutch-door – half-glass, half white-painted clapboard – that opened on to a tiny enclosed balcony. Reproductions of sylvan scenes that might have graced any English seaside boarding-house decorated the walls, and a shaggy yellow pillow with a maple-leaf motif imprinted upon it enlivened the gloomy sofa. In the kitchen a cropped reproduction in a cheap frame of Van Gogh's sunflowers took pride of place. Out of context they looked as kitsch as everything else. All in all, the accommodation was very much to my liking.

The apartment was also well situated. Not only did I have a wonderful view of the Tien Shan mountains, but Panfilov Park was across the road, and Gorky Park – with its old-fashioned funfair rides, portrait artists and tea houses – was only a short walk away, just beyond the bus terminal. Every city in the old Soviet Union had a Gorky Park, each with an identical semi-circle of grand pillars at its entrance and the same Festival of Britain atmosphere of dated fun. The other end of Gogol Street, in contrast, is now the height of Western chic at twice the cost, where Versace, Armani, Jill Sanders and Prada jostle for pride of position. Amidst them all I saw a witty billboard that captured the surreal nature of modern Kazakhstan: a smartly dressed Kazakh in a trendy suit and fashionable spectacles demonstrates the merits of a Visa card to steppe nomads in full warrior kit.

A five-minute walk south took me to a favourite haunt, the Green Market. Spurned by the grand and the upwardly mobile as too chilly in winter and somewhat flyblown in summer, the Green Market tends mostly to attract the city's bargain-conscious residents. It struck me as everything a Central Asian market should be. Stall upon stall of dried fruit create a riot of colour set off against billowing linen sheets strung over them to protect the produce from the sun. There are scores of vegetable stands, butchers and wet fish stalls, while in narrow alleys alongside, hundreds of small, open-fronted shops sell shoes, saws, bags of nails, electrical equipment and just about everything else. There are noodle stands and dark corner restaurants and a multitude of horse butchers. The fresh fruit is displayed like jewellery, each piece polished and carefully placed, while spring onions are stylishly trussed in their own stems, and green beans tied neatly in bundles. I first visited the market in summer, but I was later impressed to see the outdoor stalls open for business even in midwinter when old Kazakh women bundled in cardigans and hats sit in the snow, their wares skimpily covered in polythene, as indifferent to the cold as statues.

At the bottom of a flight of stairs in the market I came across an anorexic, knock-kneed mannequin wearing a 1950s bouffant wig, black stockings, garish panties and a one-piece pink-and-black corset with padded bra. The model seemed unconnected to any business at all, a provincial psycho's fantasy of erotic muddle. She remained where she was throughout the year, although whether as an art object or joke I was never able to fathom. I always sought her out whenever I was in Almaty to pay homage to her anarchic spirit.

One day, as I wandered through the market, I took a photograph of a stallholder seated beside his wares. 'Hey!' he called loudly as I moved on. I turned, worried that I had caused offence by taking his picture without permission. 'Come back! Take another – I wasn't smiling!' I took a couple more as the stallholder posed with a theatrical, ear-to-ear grin. 'I was dreaming before, not sad. I'm a happy guy!'

'I can see,' I said. 'Well thanks, Happy Guy!'

I moved off. 'Hey, Foreign Guy! Come back!' The man held out his hand and dropped three or four dried apricots into my palm. He flashed his Happy Guy smile: 'Present!'

The small gift put me in a good mood. I decided to go back to a stall and buy a handsome axe that I had admired earlier. It had a short, hand-carved wooden handle and a seriously heavy head with an edge to its blade that could split matchsticks. An odd souvenir, I have to admit, but it took my fancy. I haggled over the price, happily paid too much, and moved on to buy a broom made from straw. As I hesitated, the man dropped the price. 'It's a good broom,' he said. 'A very good broom.'

'I was just wondering whether it would fit into my suitcase.' A momentary look of unease flickered across the man's face. 'I want to take the broom to England, you see.'

'To England?' I might as well have said I would fly the broom to Mars. The old man placed the broom back against the wall and shrugged. 'It's a good Kazakh broom. I don't know about England.'

I bought it and made my way back to the apartment carrying the axe, the broom, two bananas and a bag of apples.

•

As I trudged daily up and down Gogol Street, I often thought of my dangerous neighbour, Leon Trotsky. He arrived in Almaty with his family in utter darkness in the early hours of a freezing January morning in 1928, and was taken to the Seven Rivers Hotel, a shabby establishment on Gogol Street that stood between the Hotel Otrar and my rented digs. The original building has long since been demolished and it took considerable detective work on my part to find anyone who knew where Trotsky had once lodged. Many of the people I asked had never even heard of the man the Communist Party spent so much energy expunging from history – another piece of Kazakhstan's vanished legacy.

There can have been no more important figure exiled to Kazakhstan than Stalin's bitter enemy and rival, second only in the Bolshevik pantheon to Lenin himself. Stalin had expelled Trotsky from the Communist Party, charged him with counter-revolutionary activity, and condemned him to internal exile. At the time, Stalin had not achieved absolute power so did not dare kill his enemy, but he wanted to neutralize Trotsky by sending him as far from Moscow as possible. Almaty, 4,000 kilometres away on the Chinese border at the very extremity of the Soviet empire, seemed the ideal place.

On the day of the planned deportation, when agents of the GPU – forerunner of the KGB – intended to put the family on a train bound for Central Asia, thousands of supporters thronged the station, and the militia was unable to disperse them. Meanwhile, Trotsky sat at home among twenty boxes of books he intended to take with him into exile. The time for departure came and went. Hours passed, then just before midnight there was a telephone call to say that deportation had been delayed for forty-eight hours. Trotsky and his wife went to bed exhausted, and slept until eleven the following morning.

The postponement was a ruse. The secret police had no intention of risking further confrontation with an even larger crowd, and instead of a forty-eight-hour delay, agents arrived at the apartment the following evening. Trotsky refused to open the door, forcing the secret police to break it down. The agent in charge of the arrest had served on Trotsky's famous armoured train during the Civil War following the Revolution. Faced with his former commander, the man became overwhelmed with shame and broke down: 'Shoot me, Comrade Trotsky, shoot me!'

'Don't talk nonsense,' Trotsky replied. 'No one is going to shoot you. Get on with your job.'

Dressed in carpet slippers and an old cardigan, Trotsky continued to refuse to co-operate with his captors, and obliged them to pull on his boots and drape a fur coat around his shoulders. He then refused to move, resulting in a semi-farcical scene in which agents carried him down to the street. Trotsky's eldest son, Leo – who would accompany him into exile – ran down the stairs ahead of his father ringing all the doorbells. 'Look, comrades! They're taking Comrade Trotsky away by force!' The apartment block was reserved for members of the Soviet élite. Several doors opened a crack to show pale, frightened faces, but they quickly closed. No one uttered a word of support.

Trotsky and his family were driven through icy streets to a different station from the previous day. The new plan was to take them on a circuitous route in a single carriage to a small station fifty kilometres outside Moscow, where it would be hitched to the main train bound for Central Asia. Trotsky's wife Natalya remembered: 'We found ourselves launched on a long journey without a single book, pencil or sheet of paper.'

The monotony was brightened by the arrival of Trotsky's devoted male secretaries, Syermuks and Poznansky, who joined the train surreptitiously en route. On the tenth day the luggage caught up with them, including Peter 'Tien Shan' Semenov's classic book on Kazakhstan. 'We read about the natural features, the population, the apple orchards,' Natalya wrote. 'Best of all, we found out that the hunting was good.'

Semenov had written the only detailed book on the area

published in the nineteenth century, and precious few have been added since. He was a distinguished Russian geographer who was the first European to explore the Tien Shan mountain range, which he described as 'the most majestic I had ever seen containing about thirty snow giants'. He had set off in the summer of 1856 with a small team of Cossacks on camels, and travelled deep into the range. He was the first European to set eyes on the most beautiful peak of all, the Tengri Tag, shaped like a near-perfect pyramid. A wealthy noble, Semenov collected old masters – which he donated to the Hermitage – and 700,000 insects, 100 species of which are named after him. He ran the Russian Geographical Society for forty years, and Tsar Nicholas II allowed him to add the words Tien Shan to his name, an honorific adopted by his descendants.

Trotsky reached the end of the railway line at the small town of Pishpek-Frunze – today known as Bishkek and now the capital of Kyrgyzstan, 250 kilometres from Almaty. The remainder of the journey, by bus, automobile and sledge, was taken in stages. Natalya later recalled their arrival at the railhead: 'There was a biting frost. The sun's rays pouring on the clean white snow blinded us. We were given felt boots and sheepskins. I could hardly breathe for the weight of my clothes, yet it was cold on the road. The autobus moved slowly over the creaking snow packed down by vehicles. The wind lashed our faces.'

They crossed an ice-covered, windswept plain, and then ploughed through deep snowdrifts to climb over mountain passes in a raging blizzard. At nightfall, they arrived at a mail station. 'We seemed to be in the midst of a snow-covered desert. We got out of the bus with a little difficulty, and after groping about in the dark for the doorstep and the low door, walked inside and shed our sheepskins with relief. But the hut was cold and the tiny windows were frosted right through. In the corner was a huge Russian stove cold as ice.'

The mail station was looked after by a Cossack woman who gave them hot tea and something to eat. Trotsky asked about the local hunting while two men from the escort went off to find accommodation. They returned in embarrassment to say that the sleeping quarters were not very good. An understatement. The family moved to a deserted hut consisting of a low, cold room with a dirt floor and furnished only with a bench and a large, rough table. Leo bedded down on the bench, while Trotsky and his wife slept on the table between sheepskins. Natalya burst out laughing: 'Quite unlike the apartment in the Kremlin.'

At dawn the following day the party set off to cross the Kuday mountains, the most difficult section of the journey. 'Bitter cold,' Natalya wrote. 'The weight of my clothes was unbearable – as if a wall had fallen on me … The road was difficult for the automobile – snow had drifted over the glassy surface.' The chauffeur was a local with expert knowledge of the treacherous mountain roads. He drank vodka throughout the trip to keep warm, and railed against the system and the incompetents who ran it, unperturbed by his august passenger and secret police guards.

The day after their arrival in Almaty, Trotsky and his wife ventured out for a walk. 'A fine thing in Alma-Ata was the snow – white, clean, and dry,' Natalya wrote. 'As there was very little walking or driving, it kept its freshness all winter long.' The town, famous in Moscow for its gardens and orchards, was then wholly Eastern in nature, the Russian influence but a veneer. The native accommodation was little more than a series of ramshackle slums, and there was no running water, no lighting and no paved roads. 'In the bazaar at the centre of the town,' Natalya wrote, 'the Kirghizes [Kazakhs] sat in the mud at the doorsteps of their shops, warmed themselves in the sun, and searched their bodies for lice.'

On the fourth day of exile the secretary Syermuks arrived at the hotel. His stay proved to be a brief one. At ten the same evening Natalya recorded: 'We heard the soft, cautious padding of felt boots in the hall, and listened intently … We could hear someone enter Syermuks' room without knocking, and say, "Hurry up, now!" and Syermuks reply, "May I at least put my boots on?" … Again the soft, almost noiseless steps and the deep silence. Later the doorman came and locked Syermuks' room. We never saw him again.'

Syermuks had been arrested by the secret police. The second secretary, Poznansky, never arrived in Almaty but was arrested en route. They disappeared into the Gulag, where after a decade of hard labour they were reduced to human wreckage and finally shot.

The rooms in the hotel on Gogol Street were clearly inadequate for an indefinite period of exile. 'Only as a result of the telegrams I sent the most exalted personages in Moscow were we at last given a house,' Trotsky wrote in a letter. They moved to a four-room apartment in the centre of town, at 75 Krasnin Street. 'We had to buy some furniture, restore the ruined stove, and in general build up a home.'

There were the usual hardships that went with Soviet life, always worse outside Moscow. Meat and vegetables were scarce, and it became increasingly difficult even to buy bread as the anti-kulak policy – originally championed by Trotsky – led to greater and greater shortages of grain. But he was allowed to have his dog Maya sent from Moscow, and given permission to go on hunting trips.

The advent of spring gave exile in Kazakhstan an idyllic quality, when the deep snow was replaced by endless fields of red poppies. 'Such a lot of them – like gigantic carpets!' Natalya wrote. 'The steppe glowed red for miles around.' It was the first time Trotsky had relaxed in many years, and soon after his arrival he began to go on extended hunting expeditions. The spring migration of animals and birds along the Ili river provided good hunting, and he wrote to friends in Moscow that still more exciting game could be found further afield in the region of Lake Balkhash, even snow leopards and tigers: 'I decided to make a non-aggression pact with tigers.'

Trotsky's obsessive and voluminous political correspondence during this period is leavened with poetic descriptions of the country-side and vignettes from his hunting and fishing trips. 'My son and I made a trip to the Ili river, taking with us tents, skins, fur coats etc. Our boots froze at night, and we had to thaw them out over the fire to get them on our feet.' The men hunted in swamp and open lake, spending up to fourteen hours a day among the reeds. Not since childhood in the Ukraine had steppe, lake and mountain played such a part in Trotsky's life.

Some of the expeditions lasted up to ten days. 'One does not often have such experiences as spending nine days and nights in the open air, without having to wash, dress or undress, eating venison cooked in a pail, falling from a horse into the river (this was the only time I had to undress under the hot rays of the noon sun), and staying days and nights on a small log in the midst of water, stone and reeds.' Trotsky wrote that he enormously enjoyed his temporary 'relapse into barbarity' – an unfortunate choice of words.

In between hunting trips, he wrote for fourteen hours a day. 'I have not left the house,' he told a friend. 'I have simply been sitting over a book, working with my pen from about seven or eight o'clock in the morning until ten at night.' To earn a living he translated and edited obscure works by Karl Marx for a Moscow publisher, and he began his autobiography, *My Life*.

In Almaty, summer brought a variety of perils: malaria was rampant and rabid dogs roamed the streets, while the newspapers reported an alarming number of leprosy cases. The family moved into a cottage in the foothills of the mountains. 'We rented a peasant house from a fruit grower,' Natalya wrote, 'with an open view of snow-capped mountains, a spur of the Tien Shan range.' When it rained the roof leaked and a collection of pots and pans were laid out in the loft to catch the water.

'With the owner and his family, we watched the fruit ripen – the famous Aport apples, huge and red – and took an active part in gathering it. The orchard was a picture of change. First the white bloom; then the trees grew heavy, with bending branches held up by props. Then the fruit lay in a motley carpet under the trees on straw mats, and the trees, rid of their burden, straightened their branches again. The orchard was fragrant with the ripe apples and pears, and loud with the buzzing of bees and wasps.'

Natalya made jam to the accompaniment of the incessant distant clatter of her husband's typewriter. Trotsky worked in a thatched hut in the orchard and happily watched a shrub grow through a crack in the floor until it was knee-high. His small workroom was littered with manuscripts, files, newspapers and clippings. Leo worked in a room beside the stables, doing research for his father and dealing with the post.

Three times a week a crippled postman arrived on horseback to deliver a bulging postbag of letters, books and newspapers. A great many letters went out to exiled supporters all over Russia, censored and delayed by a special department set up by the local political police. Every letter was read, analysed and copied, and a summary sent each month to Stalin himself.

At the end of a day's writing, Trotsky would often walk up into the mountains, gun under arm, accompanied either by his wife or his son, but always with his dog, Maya. 'We would come back with quails, pigeons, mountain-fowl, or pheasants,' Natalya wrote. But towards the end of summer Trotsky's health began to deteriorate. His malaria returned, accompanied by severe headaches, and he suffered bouts of the chronic stomach trouble that would plague him for the rest of his life.

Delayed tragic personal news also caught up with the family. Trotsky's daughters from a previous marriage, Zina and Nina, were under constant persecution from the authorities because of continued support for their father. The youngest, Nina, had broken down completely on the deportation of her husband, and both lived in utter poverty and suffered from consumption. News of Nina's breakdown had reached Trotsky in the spring, but he remained unaware of the severity of his daughter's illness. Zina, herself wasted by consumption, nursed her sister day and night, and also grew seriously ill.

Trotsky had sent Zina a telegram: 'Am grieved that cannot be with Nina to help her. Communicate her condition. Kisses for both of you. Papa.' There was no reply. Further telegrams also went unanswered. Trotsky only learned that his youngest daughter Nina had died when a letter she wrote from hospital was delivered ten weeks after her death.

The usual torrent of letters and telegrams was slowly reduced to a trickle until communication with the outside world ceased abruptly in October. Trotsky's correspondence had served the opposite purpose to the one intended. Supposed to keep the opposition connected and alive, it had actually identified followers and provided his enemy with ammunition. Stalin now read out damning extracts from the letters to the Politburo and ranted: 'The degenerate was kicked out of the Central Committee and the Party, but he hasn't learnt his lesson. What, are we going to sit and wait for him to start organizing terror or a rebellion? I propose we deport him abroad.'

Stalin had acquired vast power by this time and stood poised to become a total dictator, but still he hesitated before imprisoning or killing such an important figure as Trotsky. Instead he decided he should be permanently exiled outside the USSR. Instructions were sent from Moscow for Trotsky's deportation, and armed guards surrounded and occupied his house. The provincial agents were somewhat in awe of their illustrious prisoner, listened politely to his protests and apologized courteously for ignoring them. They willingly lent a hand packing his many cases of books, and Trotsky mentions in his autobiography how agreeable they all were.

At dawn on 22 January 1929, Trotsky and his family, together with the escort of secret policemen, once again set off in convoy to cross the Kuday mountain range. On the journey out they had forced their way through a blizzard, but now the weather was even worse – the harshest winter for a century. 'The powerful tractor which was to tow us over the pass got stuck up to its neck and almost disappeared in the snow-drifts, together with the seven motor cars it was towing behind it,' Trotsky remembered. 'Seven men and a good many horses were frozen to death ... We had to change to sleighs. It took us more than seven hours to advance thirty kilometres. Along the road we encountered many sleighs with their shafts sticking up.'

At the railhead they boarded the train and it was only well into the journey that Trotsky was told the destination of his exile – Constantinople, a city full of enemies. He protested to Moscow against the choice and the train was diverted into a siding out in the middle of the steppe to await a reply.

'The train stops on a side-line near a dead little station, and there sinks into a coma between two stretches of thin woods,' Trotsky wrote. 'Day after day goes by. The number of empty cans about the train grow steadily. Crows and magpies gather for the feast in ever-increasing flocks. Wasteland ... Solitude ... The fox has laid his stealthy tracks to the very train. Grippe rages in our car. The cold reaches 53° below zero. Our engine keeps rolling back and forth over the rails to keep from freezing. We were brought here at night, and we ourselves don't know where we are.' The exiles were imprisoned on the train for twelve days and nights until a decision eventually arrived from Moscow – Constantinople remained the destination.

Trotsky would never return to Russia, but spent the next eleven years in exile in Turkey, France, Norway and finally Mexico, where in 1940 one of Stalin's assassins murdered him with an ice-pick. The man who had been one of the founders of the most ruthless and sinister state machine on earth came to recall his exile in Kazakhstan as one of the most pleasant times of his life. He had shot duck on the Ili river and hunted wild game in the mountains, fished in the rivers and lakes, and written endlessly. Natalya recalled the Kazakh interlude as a golden period, a year at the foot of the Tien Shan range on the borders of China, 250 kilometres from the railway and 4,000 from Moscow, a year with letters, books and nature.

The portrait of Trotsky in exile, stripped of his power, suggests a bookish, left-wing intellectual with a love of hunting, more sinned against than sinning. In power, he had displayed different traits. I asked my Kazakh friend, the professor of philosophy with a soft spot for Lenin, if things might have turned out differently had Trotsky triumphed over Stalin. 'Much the same, I'm afraid,' he said. 'Much the same.'

◆

Young Kazakhs seem to have taken the horrors of the Stalinist era in their stride. Just as Che Guevara is mostly remembered as an emblem on a T-shirt, so Lenin and Stalin are now motifs in a trendy Almaty restaurant. The philosopher's son invited me to join him for dinner in this nook of Soviet nostalgia, before going out on the town with his groups of friends – his 'boys'.

We met at the Revolutionary Military Council, a Post-Modernist, capitalist eating-house heavy on irony and light on politics. The place was decorated with Soviet Russian posters, with murals of the history of the sputnik on one wall, and the Red Army band on horseback on another. A large hammer-and-sickle was cut artfully into the plaster of the ceiling, and there were matching light fittings. A bust of Lenin – 'Our Beloved Leader' – sat on a shelf, unbeloved and irrelevant in the cold judgement of the history in which he believed. Lenin was also depicted on placemats advertising Coca-Cola. The waiters and waitresses wore red USSR T-shirts and white Young Pioneer neckerchiefs, and handed out Soviet-era postcards with the menus: there was one of dear old Lenin exhorting the masses, while 'Uncle Joe' Stalin sat at a desk, cuddly as a koala, burning the night oil.

'Strange, really,' I said. 'How everybody accepts all this as harmless nostalgia, just a joke. And yet Stalin was a mass murderer – worse than Hitler. And Lenin invented the terror state. It's inconceivable to think of a Nazi beer cellar in Berlin hung with swastikas, with the waiters dressed up as SS officers handing out postcards of Goebbels, and a bust of "Uncle Adolf" in the corner.'

'They don't have a place like that?' my friend asked, dramatically missing the point.

'No, they don't. An Indian opened a café in Bombay called "Hitler", with a picture of the Führer in the window, and there was hell to pay. In Germany it would be against the law.'

'Against the law?' My friend seemed genuinely puzzled. 'The German government controls history? What about Western freedom of speech?'

We were entering deep water. I sighed and studied the menu. A Young Pioneer arrived at our table and we ordered food and vodka – 'Two hundred grams'. The vodka arrived in a carafe together with a plate of herring, potato and onion. The combination lined the stomach, my friend said, and made intoxication virtually impossible. Furthermore, he added, vodka should not be sipped in the manner of a Western cocktail but banged back in one. Constant, birdlike sipping made you drunk. We toasted each other, downing our vodka in one, confident of perpetual sobriety. 'Another two hundred grams!'

A great deal of food arrived, with the dishes served all at once so that courses overlapped one another. More toasts were made – to Kazakhstan, England, wives, friendship, health, newborn babies – and I banged back half a dozen glasses. 'Another two hundred grams!' Before one toast I forgot to have a mouthful of herring and potato. 'Be careful,' I was warned, 'you'll get drunk.'

We moved on to meet 'the boys' in a pleasant open-air bar called 'Soho' that had tables in a wooded garden and was packed with well-dressed young people out on the town. A typical Kazakh mix – two ethnic Kazakhs, one half-Kazakh half-Russian, an ethnic Russian and an ethnic Korean – the boys spoke Russian and displayed the playful camaraderie of many years of friendship. They were all fashion-conscious, wearing expensive designer jeans and shirts, and carrying the latest sleek models of mobile phone. Everyone seemed to have invested heavily in their watches. 'Girls expect a guy to wear a cool watch,' one explained.

The philosopher's son had recently had a baby boy, and this seemed to be a source of envy for the others, although they teased him about his loss of freedom. But fatherhood confers status in Kazakh culture, and the government encourages young people to have large families. 'All Kazakh babies are born with a birthmark at the base of their spine, like a purple bruise,' my friend told me. 'This disappears in a few days. Korean and Japanese babies have this too, but not Chinese. Strange, huh?'

The Kazakh rituals of birth were explained to me. The first thing the proud father did was to call up his 'boys' and take them all out for a drink. Not to do this was considered very impolite. A grandmother usually moves into the home to help, and only close family are allowed to see the baby for the first forty days of its life, after which a big party is thrown for friends and relatives. 'There were a hundred people at the party for my son and I got this chef to come in and cook a *plov* with this special rice. Very expensive. It takes in just the right amount of water and never gets soggy.' *Plov* is a delicious mixture of rice, onions, carrots and raisins, and is always served at serious feasts, often with *shashlyk*, marinated kebabs of lamb or beef.

I asked the Korean and the Russian when their families had arrived in Kazakhstan. They looked at one another for support. 'I don't know,' the Korean said. 'A long time ago.'

'Yeah, my grandparents were born here,' the Russian said. 'We've always been here.'

I asked if there was any friction since independence because of their different ethnic backgrounds.

'Why?'

'Well, history maybe ...'

'Not really,' said the Russian, shrugging. 'I don't speak Kazakh, though. But I suppose my kids will. That's about it. In the future Russians will need to learn Kazakh.'

The boys were of a generation that remembered Soviet times not as a criminal and moral hell, but simply as a period of privation and lethargy. By the time these 30-year-olds were in their teens the moribund system had lost even its ability to cause fear, and had sunk into a stagnant, all-embracing bureaucracy dedicated to incompetence. They looked back on the Bad Old Days with good humour, seeing them as a source for a hundred shared anecdotes: 'I remember sitting on the back of a truck in winter and my feet were freezing,' one of the boys said. 'My friend had been in Moldova and come back with a new pair of felt boots. There had been no felt boots in Almaty for ages. So he let me borrow his boots for part of the journey to warm my feet up, and then I gave them back to him.'

Everyone laughed. Other hardships were cheerfully remembered, such as student graduation parties where people scoured the town and queued for hours to buy a few bottles of beer, and the occasional bottle of vodka, which were then hoarded until there was enough for a decent celebration. 'Yeah, once I queued for three hours at a place for beer, and when I got to the front they only had apple juice! But even bottled apple juice was scarce, so I bought six bottles for my mother.' It was cheerfully agreed that the Soviet system was such that it could create a shortage of sand in the Sahara.

A series of New Russian jokes followed, mocking the nouveau riche class that has risen from the ashes of Communism: 'Ivan is doing really well at the bank and buys a new three-bedroom apartment in a great new building, and a brand-new car. He is always well dressed in the latest fashions of the most expensive designers. He has a Piaget watch and Italian shoes. He invites a friend over for dinner to show off his new furniture, his stereo, his plasma TV. Everything is great and his friend is really impressed. Then the friend goes to the bathroom and is shocked to find only squares of newspaper on a nail instead of lavatory paper. When he comes out he says, "Ivan, what's the matter? You've got everything, a great new car and this beautiful apartment – why newspaper in the lavatory?" Ivan's eyes fill with tears: "*Nostalgia!*"'

The talk turned to where to go next. It was Friday night and the town would be hopping so it took a while to reach a consensus over a club. Mobile phones were snapped open and assignations made. Nothing really got going until after midnight, when coiffed and scented Kazakh beauties thronged the fashionable spots. Eventually, a decision was made. 'Best place at the moment,' my friends said, 'is the Admiral Nelson.'

'The Admiral Nelson?' I was incredulous. 'You must be joking?'

The streets around the club were full of new cars driven by smart-looking young men with pretty girls. 'Almaty on a Saturday night is like a car show,' one of the Kazakhs said. 'You name the make – it's here. Ferrari, Maserati, Lamborghini ...' The chic thing in town is to have a personalized plate with special numbers on it – like 777, considered very lucky, or 007, considered droll. Or even 911, which I considered sinister. Apart from the name, the Admiral Nelson was mercifully restrained in its nautical, horn-piping theme, and not on the foreign businessmen's beat. There was something depressingly seedy about most of these places, I would later discover, with their inevitable congregations of noisy, drunken men and accompanying hustle of hookers.

The girlfriends of the single men of our party arrived, and the couples peeled off to dance. I stood at the bar with the remainder of the boys drinking vodka. I think I proposed a joke toast to Trotsky, which elicited no reaction whatsoever. 'Another Enemy of the People exiled to Almaty,' I said. 'He liked to go duck hunting on the Ili river.'

There was a brief conversation about hunting. All the boys liked to hunt with rifles or shotguns, and in winter they shot rabbits on the steppe at night. They also went on long weekend expeditions into the wilds after bigger game, and I was given a sure-fire remedy to stop diarrhoea when out in the sticks: a shot glass charged with a fifty-fifty mixture of vodka and salt – 'Like swallowing a sack of cement.'

After midnight the beautiful people of Almaty began to show up in force. And they really were beautiful. The girls were elegant, well turned out and of extraordinary variety. I tried to differentiate between them.

'That one Kazakh?'

'Yeah.'

'That one Kazakh?'

'Maybe half-Korean.'

'That one Kazakh?'

'Yeah, but you know, a potato nose.'

'Potato nose?'

'That's what we call Russians.'

Our Russian friend said nothing, neither upset nor amused – it was obviously accepted local argot that offended no one. I asked what the Russians called the Kazakhs but nobody answered.

'I'll tell you what Russians call Kazakhs,' one of the ethnic Kazakhs said to me when we were alone. Baurzhan, although one of 'the boys', was actually in his early forties – ten years older than the others – and a successful businessman. He was exceptionally tall for a Kazakh, and as a 13-year-old had played basketball all over the USSR, and been paid a good salary. 'Later I went to Moscow University,' he said. 'And I learned what Russians call us. "Black Arses." Everybody darker than them is a "Black Arse". At university I tried to join basketball teams and they would say, "Wrong colour!" One of the other students called me a gook and I got into a fight and hurt him badly. It was a big scandal, and I got kicked out.'

Baurzhan, the philosopher's son and I decided to leave the couples and move on to join another group of friends at a nightclub they were thinking of buying, called 'Heaven'. Although there are plenty of taxis in Almaty, it is usual to hail any passing car that looks empty. The drivers, happy to earn petrol money, often stop and take on passengers. We piled into an ageing Volga and, after haggling briefly over the fare, drove to the club.

There was elaborate security on the pearly gates of Heaven in the form of a 300-pound Kazakh St Peter, who questioned our suitability for entrance. After some indignation and argument we were allowed upstairs. Our host stood at the top to welcome us. Suddenly, two Kazakhs burst out of the bar area in a fight and reeled towards us. They were well-dressed young men, very drunk and very angry. And possibly very rich, for the bouncers were surprisingly gentle in the way they dealt with them. My friends immediately pushed me against the wall, shielding me with their bodies. 'Sometimes these guys get out knives.'

The club seemed practically deserted. We avoided the bar and went directly to a VIP booth in a side room where three young men sat at a table with an iced bottle of expensive-looking vodka on it. My host introduced me with a toast. I threw back a glass of vodka. And after a couple of minutes I did the right thing by responding with a toast of gratitude. It seemed as if no sentiment could ever be considered sincere unless it was followed by a shot of vodka. I began to wonder how many more toasts I could bang back without dying.

I took a spin around the club and passed a couple of lap dancers. Idle through lack of custom, one girl was sitting on the bar, naked except for a cowboy hat and thong. She tipped her hat in my direction in a gesture of absolute boredom. A second girl, naked except for a pair of red panties, sat beside a pole in the centre of a tiny ebony stage, filing her nails.

On my way back to the booth I passed a couple of potato noses with exposed belly buttons, dressed in tight jeans and flimsy tops. They whooped at me loudly. It was the global cry of the airhead, the crass modern holler of phoney enthusiasm and synthetic fun. Back at the booth, I remarked on the lonely lap dancers and the airheads reduced to whooping at foreign drunks.

'Not much action here,' our host said. 'I don't think we'll be buying this club.'

Baurzhan began to tell me about doing business during the wild times directly after independence. 'At first I felt nothing about independence. There had been no hope before, and I assumed there would be no hope again. It wasn't like in Stalin's time when you got killed, it was just that nothing was possible. People were resigned to nothing. So I thought: "Make some money while you can. It might all go back again." When the Soviet Union collapsed everybody had a horrible time. No meat, no sugar. At eleven o'clock in Almaty it was so dark it was like you'd closed your eyes.

'Inflation was running at 30 per cent a month at least. So you took a loan from a bank in local currency, used it to buy dollars, and waited. You'd pay off the loan and borrow twice as much the next month. And buy more dollars. And so on. Easy money!

'I'll give you an example of the sort of deals we used to strike in those days. A guy says he has three lorryloads of metal. I say I'll take five – and we make a deal. Then he goes off to find the metal and I go off to find the money. Another deal – I would buy a Lada car for 3,000 roubles and drive it to Balkhash and exchange it for ten tons of copper ingots. I'd bring the copper back to Almaty and sell it to Chinese traders from over the border for cash. Six hundred kilometres of horrible roads – but 300 per cent profit in a week. Yeah, you had to bribe the police – and yeah, you had to deal with the gangsters. The gangster problem was ridiculous and quite dangerous. Walking through Panfilov Park in those days was a heroic act. But you had to show you could stand up to them. If you didn't, you were finished.'

This anarchic style of business, along with the worst excesses of corrupt police, blackmailing gangsters, and muggers in Panfilov Park, came to an end around 1996. 'You go to Uzbekistan or Kyrgyzstan and there are a few very rich people,' Baurzhan said. 'Richer even than our rich – and we have half a dozen billionaires listed in Forbes. But in these other countries it's unbelievable. Crazy rich. But they have no middle class. People have no hope for a better life. Ever. So it's a mess. A middle class was made here – you make a middle class, you make a country.

'I came to realize that suddenly it was now possible to do real business. Not cowboy stuff. I was trying to sell some kind of metal concentrate to an Italian company and they said they would only buy it if this English company from Liverpool guaranteed the quality and quantity. And I thought that would be a hell of a business for Kazakhstan. So I met the Englishman who ran the business and said I wanted to open an office here. I had zero English. We shook hands. And it was done. He took a big risk, and he did everything for me.

'I was making maybe ten thousand a week cowboy style then, and this guy offered me five hundred a month. I said okay. My friends thought I was crazy. But I saw it as a big opportunity. In four years he made me a partner. And today I have one hundred and fifty staff and offices in twenty regions of Kazakhstan, three offices in Uzbekistan, three in Kyrgyzstan, seven in Russia, two in Mongolia, two in Ukraine and two in Germany. All done on a handshake. This guy did everything for me – on trust. So I have really come to respect English people.

'He lives in Liverpool. I like Liverpool. First time I went to England I was told I would be taken into a pub, given a pint of warm beer and told that the beams were three hundred years old. So I arrived and my partner took me to a pub in Chester. He bought me a pint of warm beer and pointed at the beams and said they were three hundred years old. It was very nice.'

There had been a number of toasts interrupting this discourse, and suddenly it was my turn again. I raised my glass, spilt half its contents, and had to be recharged. I raised my glass again, so carefully it seemed like slow motion, and declared that in the spirit of scientific research I wished to announce that, whereas it might be true that banged-back vodka possibly made a person less drunk than the same amount sipped, I had discovered that two bottles of the stuff drunk rapidly, regardless of potato and herring intake, made you very, very drunk. Nevertheless, before my sad and early death, I wished to propose a toast to the boys, Baurzhan, Liverpool and warm beer. This twaddle, which I considered mildly amusing at the time, was received with polite bemusement and a collective mental shrug. I think they thought I was drunk.

I don't remember going anywhere else. And I'm not sure how I got back to the apartment, and God only knows how I managed to punch in the code and unlock the door. I *do* recall reeling around and groaning a lot. The floor moved, the ceiling spun, and I told myself that I had not drunk so much in, oh, *years and years*. In the manner of an old campaigner I downed Vitamin C tablets and drank glass after glass of water in an attempt to take the edge off the imminent and inevitable hangover. I tried to figure out how many toasts had been drunk, the alcoholic equivalent of counting sheep, and soon nodded off – or, more accurately, passed out cold.

The philosopher's son rang late the following morning to ask how I was. 'Alive. But off my food. How about you?'

'A bit hung over.' He sounded surprised.

CHAPTER THREE

◆

NATIONAL TREASURES

I was in Almaty for the first snow of winter. The fall began at night and was so fine it seemed like a trick of the light, no more than frozen air. The snow continued lightly all the following day, and by evening it was coming down hard. Within twenty-four hours the town was under a thick blanket of white.

Kazakhstan in winter is a different country to Kazakhstan in summer, another reality. And yet everything continued as usual. Beaten-up Ladas with bald tyres slid and shuddered at traffic lights but somehow found traction to pull away, while heavy lorries about to jackknife skidded skilfully back on track. Skinny domestic cats took on the appearance of miniature Siberian tigers, bounding with delicate distaste through snowdrifts. I saw a tabby curled up fast asleep on one of the fat, above-ground heating pipes that deliver warm air to the older buildings, oblivious to the falling snow, dreaming of fish.

On foot the citizenry demonstrated a peculiar gait for negotiating the packed snow and black ice underfoot – a geisha trot of small, determined steps allowing them to correct a sudden loss of balance without pause. Women in long fur coats and high-heeled boots, with mobile phones glued to their ears, automatically adopted this oriental shuffle, while men with hands dug deep into pockets, cigarettes stuck between lips, demonstrated the masculine version of a sudden boxer's bob. The whole Almaty icecapade was a wonder of rapid, instinctive human adjustment to altered conditions.

There is one new winter hazard in Kazakhstan, however, that defeats even the inner gyroscopes of the ice-canny natives, and it is taking an ever-increasing toll all over the country. Prosperity has led to the widespread and inappropriate use of marble on the floors of swanky new buildings, a hazard that has caught both nomad and Russian unprepared. As people come into the heated buildings, stamping snow from ice-encrusted boots, small puddles of melting slush form on the stone surfaces, turning them into disguised and treacherous ice-rinks. I rarely saw anyone fall on the street, but the pratfalls inside these ice-rink foyers of nouveau riche mansions were numerous and spectacular.

Slithering and juddering through the icy streets in boots with a tread like tyre, I attempted to imitate the local gait as I made my way to a compound surrounded by a high wall of corrugated iron in a rough part of town. Known as Treasure Island, this is the workshop of Krym Altynbekov, who is something of a national treasure himself. In Soviet times Krym studied at the Moscow State Institute for Restoration and worked at the Hermitage, in St Petersburg. Since independence he has investigated the methods of restorers all over the world. Almost every archaeological treasure discovered in Kazakhstan over the last twenty-five years has passed through his hands and been lovingly restored by those same hands – fabulous jewellery of the Huns, weapons of the Mamelukes, priceless artefacts from the Ahmet Yasevi Mausoleum, silverwork inside Almaty Cathedral, and the wondrous objects of ancient Scythian culture.

I was taken to this magical place by Yermek Zhangeldin, a small, compact Kazakh of quiet charm, who when first introduced handed me a card bearing the words 'Art Critic'. Resisting an urge to bolt, lest I become overwhelmed by waves of steppe-style opaque language and convoluted thought, I soon understood that Yermek's interpretation of the critic's role was to discover and enthuse about gifted Kazakhs in the plastic arts. And he certainly enthused about Krym, whom he described as a genius. (I later discovered that Yermek, who was always selflessly promoting others, was one of the country's leading scholars. He had been curator of the National Museum, and displayed an encyclopaedic knowledge of every aspect of Kazakh history and culture.)

It was quite a business entering Krym's compound and involved several calls on Yermek's mobile phone. Eventually there was a rattling of chains from behind the metal fence, and the sound of bolts being pulled back, and I wondered if the National Treasure might be a tad paranoid. A slight, smiling man greeted us with a peal of delightful, childlike laughter.

Inside it soon became clear why Krym was serious about the security, for we had entered a genuine treasure house. The space was a workshop, office and museum. Antiquities were everywhere. Krym casually handed me a small gold snow leopard. 'That is two, three thousand years old,' he said.

Pinned on the door of Krym's office is a strange, flowing chart published by the government's Office of Ethnography, which places distinguished Kazakhs directly descended from Genghis Khan in an elaborate family tree. In old Kazakh society, from the sixteenth century, those descended from Genghis Khan formed an aristocracy known as *Tore*, the White Bone, and bore the title Sultan from birth. They were beyond the law and immune from corporal punishment. A second tier of aristocrats, greatly respected by the people but with fewer rights and privileges, were descended from the original Muslim teachers, the *khoja*. But the most important figure in any Kazakh group was the *bei* – a judge renowned for his wisdom and knowledge. *Beis* were democratically elected, and only the most respected men versed in the law were chosen. They tended to be men of natural authority and their importance in Kazakh society was enormous. Next in importance were the *batyrs*, or warriors. The most numerous middle caste, the

Black Bone, were answerable to both *bei* and *batyr*. A lower caste was made up of slaves taken in battle.

The portraits of seven Kazakhs were embedded in the official diagram of Genghis Khan's family tree, and Krym was one of them, a bona fide member of the White Bone. The National Treasure did not take his aristocratic lineage as seriously as he might, and after Yermek respectfully explained its significance, Krym did a little jig, punched both arms in the air like a footballer after scoring a goal, and laughed. 'Genghis Khan had an empire that stretched from Mongolia to Ukraine,' he said. 'Alexander the Great only controlled a quarter of the territory Genghis Khan did. And you know why he managed to take over the world?'

I muttered something about advanced military techniques and the use of heavy cavalry, but Krym waved his hand dismissively. 'Yeah, yeah, yeah ... maybe. But Genghis Khan had a great tax policy. Half a per cent. With a tax policy like that people sign up. Who wouldn't love a guy with a tax policy like that? You know what we pay here now? Forty-five per cent! It's terrible! No vast empire for us.'

Krym was clearly a lateral thinker. As he contemplated the horrors of modern Kazakh tax policy, he laughed. It was a wonderful laugh – light, infectious and fun. Krym applied it to all aspects of life, even tragedy I would discover, and used it to put things in their place. The laugh was employed to deflate the pompous, defang the dangerous, and oil the grinding cogs of daily life. It was tonic, charm and weapon. Don't let the bastards get you down, the laugh communicated – *ever, over anything!*

Krym's ancestor of course had taken over half the world, and not just by adopting liberal tax policies. Genghis Khan was a military genius who led a disciplined army of hundreds of thousands of the most fearsome mounted warriors ever encountered. The great sweep of Mongolian conquest began in Kazakhstan in the thirteenth century when an army, led by one of Genghis Khan's sons, laid siege to the Kazakh city of Otrar, situated in the south, close to the border with what is now Uzbekistan, reduced it to rubble and massacred its inhabitants. The Mongols went on to take Bokhara, Afghanistan and India in the east, then they moved westwards to overrun Hungary and Poland. After Genghis Khan's death, the lands of the empire, which stretched from Poland to the China Sea, were shared among his three sons. Most of modern Kazakhstan went to one son and became known as the Golden Horde; a second son took the lands of the Seven Rivers region – a large area of southern Kazakhstan spreading from modern-day Almaty to Turkistan in the east – known as the Blue Horde; and a third took China and Mongolia.

I told Krym and Yermek about an earnest young Kazakh intellectual I had met who gave me a hyper-nationalist view of the nation's history – stories of giant stone cities lost in the steppe and so on – and wondered why this version was so completely unknown. Krym and Yermek listened politely as I told them the history of their country, and I saw them eye one another. 'In answer to your question,' Yermek began, 'maybe some of these facts ...'

'You have been told rubbish,' Krym interrupted, and he laughed. 'We Kazakhs were under the shadow of the secret police for so long that it was wise to keep quiet about our history, which the Soviets condemned as feudal, primitive and reactionary. So when we got independence some people rushed to make things up. It is a pity, because the real history is truly extraordinary.'

The exact origins of the Kazakhs themselves are a muddle of fact, possibility and conjecture, based largely on oral history and legend. My favourite story is of a beautiful white steppe goose that turned into a princess and gave birth to the first Kazakh – kaz is Turkish for goose, ak means white. The most popular legend is of Alash, whose three sons established each of three Kazakh hordes.

Historians agree that the Kazakh people did not form until the mid-fifteenth century, when the great-grandsons of Genghis Khan, Janibek and Kerei, moved with their supporters to the western part of the Seven Rivers region of Kazakhstan. Their numbers increased over the years and the territory they controlled expanded. The name Kazakh came into use around this time, possibly derived from the Turkish word *qaz*, to wander – more likely, I must admit, than white goose. By the end of the fifteenth century the Kazakh khanate encompassed all of the area that is Kazakhstan today.

The next century saw the evolution of the three Kazakh hordes – known as Juzes – which survive to this day. The hordes were defined by geography rather than common ancestry, and gave stability and order to a vast and borderless territory. The Great Horde took the Seven Rivers region, the Middle Horde territory to the north as far as Siberia – using central Kazakhstan as summer pasture – while the Small Horde took the low and dry region west and north of the Aral Sea. Each spoke the same language, and today, despite the thousands of kilometres over which their territory stretches, there are no regional dialects and scarcely any difference in accent. The first question a modern Kazakh still asks of another is what horde he is from. But tribal rivalries have been exaggerated and misunderstood in the West, and while Kazakhs from the same horde feel an automatic affinity for one another, there is no hostility to somebody from one of the others.

'Our people have many epics and legends, oral testimony of historical events, but little physical evidence exists to corroborate them,' Krym said. 'And without this they are only legends. This is why I find restoration work so exciting. In order to study and understand our history, we need to preserve these material treasures which carry the spiritual message of the past and bear witness to the ancient traditions.

'To make things "speak" they must first be "healed". The work requires a huge commitment and intense research. The job is physically hard and dirty, and a lot of people don't want to do it. But I've always believed these ancient objects hold a great secret. As you work with them, they start to reveal their secret – like a flower opening in spring. A very exciting moment.' He handed me an ancient Scythian pillow of solid black wood with an indentation for the head. 'That's twenty-five centuries old – it took five years to restore.' Suddenly, the block took on mysterious and magical properties.

The most famous restoration work Krym has undertaken is of the Scythian Golden Man, who has become an unofficial symbol of the country. 'The Golden Man was found buried in a kurgan [burial mound] in 1969,' he said. There are thousands of kurgans all over the country, even in downtown Almaty – one was found as late as 2004 in the middle of an apartment block. Naturally, most of them have been plundered.' The miracle about the kurgan of the Golden Man was that while its outer chamber had been entirely ransacked, an inner chamber full of price-less gold artefacts remained hidden for thousands of years. The corpse of the warrior chieftain was covered in chain mail consisting of 4,000 cast platelets of gold attached to a garment of leather like the scales of an armadillo, and each platelet was inscribed with intricate decoration. The figure lay next to a gold-tipped spear and held a whip with a haft bound in gold.

'The Soviets didn't pay much attention to the discovery. They were interested in the gold, but not in the wooden artefacts that were 4,000 years old – it was just rubbish to them. So much soggy wood. And then of course the Golden Man didn't fit with Soviet culture because the Sak, or Scythians, only buried people from the highest strata of society in kurgans. Warrior chieftains and suchlike people. No proletarians in the kurgans! So the Golden Man was politically incorrect.'

Krym worked on the Golden Man for twenty years with a large team of people under him, and top restorers from France, Germany, England, Italy and Russia contributed their talents. 'The level of workmanship on the Golden Man was as great as that of ancient Egypt under the pharaohs. It revealed a people with a very high level of culture in terms of philosophy and mythology – a people who observed the cosmos. And it revealed a very high level of skill in regard to working with metal, and of physics and chemistry. The work is perfect – perfect!'

The objects found with the Golden Man were either solid gold or made of wood and covered in gold. Krym first needed to conserve the ancient, sodden wood before tackling the delicate task of restoring the object. He had discovered that the best laboratory in the world to restore wood with the consistency of sponge was in Grenoble, in France. 'But the technology employed was very expensive. Kazakhstan was going through a difficult transition period after independence, and there was no money for anything. So I developed my own method. I use a polythymolglycol and alcohol solution to replace the water at a controlled temperature. The process is very complicated and takes time. A centimetre of wood takes eight months to restore. But what would cost a thousand dollars in the West only costs me twenty.'

Peter the Great was the first to recognize the artistic value of the artefacts of the steppe nomads, and he ordered that looted art from the kurgans should be bought up and sent to St Petersburg. This formed the basis of the great collection in the Hermitage, made even more spectacular when in 1929 the Soviet archaeologist Sergei Rudenko investigated kurgans in the Pazyryk valley, north of the Altai mountains. Over the next twenty years Rudenko found more than a thousand perfectly preserved objects, dating from 400 to 200 BC, in five kurgans in the same valley. All the burial mounds had been looted of their gold, but they still contained human and animal remains, wall hangings, pottery, furniture, saddles and sacred objects.

'It seems that the high point of our national Kazakh art lies in the distant past,' Krym said. 'Wax casting is considered a modern innovation but these ancient craftsmen were masters of it. They also performed perfect micro-soldering without a magnifying glass or special instruments, something even modern jewellers cannot do. And yet this was a secret possessed by our ancestors.'

The Ministry of Culture only funds a small part of Krym's work. The rest he pays for out of his own pocket by creating and selling exquisite reproductions of the ancient jewellery in Europe – golden Scythian deer with turquoise eyes, beautiful snow leopards and strange mythical beasts. All his money goes into running the laboratory. He has never owned an apartment and still lives with his wife's parents. He jokes that much of the work is done by slave labour, by which he means his family: his wife Saida is in charge of the archive, while his daughters Dina and Elina, who graduated from the Hermitage school of restoration, help him in his work. Talented nephews undertake the complex casting of the reproductions. Krym handed me an exquisite silver eagle that seemed as old as time: 'Made that last week,' he said.

Krym spends endless hours in the workshop, and he also accompanies archaeologists on digs as a restorer. 'They call me in to take out the mummies and artefacts, like a paramedic in an emergency ambulance – the wood crumbles within fifteen minutes of being exposed to the air but we have the technology to save it. The Scythians mummified people and horses. But while the ancient Egyptians dried out bodies to mummify them, here in Kazakhstan they developed a form of artificial refrigeration, using ice from the mountains and some chemical technology. They kept the bodies frozen until they were ready for burial in the kurgans, and used layers of wood and bushes as insulation to create icebox conditions. Most mummies have been destroyed by grave robbers over the centuries, but we have been able to save a few.'

Another of Krym's great achievements has been his work on the fabulous Berel treasure, named after the place where it was found. The remains of a nomadic chieftain and a woman, preserved by permafrost and lying in a carved larch sarcophagus, were discovered by a Russian archaeologist in a *kurgan* in the Altai mountains. Laid out in a semi-circle beside them were thirteen horses, each one complete with fabulously decorated red saddles, bits and bridles. Every inch of the tack had been decorated with multi-coloured mythical animals.

'We found out through DNA that they are mother and son. They had been buried with the same ritual, as Scythian men and women had equal rights and fought alongside one another as warriors. But the bodies had completely different decoration. The nomads have a saying that a person comes into the world riding a horse and leaves the world riding a horse. So the sacrificial horses would have been placed there to take them into the next world. And the beautiful items of jewellery were coded messages to the gods. This is why the Kazakhs, though they are Muslims, are slight in their religion and still pray to the spirits of their ancestors, to fire, to the sun, to the sky.'

The finds in the *kurgans* have radically changed the way in which scholars think about the ancient steppe nomads. Though in the popular imagination of the West they are still regarded as savage barbarians, all the evidence now points to the contrary. Nomad mastery of the horse around 1000 BC was in itself a great technological leap forward, enabling mankind to travel long distances over short periods of time relatively effortlessly. The first horsemen were the Cimmerians, a mysterious nomadic race from the steppe north of the Caucasus, recruited by the Assyrians as mercenary cavalry as early as the eighth century BC. The Cimmerians were pushed from the steppe by the Scythians (broadly speaking, anyone who called the steppe, or Sea of Grass, home was considered Scythian by the ancients), and the Golden Man would have been one of their leaders.

The Scythians of early classical antiquity, and their kinsmen the Sarmatians and Alans of late classical times, were an Aryan race of blond, blue-eyed nomads from the Central Asian steppe, who at their zenith roamed from the plains of modern Hungary to those of western, or possibly central China. By the sixth century BC the Scythians had become one of the most militarily and politically powerful peoples in the world, masters of mobile warfare. Herodotus travelled to the northern shores of the Black Sea in the fifth century BC to interview the descendants of the Scythians living on the westernmost edge of the nomads' world. He used the term 'barbarian' in his book, The Histories, to describe all non-Greeks who spoke the 'babble' of a foreign tongue. For him, the term had no pejorative meaning.

The Scythians were greatly feared in the ancient world. In the sixth century BC, after the Persians defeated them in battle, their queen, Tomiris, waited nine years to take a terrible revenge. The Persian emperor, Cyrus II, was tricked into leading an army 200,000 strong into a Scythian ambush. They were slaughtered mercilessly and not a single man survived to take news of the disaster back to the Persian capital. Instead, Queen Tomiris sent back the severed head of Cyrus sown into a leather bag full of blood from his slain warriors: 'Be satiated now with the blood you thirsted for and of which you could never have enough.'

In time, the Scythians – including the Sarmatians and Alans – were driven west by the Usuns, whose culture had prospered for 4,000 years. They in turn were pushed out by the Huns, Turkic people of different racial stock who looked like Mongols and who are the direct racial ancestors of modern-day Kazakhs. It was to protect themselves from the Huns that the Chinese built the Great Wall. Under their leader Attila (Little Father), the Huns also swept across Central Asia and into Europe, and brought about the collapse of an already shaky Roman empire. But again, they were far from barbaric or primitive – the Huns developed a complex bureaucracy, codified laws, introduced taxes, spread literacy and were the first to develop a feudal land system. Attila's death in AD 453 led to the disintegration of the Hun empire and plunged the steppe into chaos.

To the city dwellers of Athens, and later Rome, the endless waves of attacking horsemen from beyond the known world came to engender terror. The steppe seemed to be an evil cauldron periodically unleashing forces bent on destroying 'civilization' – in time Scythians, Sarmatians, Huns and Mongols swarmed out of the Sea of Grass, overturning everything settled people had created. As the nomads built no great cities or lasting monuments, they were seen as savage and primitive, destroying all and creating nothing. Even today mention of the Mongol army of Genghis Khan suggests mindless slaughter and rapine. The concept of the 'barbarian at the gate' has been passed down to us in Europe through the ages: in the First World War the black propaganda of the British dubbed the Germans 'Huns', in other words brutal and cruel; in the 1990s the term was used to describe ruthless and uncaring corporate raiders.

'It's all a bit muddling, these Scythians and Huns and Mongols, roaring across the steppe,' I said.

'The Scythians, the Sarmatians and the Alans are vanished races,' Krym said, 'so we are having to recreate them. As for the Huns, they are supposed to have had no written language, but they did. We have found a sixth-century text in Turkic, but we have no Rosetta Stone to break the code. Perhaps you can see why it captures my imagination – why I find it so exciting, bringing all this back to life.'

•

Earlier, I had expressed a desire to meet the men who hunted with eagles – the berkutchi, or eagle rulers – and now Krym told me he was going to take me to one of the greatest. 'You can put on a Kazakh hat, pay a thousand dollars a day, and go as a tourist,' Krym said. 'Which is not so bad ... maybe nice. Or you can pay for petrol for Yermek's car and come with us.'

We piled into Yermek's battered Lada and took off in the snow. There was an exchange in Kazakh, which I later guessed went something along the lines of 'I hope you know where you're going this time, Krym.' And a riposte from Krym that it didn't really matter with Yermek driving a beaten-up Lada through deep snow, as we'd never get there anyway. Either way, early on I thought the expedition doomed.

On the edge of the city we barely made it up a small hill, and Yermek lost control of the car as we crested it. The Lada slid down the road on the other side at a 45-degree angle for a hundred metres, as he turned the wheel this way and that without any effect. 'Wheee!' Krym trilled happily.

The car righted itself and we ploughed on through fast falling snow. Yermek now had his nose almost resting on the windscreen and was either giving himself a muttered pep talk in Kazakh or praying. I chatted to Krym to take my mind off the hazards of the journey. Inside the office I had noticed a photo of him standing in front of a massive hammered metal mask of Lenin, and I asked if he had made it himself. 'Yes, yes ... Lenin. You like it?'

It was an extraordinary and original likeness, I said. A work of art. But there was something hard and cold about it. Both men gurgled with laughter. 'Yes, yes ... hard and cold,' Krym said happily. 'Lenin. Metal monster. Thank you!' He pretended to spray the inside of the car with machine-gun fire and laughed. 'Before the Revolution my uncle was head of Alash Orda, the first Kazakh political party, and then he was in the Duma. In 1936 he was declared an Enemy of the People and shot. His body was never returned so my father buried his hat in the cemetery instead. My grandfather was hanged in a prison near Karaganda in 1965 for saying the First Secretary was a fool – a fact secretly agreed upon by everyone in the country. After that the family changed its last name to try and avoid trouble. But grandfather's brother could not resist making anti-communist remarks, and when the authorities found out who he was they threw him out of his apartment with four children in midwinter. And in 1975 he was also hanged in prison. Other members of the family were put into psychiatric hospital for being crazy enough to be members of such a family. So after that my parents prohibited me from talking about the origins of the family.'

Krym laughed. 'We restricted ourselves to kitchen politics –

that is when you go into the kitchen, run water and bang pots, and say everything about the lousy government and the lousy ideology and the lousy communists. But as soon as you leave the kitchen you have to be very quiet. Outside the kitchen I said in a loud voice that Lenin was the best person in the world, that nobody was better than the communists. And so I was allowed to carry on with my work. My life was okay because I didn't stick my nose into other stuff. The communists thought the hard metal mask of the Lenin monster was great. "Well done, Krym! You are one of us." '

At first, Krym's accompanying laughter to all these terrible stories sounded incongruous and disrespectful, but I soon realized it was an act of defiance, a way of putting himself beyond the reach of the world's metal monsters. 'And now those days are over,' he said. 'Okay – I'll say something, not so very terrible, but before it would have got me ten years' hard labour. Sometimes we have international conferences in Almaty and invite all these famous professors to come and give lectures. They talk and go away. No practical help at all. And then the heads of departments of our museums go to Egypt with their wives – a tourist trip. Of no practical use whatsoever. A waste of money. Twenty years ago I would have ended up in the Gulag for saying that!'

It was now snowing so hard it was almost impossible to see. Yermek wound down the window to look out and a small blizzard entered the car, filling it with a flurry of snow. A ridiculous image came to me of a Kazakh Christmas gift – instead of a glass ball shaken to reveal Santa in a snowstorm, a toy Lada shaken to reveal a blizzard enveloping driver and passengers.

Krym began to give contradictory and confusing directions, in between bursts of laughter, until even his placid friend started to get rattled. The expedition was on the verge of being defeated by the elements, and we seemed to have reached a point where we couldn't go forward or back. Krym suddenly insisted that Yermek turn right and climb a hill, which he did, skidding from side to side. We were then presented with openings to five snow-filled lanes.

Yermek declared authoritatively that to go any further would be courting disaster. He refused to commit the car to any of the narrow lanes ahead unless Krym was sure – *absolutely sure* – it was the right one. Krym said that this was a very wise decision. He opened the door, climbed out, and set off on foot. Yermek and I exchanged glances. 'Does he know where he's going?' I asked.

'Possibly,' Yermek said. 'Possibly not.'

Krym had disappeared from sight, so we had little option but to follow the trail of deep footprints left in the snow. We plodded on for what seemed like a very long time and a very long way. The snow piled on our hats and shoulders, and it was bitterly cold. Suddenly, the sound of shouting in the distance reached us, followed by Krym's unmistakeable laugh.

'He has found the *berkutchy*,' Yermek said.

We came upon a wooden house surrounded by farm buildings where a piebald horse tethered to a hitching post stood in swirling snow. Krym was standing with the *berkutchy*, a tanned, rugged man in his sixties who exuded confidence and serenity (the *berkutchy* is renowned in Kazakh life as someone with great inner resource and dignity). An excited Krym conducted a series of rapturous introductions.

The *berkutchy* told me he was a Kazakh born in China who had become a victim of Chairman Mao's Cultural Revolution. To escape he risked and survived the dangerous journey over the mountains into Kazakhstan, only to be arrested by the Soviet authorities. 'Out of frying pan into the fire,' Krym said. The *berkutchy* nodded solemnly. He had been imprisoned for a year, he said, and he spent a further three under the cloud of official investigation, a condition that made life almost impossible. He related his story without bitterness or emotion: 'That was how it was then.'

We walked to a small log cabin beside the *berkutchy*'s home where the eagles were lodged. He disappeared inside and emerged minutes later with a magnificent creature on his arm. My inner excitement was matched openly by Krym, who clapped his hands in spontaneous appreciation and pleasure, and smiled from ear to ear. We were a couple of schoolboys on an adventure, having a grand old time. The golden eagle was six years old and one of the *berkutchy*'s most prized birds. I asked him about the rudiments of training, a naïve question for the secrets of the profession are closely guarded. He did, however, tell me the basics.

The *berkutchy* first spends weeks among the remote eyries of the Jungar, Altai or Tien Shan mountain ranges, where he risks his life to steal an eaglet from its nest. From then on a close relationship is established. The eagle ruler sleeps beside the eaglet for nights on end and feeds it by hand for a month. 'And they have a big appetite.' The eaglet is hooded early on to make it totally dependent on the *berkutchy*, and the absolute trust which will last a lifetime is slowly built up. When the bird has bonded, the eagle ruler begins to train it to fly from his arm and return. The first kill cements the relationship. 'The bird is given all the meat so it understands that man and eagle are partners in hunting and are not in competition.'

Time and boundless patience complete the process. 'You go hunting together, and it only takes a couple of months for the eagle to understand the advantages of the partnership. An eagle properly trained is reliable and does not turn on its ruler. But if it is treated badly, or even if it is treated with harsh words and contempt, it can turn. It is like a dog or a man. Treated properly it is grateful – if not, it turns.'

There are less than a hundred registered professional *berkutchi* in the country, although many more Kazakhs hunt with eagles as a hobby. A trained eagle will catch rabbits and small deer for its ruler, kill foxes that threaten his sheep, and even confront wolves. 'If the bird is big you can hunt for a big wolf. They fly straight into the face and go for the eyes, the neck, the snout. They do not attack from behind. In the wild they take sheep and even cattle, but they fear humans.'

I was handed a thick leather gauntlet and asked if I wanted the eagle on my arm. The *berkutchy* slipped a hood over the bird's head and moved towards me. 'Brace your arm more,' he said. 'This bird is heavy.' The eagle that stepped on to the gauntlet must have weighed seven kilos and as it settled it spread its wings to display a span of around three metres.

It began to make soft noises, then turned its head in my direction, and I saw the scimitar curve of a four-inch beak up close. The eagle could have taken out my eye in an instant or ripped open my skull with ease. I wondered if it sensed the disquiet of an amateur – no eagle ruler, but eagle-ruled. And eagle-scared. It became very still and silent. I looked towards the *berkutchy* for reassurance that this behaviour was normal. He seemed unperturbed so I relaxed. The eagle was perched upon my arm for no more than a couple of minutes, but to be so close to such a powerful and noble creature was a quiet moment of communion with the eternal.

◆

The journey back to Almaty was more treacherous than the one out, but we were all in such good spirits after our time with the *berkutchy* that when Yermek skidded on black ice or ricocheted off a snowdrift, there was hardly a pause in the conversation. This ranged from the best place in Almaty to buy pizza – fiercely contested – to just-fancy-that snippets of Kazakh history.

I was amazed to learn from an offhand remark made by Yermek that the fearsome Mamelukes of Egypt, whose rule spanned 300 years, were descended from enslaved Kazakh warriors of the nomad Kipchak tribe. He related a tale of murder and intrigue as gripping as that of the Caesars.

The Mamelukes came into being when the caliphs of Baghdad decided to use nomad slaves to strengthen their armies (the word Mameluke comes from the Arabic, *mamluk*, meaning owned).

They proved to be fine soldiers and rose to high positions in the military, until in AD 870 one seized power in Egypt. In less than ten years the Mameluke sultan had conquered the Mediterranean coast from Egypt to Syria.

Although early Mameluke rule was short-lived, they regained power in 1250, and from then on grew in strength. The Mameluke sultans were not a family dynasty but warlords of a military oligarchy, plotting and struggling against one another to gain power. Their loyal troops and administrators from the steppe spoke their own Turkic language, as well as the Arabic of their masters, and their numbers were constantly replenished with nomad warriors. The greatest of the Mameluke sultans was Baybars, an enslaved Kipchak brought from the steppe to Egypt, who rose to become a general and killed his own Mameluke sultan to seize power in 1260. During his rule he crushed the Assassins in their last strongholds in Syria, drove the Crusaders from Antioch, and extended Mameluke rule across the Red Sea to Mecca and Medina. The Mameluke sultans remained in power until 1517, when their yet more powerful Turkic kinsmen, the Ottomans, captured Egypt and hanged the last of them. But the Mameluke soldiers and administrators were useful to their new masters and were allowed to live, although a wary eye was kept on their power. When it once again grew to be too great in the early nineteenth century the Ottomans massacred them to a man.

'Well, well, well,' I said. 'So the mighty Mamelukes started out as Kazakh slaves.'

'And I am sure you are aware,' Yermek said politely, 'that it is highly probable that the legends of King Arthur and the Knights of the Round Table originated from Kazakhstan.'

'King Arthur was Kazakh?!'

'It's possible he was the Roman leader of Sarmatian cavalry posted to Britain.'

'My God, the Welsh and the Cornish will go nuts when they hear this!'

'Better suppress information,' Krym said.

It was beginning to seem as if everything was from Kazakhstan: apples, tulips, the Mamelukes ... even the legends of King Arthur and the Knights of the Round Table. I wondered whether in the fullness of time I would discover that the hot dog, the hamburger and the oven glove came from Kazakhstan. 'Was Marilyn Monroe Kazakh?'

'Yes please,' Krym said.

'I am serious,' Yermek said, looking a bit cross. 'This is not patriotic rubbish to boost Kazakhstan. Although not absolute historical fact, like the Mamelukes, it is serious scholarly speculation.'

The notion that the story of King Arthur, as much a part of British identity as warm beer and the class system, was based on ancient legends from the steppe came as a shock. To dip a toe into the shark-infested waters of Arthurian scholarship is to risk losing a leg, for academics defend long-held positions without quarter, but the theory is that the Celtic legends of Arthur are an elaboration of much older stories.

King Arthur, if he existed at all, lived from circa AD 500. The earliest written references to him date from the twelfth century, by which time historical fact and folk legend had become so interwoven that one contemporary who had heard the stories through the Bretons of France described them as, 'Not all lies, nor all true, not all foolishness, nor all sense; so much have the storytellers told, and so much have the makers of fables fabled to embellish their stories that they have made all seem fable.'

Almost a thousand years before the first stories of Arthur were written, there are historical records of steppe warriors arriving in Britain. In AD 175, the Roman emperor Marcus Aurelius sent a contingent of 5,500 Sarmatian *cataphracti* – heavily armed auxiliary cavalry – to Britain from the Roman province of Pannonia, modern-day Hungary. The Sarmatians had been pressed into service in the Roman legions after defeat in battle, and they were posted in garrisons 500-strong along the length of Hadrian's Wall, which marked the limit of Roman control in Britain. Their mission was to keep out marauding Picts and Caledonians. After their service was over they settled in Bremetennacum Veteranorum, adjacent to an important Roman cavalry post near the modern village of Ribchester, in south-west Lancashire. And no doubt in their retirement the veterans repeated the legends of the old country, and told war stories of their battles under their leader.

The commander of the Sarmatian cavalry was a Roman officer named Lucius Artorius Castus, prefect of the VI Legion Victrix, headquartered at Eboracum (modern-day York). The Welsh name Artyr is derived from the Roman Artorius, and as there was no king of that time recorded when Arthur is said to have lived, it is reasonable to regard Artorius as a likely candidate. He was charged with the defence of northern England and was a *dux bellorum* – war leader – with a distinguished military career both before and after his British posting. Born in central Italy, he had begun his career as a centurion in Syria and earned rapid promotion through service in Judaea, the Danube, Macedonia, Transylvania and Hungary. He commanded a Roman fleet near Naples, was procurator of Liburnia, and is thought to have died in the Battle of Septimus Severus, at Lyons, in AD 196. His Sarmatian auxiliaries seem to have idolized him, and many took the name Lucius or Castus themselves and named their sons after him. It is suggested that Artorius' many triumphs and victories in the north and elsewhere were later transposed to Arthur in his battles against the Saxons in the West Country.

Even if Arthur did exist, the stories of the Knights of the Round Table have little connection with the reality of the post-Roman Celtic world of ancient Britain. Celtic warriors drove clumsy chariots and were not noted horsemen. Similarly, the Romans concentrated mostly on infantry rather than cavalry. The Sarmatians, as direct descendants of the Scythians, had always been mounted warriors, and there are engraved images of warriors wearing chain mail and jousting that predate medieval knights by a thousand years. They were the first great cavalry nation, 1,500 years before Europeans adopted the notion of cavalry, and they fought from horseback with swords and lances, and were able to fire bows accurately from galloping horses using deadly three-sided bronze arrows. The mounted warriors of Central Asia were also known to carry silk dragons resembling wind socks as their battle standards, which is why modern cavalry regiments are known as dragoons. Warriors were identified with individual emblems that slowly evolved into the medieval concept of the heraldic device. And the Sarmatians actually *looked* like medieval knights. They wore overlapping scale armour, conical hats and trousers, instead of the loose Roman or Celtic tunic (trousers are from Kazakhstan).

The rich Sarmatian heritage of legend, describing an epic tradition that flourished in ancient Scythia in the first millennium BC, seems to have been shamelessly plagiarized in the stories of Arthur. Just as the young Arthur draws the magical Excalibur from stone, so the Scythian god of war is symbolized by a magical sword thrust into and drawn from the earth. Similarly, just as Excalibur was thrown into a lake on Arthur's death, so the magic sword of a great warrior chieftain of the steppe is thrown into the sea on his death. And just as Arthur is said to have led his knights to the continent, so the real Artorius led an expedition to Armorica (Brittany) to put down a local rebellion. A legend on the origin of the Scythians also tells of golden objects falling from the sky, one of which was a golden cup – suggesting the Holy Grail. The numerous similarities and parallels with the stories of King Arthur begin to make the hypothesis seem obvious.

'You've convinced me,' I told Yermek.

'There are many, many more similarities,' Yermek said. 'And then, of course, there is Lancelot ...'

'Sarmatian, no doubt,' I said.

'Probably Alan – first cousins and indistinguishable from the Sarmatians, also from the steppe. They ended up in France, not Britain.'

The theory here is that Lancelot was a warrior from the Alan tribe who settled in Gaul, on the River Lot, in the early fifth century AD – Alan of Lot, Alanus à Lot ... Lancelot. A band of Alans is said to have stolen vessels from the Basilica of St Peter's during the sack of Rome in 410, including a sacred gold chalice they associated with their own legend. The vessel was taken with them to southern Gaul, the region traditionally associated with the grail legends – where it disappeared. People, including the Monty Python team, have been looking for it ever since.

'Now tell him about Marilyn Monroe,' Krym said.

Yermek looked at me and sighed, as if asking how a man could ever be serious with this character Krym, descendant of Genghis Khan, in the car. 'Modern scholarship confirms,' Yermek said, 'that Marilyn Monroe was not from Kazakhstan.'

We arrived back in Almaty to find the city buried in snow. It had not stopped falling for a moment. The friends dropped me off in front of my lodgings, and then the Lada took off, skidding crazily. As Krym wound down his window to flap a hand out of it in farewell, the car filled with snow.

CHAPTER 4

CITY OF THE PLAIN AND THE VANISHING SEA

The Arkansas romantic had told me that the Kazakhs had built themselves 'a shiny new capital out in the middle of the prairie, pretty as a picture'.

Astana – Kazakh for 'capital' – is bang in the middle of nowhere. It takes twenty-eight hours to reach by regular train from Almaty, or nine hours by a special high-speed Talgo train built by the Spanish. Even by air it's two hours, and every flight is packed or, more precisely, stuffed in winter when passengers bulk up in fur coats and felt boots. The experience is like travelling in a clothes basket. Men and women go through the elaborate ritual of wrapping their fabulous mink hats in newspaper – usually *KazakhPravda* – and placing them in plastic bags for the flight. The overhead compartments are filled to bursting point.

Just as Peter the Great built St Petersburg in a swamp, and Philip II of Spain turned a dusty village into Madrid, so President Nursultan Nazarbayev has transformed a rundown, rusting steppe town into a capital. Astana, surreal city of the plain, is a confection created by presidential decree over the past decade at a cost of 10 billion dollars and climbing. The town chosen for the world's greatest architectural makeover had previously long been in decline, inhabited largely by a Russian population of impoverished agricultural workers. Its concrete tower blocks were crumbling, the workers' housing slum-like, and the infrastructure chronically rundown. Not to put too fine a point on it, the place was a dump.

There had been plans once before under the Soviets to develop the town as the capital. Nikita Khrushchev had hoped to transform the surrounding uncultivated steppe into the breadbasket of the Soviet Union. On paper the idea looked terrific. A hundred million acres of wheat were duly sown, and Russians in their tens of thousands were encouraged to move to the region and settle.

My drive into town from the airport passed through part of the land that had inspired this grand agricultural folly, known as the Virgin Lands project. The Kazakh would have pointed out, had they been asked, that the soil could not sustain the sort of intensive cultivation planned (the original Kazakh name for the city was Akhmola, 'white grave', because of the colour of the earth). But in the 1950s, swarms of Russians and Ukranians flocked to the area around Astana to work the land, which had been traditional nomad pasture for a thousand years. At first the project seemed to be a great success and the city boomed. Then howling east winds stripped the soil from the fields, and constant irrigation poisoned what remained with a build-up of salt. The project slowly wound down and Moscow's idea of making the city the new capital was quietly abandoned.

President Nazarbayev's decision to revive the idea was taken in July 1994, and the move began three years later. The plan was universally unpopular at first, and deeply resented by the many thousands of government employees who were now obliged to leave their families and homes in pleasant Almaty to live a thousand kilometres to the north, amid the mud and clatter of a building site in the middle of the wind-swept steppe. The president justified his decision by saying that Almaty had grown from a manage-able population of 400,000 to 1.5 million, and had simply run out of space to expand. Though the mountains surrounding Almaty provide a beautiful backdrop, they trap pollution, and the area is also prone to earthquakes. Situated as it is in the extreme south-eastern corner of the country, near the border with China, the city is also a long way from the rest of the republic – the rich oilfields of the Caspian Sea are 3,000 kilometres to the west, and Kazakhstan's unstable southern neighbours are too close to Almaty for comfort. Astana, on the other hand, is in the centre of the country.

The explanations were taken with a large pinch of salt. However sound the reasons put forward, there was also an undeclared political agenda. One and a half billion Chinese live cheek-by-jowl over the mountain border, while on the Kazakh side a population of a mere 15 million have limitless space. There is nothing paranoid in the Kazakh concern over the Chinese need for living space, and their age-old claims to swathes of Kazakhstan and Siberia – to say nothing of their growing appetite for oil and gas. 'If you see a few ants in your home it is not such a problem,' a Kazakh said to me. 'But an infestation of millions and millions – then you have a problem.'

To the north, Kazakhstan shares a 7,500-kilometre border with Russia. Most of the ethnic Russian Kazakhs live in the north, and form a majority there. Today relations between the two countries are excellent, and the long border has been ratified, but directly after independence Russian hyper-nationalists laid claim to vast areas of northern Kazakhstan. There was a real fear that the Russians might revive old imperial ambitions and push south. Astana's position in the centre of the country – and its rapid influx of ethnic Kazakhs – makes any sudden land grab less likely. Neither China nor Russia poses an active threat today, but it makes good political sense to take a long view to protect Kazakhstan's future.

And so, reluctantly, like small boys on their way to school, tens of thousands of government employees moved to Astana as the various ministries transferred sections of their operation to the city. The move, which took two years, presented fewer problems from a practical point of view than originally anticipated. There was room for the country's entire government, parliament and presidential apparatus in the grandiose Soviet buildings of the old regional Communist Party. But the place was no fun, and in bad weather the winds from the steppe were an endurance test. Even the president, when planting a tree in the early days of the city, conceded: 'It is windy up here, isn't it? It certainly is windy.'

'I was among the first batch,' a senior official told me. 'There was no pressure to go, but people knew it was a career move and that those who stayed behind would be left behind in their careers as well. So the message was, "If you are excited by the idea, join us!" And we were warned that at first it would not be easy.'

And it wasn't. 'Astana is very cold and I found it a great torture,' the official continued. 'I was born in Central Kazakhstan and taken to Almaty when I was two months old, so that was my home. Just moving to Astana was a feat – you were going nowhere and didn't know what to expect. The first winter was terrible because people from Almaty were not used to such harsh weather. Not that we were spending much time outside. People looked forward to summer, but this brought new tortures – dust and mosquitoes. Even locusts! The mosquitoes were so bad that a special effort had to be made to control them. My own theory is that government personnel proved so untasty the mosquitoes moved away.'

Conditions demanded a pioneering spirit. The offices were old and shabby, accommodation was scarce, and for the first year families remained behind in Almaty. Even senior members of the administration were expected to share cramped apartments, while the young lived in barracks. 'It was like the Army. People had to sleep ten to a room. It was unpopular but people understood. They were prepared to face the hardships, but it was difficult for the middle-aged. In Astana people put in twelve-hour days, arriving at the office by nine and leaving at nine at night. No overtime. And no one grumbled. Of course, one reason people worked such long hours was that the offices were warm and there was nowhere else to go!'

There were no bars or restaurants and only one hotel in the whole town. 'A provincial Soviet hotel with a provincial Soviet restaurant, serving one starter and one main course. The local standard of food was terrible. They were used to a dozen customers a week, not the army of arrogant Almaty residents who sniffed at the quality of the food and service. The locals didn't understand what service is. If you asked for something they would shout at you. "Fuck off!" was in the air.'

People began to revert to the behaviour of their student days, even the most senior officials. 'We would spend twelve hours a day shouting at one another in the office, and then go home and have a party. There were fantastic feasts! The ladies were cooking, the men provided the booze. There was a lot of booze, I'll tell you! And the next morning, with party eyes and hangovers, we had to go back to the office. Actually, it was great fun, a romantic time.'

The infrastructure gradually improved, and within six months a dozen small cafés offering home cooking opened in ground-floor flats. 'I remember going to one and being asked, "Still or sparkling bottled water?" It was a shock.' Sauna baths and billiard halls opened – which in Kazakh/Russian culture always contain a decent restaurant. More housing became available, offered for sale in the private economy but subsidized 80 per cent by the government. 'I got a three-bedroom apartment, something I could only dream about in Almaty. It was fantastic! In the old Soviet days getting an apartment was the equivalent of winning the jackpot. A family of four would wait all their lives for twenty-four square metres of living space. So imagine, children of parents with that experience moved to Astana and within three years got a nice flat almost free. Parents who might have been against the move visited the kids and saw this. Housing was a great attraction.'

The newly emerging, upwardly mobile young of the middle class found the move an adventure. 'I didn't mind leaving Almaty, even though I was born there and my family is there,' a young man from the foreign ministry told me. 'I felt very good about being at the beginning of something, being part of building a new capital for my young country. It felt like being part of the future rather than the past. At first I missed Almaty and found Astana boring.

But the place gets better all the time. And now I really like it. It's home.

'One of the secret reasons for the move, in my opinion, was to get rid of the old farts. The old Soviet bureaucrats were set in cement. New people were needed to produce the new face of Kazakhstan. There was no point trying it with the old generation – new things can only be done with new people. Suddenly the average age in the foreign ministry was 30. So the move to Astana rejuvenated the government enormously in terms of this great influx of young blood.'

The pace of change in the new capital was spectacular and visible. 'When I first went you would barely see any prams on the streets. Within a year they began to appear. After two years the whole embankment was full of prams.'

Although embassies were given prime locations at good rates (the British Embassy was dedicated by the Duke of York), and businesses given every encouragement to set up shop, there was profound scepticism about the whole project among the foreign community. 'When I first went there the whole place seemed to be one great building site,' said Lord Kilrooney, a British parliamentarian who has visited the country on several occasions over the years. 'Just an ocean of mud. I thought it was folly and that they would never pull it off – the Kazakhs had bitten off more than they could chew. Frankly, it seemed impossible. And then I went back three years later and there it was – a new city. By anyone's standards, it's an extraordinary achievement.'

Astana snakes along the River Irtysh, gleaming and brash, lacking atmosphere and patina. Its population has already doubled to 600,000 and it is expected to grow rapidly to 1.5 million. The remains of the old city are fast disappearing under the relentless advance of bulldozer and wrecking ball. Building goes on day and night, and even in the early hours of a winter's morning when it was minus 30 degrees centigrade, I saw men working in artificial light high up on the scaffolding of an apartment building. The few remaining down-at-heel districts, with their unpaved streets and clumsy, above-ground heating pipes, seem hopelessly sad and dated beside the gaily coloured (and expensive) houses of the suburbs.

The city is so spanking new, so lacking in a settled identity, it seems unreal. The oriental Post-Modernist style takes some getting used to, although the locals have softened the effect by giving many of the buildings homely nicknames: a canary yellow skyscraper is known as 'The Banana Building'; three squat cylindrical structures are called 'The Beer Cans'; and 'The Cigarette Lighter' was so called *before* it suffered a catastrophic fire. (Inevitably, such an ambitious building project has had its failures: one building is known as 'The Titanic' after a huge crack appeared in its foundations; another, threatened by a crumbling riverbank, has been dubbed 'The Kursk'.) The Ministry of Finance actually looks like a dollar sign, while the sweeping curves of the Sports Centre look, well, sporty. New religious buildings stand among government ministries and banks – a spectacular mosque donated by Qatar; a big blue synagogue paid for by a Jewish Kazakh aluminium billionaire; and a large Russian Orthodox church built by public subscription.

I dropped into the central planning office, where a scale model of the entire city spreads across the whole of an upstairs floor, built to a master plan by the Japanese architect Kisho Kurokawa. A city official pinpointed all the various buildings for me with a laser beam: the presidential palace, ministries, corporate skyscrapers, churches, mosques, apartment buildings and shopping centres, all built in less than a decade.

The jewel in the crown is the Palace of Peace and Harmony, a gigantic 200-million-dollar pyramid designed by the British architect Norman Foster. Conceived by the president as a meeting-place for the world's religious leaders to promote tolerance and understanding, the pyramid has been built on a site of 90,000 square metres in the heart of the capital. A rapid building schedule was imposed on the architects, whose design team developed a construction plan using prefabricated components manufactured in

Turkey during the harsh winter months, and later erected during the summer.

The pyramid was opened in September 2006, and an architectural journalist who visited the site a week before described hundreds of workers – many of them women – and contingents of the Kazakh Army furiously working to transform a 'shrieking, fiery pandemonium into a mysterious kind of heaven ... The interior, all swirling smoke and deafening clamour, shot through with torrents of sparks, was William Blake crossed with Piranesi ... more Inca than Egyptian; like a temple ... a place to wonder at.'

The pyramid is a tubular steel frame sixty metres high built on a man-made hill concealing a 1,500-seat opera house. The base is clad in pale granite, and the entrance at the side of the hill leads into a black granite foyer and then the floor of the main hall. This has triangular glass panels set into the floor that look down into the opera house below, a two-tiered, horseshoe-shaped room lined with wood. (The architect for this was Anne Minors, who worked on both the Royal Opera House and the new theatre at Glyndebourne.) Funicular elevators, like those of the Eiffel Tower, rise up the inward leaning walls to the floors above. Two of these have been set aside to provide offices representing every one of Kazakhstan's different ethnic groups. Above them are floors housing chapels for eighteen of the country's principal religions – which number forty-six in all. At the top, a ramp surrounded by a hanging garden leads to a chamber where the world's religious leaders meet in a triennial congress. A massive lens in the floor floods the atrium below with light, filtered through an apex of blue and yellow stained glass, with a motif of giant doves in flight – the work of a British artist, Brian Clarke.

The pyramid is extraordinary both in concept and in structure, a modern multi-faith cathedral, described by Lord Foster as 'A contemporary reconsideration of religious architecture ... dedicated to the renunciation of violence and the promotion of faith and human equality.' The architect directly in charge of the pyramid's construction, Lord Foster's colleague David Nelson, said: 'It was one of those things that captures the imagination. We felt that if someone wants to bring together the world's religions, that is something that's well worth doing at the moment. As a symbol, the pyramid's not owned by any of today's religions.'

In the centre of Astana there is a tall, spiky tower with an aluminium and glass cap perched on top of it. It is a place that Kazakhs insist the outsider visits for a view of their new city. I did as directed, entered the tower, bought my ticket and rode the lift to the bubble at the top. A guide of great beauty and passivity droned the story of the tower's creation in a robotic monotone. I learned, among other things, that the tower was ninety-seven metres high to reflect the move to Astana in 1997. The guide then recited the legend behind the tower, perhaps for the hundredth time that morning. No wonder her eyes had the faraway look of an alien species.

The legend, according to Kazakh folklore, tells of a holy tree in which every night a mythological bird laid a beautiful egg bright as the sun. And every night, sure as eggs is eggs, an evil dragon devoured it. Over time, good Kazakhs grew tired of this routine and slew the dragon. And ever since, the guide droned, the sun has shone eternally, a symbol of the eternity of creation.

'But the sun doesn't shine eternally,' I said. 'It goes down every night.'

The guide ignored my comments, and led me to a raised podium in the centre of the bubble where the upturned palm of a golden hand lay on top of a pillar. It is a cast of the president's hand, I was told, and I was invited to place mine upon it. I did as instructed – and almost jumped clean out of my felt boots. The tower was suddenly filled with a roaring choir backed by a mighty orchestra, as the national anthem was belted out at full patriotic throttle.

A group of schoolchildren standing nearby giggled at my

reaction. I had the impression that they had spent most of the morning amusing themselves watching one mug after another jump in alarm as they triggered the unexpected blast of musical gelignite. I decided to stand with the children and enjoy the joke. The next person out of the lift was a sombre-looking old Kazakh accompanied by his wife. They dutifully admired the view, circled the floor, and were then led to the presidential hand.

The children and I waited, exchanging sly, conspiratorial glances. The man placed his hand on the cast. The music blasted. He stumbled back several paces, while his wife put her hand over her mouth in shock. We sniggered with pleasure.

In the lift I meditated upon what made Kazakh children so appealing. They were certainly a mixed bunch, as you might expect in a country with so many ethnic groups – but any schoolyard in London is mixed. It struck me that they were behaving as children used to behave – like children. There was none of the spoilt moaning or supercilious precocity that has become the norm in the West. These kids still had a sunny sense of fun unclouded as yet by the rigours of modernity.

My Kazakh snooker partner, Umbetov, whom I had met in London, lived in Astana and was eager to show me the town. When he understood I was serious in my plan to write about the country, and had a publisher, he told me he might be able to arrange a meeting with the president. I was asked to jot down a description of the sort of book I intended to write about Kazakhstan and my friend would see what he could so. I took this with a pinch of salt. I had read that the Wall Street Journal correspondent for the region had waited ten years for an interview. But Umbetov said that President Nazarbayev was a voracious reader, had written a couple of books himself, and was known to have a soft spot for musicians and writers. Even so, I did not hold out much hope that the most powerful man in the country would give me his time.

In the meantime, Umbetov exhibited the generosity and hospitality on which the Kazakhs pride themselves. His manner in Britain had been sophisticated and urbane, but on home ground he became a proselytizer for all things Kazakh. We visited the newly opened National Museum where the ground floor was dedicated to a self-conscious display of the symbols of Kazakh independence and the forging of a national identity. There were flags and plaques, coins and bank notes, all aimed at reminding a people who they once were and what they had become.

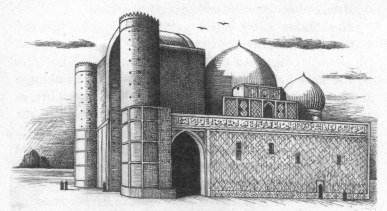

On the first floor there was one of Krym's superb reconstructions of the Golden Man. There was also a large model of the mausoleum of Sheikh Akhmed Yassawi, a twelfth-century mystic and poet, and founder of a powerful Sufi order. Made splendid by Tamerlane in the fourteenth century, it lies on the edge of the Kyzylkum desert, in the Kazakh town of Turkestan, and is Islam's second holiest place of pilgrimage after Mecca. It was closed by the communists and left to fall into ruin but has since been restored to its former glory.

Today the tomb ranks as one of Islam's architectural wonders. The entrance is monumental, flanked by tall, round towers, while behind it is the mausoleum's great aquamarine dome. Behind it a second, smaller, ribbed dome caps the tomb chamber itself, exquisitely tiled in shades of blue and white. Inside the mausoleum, in the centre of the main chamber, is a massive cauldron weighing 2,000 kilograms, hammered out of bronze, gold and zinc by

Persian craftsmen, which once held holy water. It was stolen by the Soviets in 1935 and taken to the Hermitage, where it stayed for fifty years, before it was returned in 1989 during the Gorbachev years. One of Yassawi's verses is inscribed on the wall of his tomb:

The prophet has this wish:
When one day you meet a stranger,
Do not do him wrong.
God does not love people with cruel hearts.

The surreal contrast between the old world of Kazakhstan and the new, however, was best experienced in the state-of-the-art aquarium. A peasant family posed in rigid delight in the lobby for a photo beneath a plaster replica of a giant squid. Inside, we followed in the footsteps of a file of Second World War veterans in Kazakh hats, looking impoverished and frail in threadbare suits adorned with row after row of medals, a gallant crew enjoying a subsidized day out. They wandered awestruck through glass tunnels, surrounded by an artificial ocean, while hammerhead sharks swooped overhead. There was something ancient and dignified in the wonder of these descendants of

landlocked steppe nomads in the midst of such strange, aquatic mysteries.

That night Umbetov took me to a very smart, expensive and packed restaurant with a wine list thick as a telephone directory. The waiter brought me a menu in English and my friend watched me as I read it, his eyes twinkling with mischief. Looking for traditional dishes, I came across the following: Tasteful Fingers, Pork Legs Italian, Verdure Wrapped in Dough, Whimsical Salad, Goose With Love, For Lazy Fellow, Enigmatic Dumpling, Fried Crucial Stuffed With Onion, Two Quails with Jolly Sause, Close Your Eyes and Open Your Mouth, Water Melons of Mother-in-Law, Herring Under Fur and – the near-mystical – Porridge made With Axe.

'Spoilt for choice,' I said.

'The owner is an amusing fellow whose English is not up to his sense of humour.'

'Or vice versa. I'm torn between the Lazy Fellow and the Fried Crucial.'

'Take the duck. What would you like to drink?'

'Perhaps I should try Kazakh wine.'

'Perhaps you should,' my host said. 'I'll stick to Bordeaux, if you don't mind.'

I was served a delicious wild duck, tender and tasty, and we finished off a couple of bottles of good claret. At some stage during the meal, I asked, without much hope, 'Any luck with the president?'

'I'm working on it,' said Umbetov.

Ah well, I thought, at least I got to see the aquarium.

The following day Umbetov insisted on driving me around to various sights. Something I learned quickly about the Kazakhs – especially ethnic Kazakhs – was that they respond extravagantly to anyone taking a genuine interest in their country. Instead of shaming the outsider for his ignorance, they accept it as the natural fate of a young nation, and they are happy to fill in the gaps.

In between patriotic outbursts of enthusiasm, Umbetov

spent his time on his mobile phone. It was disconcerting, especially as he became increasingly excited and distracted with every call. During a ten-minute stretch when the phone did not ring, he became distant and furtive. Then the damn thing rang again. I groaned quietly to myself. It was only a short call but when Umbetov snapped the phone shut, his face was radiant.

'It's fixed,' he said in triumph. 'You'll get to see the president.'

•

Nursultan Nazarbayev's life mirrors the post-war history of his country, a significant amount of which he has made. The son of a shepherd who worked for a Stalinist collective, Nazarbayev worked his way up from a foundry worker in a steel mill to become the republic's leader under the Soviets. Upon independence, he was elected president, and after eighteen years in power is now enjoying a third term, elected by an overwhelming percentage of the vote. Even those who question the accuracy of the numbers admit his widespread popularity.

Yet in the West Nazarbayev's image is muddled and contradictory, like almost everything about Kazakhstan. The Western media tends to lump him in with the clutch of unpleasant despots to the south, and call for regime change. Opponents within the country accuse him of stifling opposition. To the most extreme of his critics he is a megalomaniac dictator with a lot of oil and a pharaonic building complex, rigging elections and feathering his own nest.

My own unscientific research on the street confirmed the president's popularity. The blanket, universal approval became tedious. Most Kazakhs of all ages and ethnic groups genuinely seemed to like and respect Nazarbayev as a man who makes them proud of their young country. Even diehard communists spoke of him with respect for the way in which he had always fought for Kazakhstan's interests when it was a part of the Soviet Union, even if they did deplore his conversion to capitalism. The young seemed to like him most of all, particularly women.

His opponents tend to be either disaffected members of the administration who have been dropped along the way, or those who believe the government is a corrupt élite that has been in power too long, or old communists wedded to Gosplan statistics. Despite all the evidence, the communists insist that the economy was stronger in the old days, a looking-glass argument that even the most committed Marxist-Leninist would find hard to accept. More persuasive voices argue that the country's oil riches should be poured more quickly into health, education and infrastructure, and complain that the president's family is too powerful. Either way, Nursultan Nazarbayev is unquestionably the power in the land and runs the place with a firm, paternalistic hand.

Umbetov had given me a rapid lesson in diplomatic etiquette before I went to see the president. I was expected to behave myself, dress appropriately and keep the weak jokes and half-baked opinions to a minimum. Nazarbayev did not suffer fools gladly. And a final word of advice – avoid any invitations to play Russian billiards. The president was a killer!

At the hotel I changed into a jacket and tie for my meeting, and an official car drove me to the Presidential Palace. This is a vast wedding cake of domes and pillars, a place of work rather than a residence, designed to impress by its sheer ostentation and scale. Like everything else in town, it is a work in progress, and an army of workers in overalls was clearing the grounds to prepare gardens.

A foreign ministry official took me into the palace and led me through the main hall, which is flanked by hundreds of cream-and-gold pillars and hung with crystal chandeliers each the size of a small house. The interior has the proportions of a city square, and small armies are able to parade here in winter when ceremonial occasions cannot be held outside. I was deposited in a reception area hushed as a church and manned by a smartly dressed waiter serving refreshments.

My appointment was for 4.15. Powerful men in Asia do not usually exercise the courtesy of kings, so I prepared for a long wait. Or a last-minute cancellation. At 4.05 the head of protocol introduced himself and sat down. We made polite conversation: he had written the book on protocol for the new nation, no mean task. Every detail had to be delineated, from the procedure in receiving dignitaries to the size and design of the pennant on the presidential limousine. At 4.10 the head of protocol's mobile phone rang: 'The president will receive you now. Please follow me.'

We clattered back across the length of the mostly deserted hall to a doorway at the far end. A clutch of press photographers and TV cameramen were slumped on chairs beside it in a Zen-like state of professional boredom. I tried to look important, but they didn't give me a second glance. Thorough and polite security men removed my mobile phone, searched me and directed me into the president's outer office. Almost immediately an inner door opened and I was ushered through. It was 4.17. I was two minutes late for the president.

The office was an elegant room of medium size containing the president's desk and a conference table at which he was seated with a single aide. President Nursultan Nazarbayev rose, offered his hand – and subjected me to the most penetrating gaze I have experienced since boyhood. It was a hard look of evaluation, experienced and unforgiving. The last time I had been exposed to such naked character assessment was when I left my preparatory school for the senior school with a dubious reputation. Unsmiling in black robes, the new headmaster had inspected me closely and found me wanting. I feared the president might feel the same.

As a first encounter, it was unnerving. When I sat down the president asked me to describe my 'vision' of the book I wanted to write. I began to waffle. Then rabbit. Flattery and flannel would surely have followed, although I did have the sense to realize I was in the presence of a man unlikely to be susceptible to either. Instead, some self-destructive urge pushed me to desperate and pompous self-promotion. I heard myself solemnly intone: 'I would like to write a book on Kazakhstan that will be read for many years to come.'

A faint smile of disbelief played upon the president's lips. It was the response of a writer who knew the odds, rather than a president. I risked a joke: 'The president looks sceptical.'

'No, no,' he said. 'It's natural that a writer hopes his books will last. I wish you every success.'

I decided to put my cards on the table. 'In honesty, I know very little about your country, Mr President. But a stranger on a plane once made an offhand remark to me that apples came from Kaza-khstan, and somehow it captured my imagination. It made me want to know more.'

The president nodded and addressed his aide in Kazakh. I hoped it was not something along the lines of 'Get this bum out of here.' But the remark about the apples seemed to have broken the ice. 'Not much more than a decade ago,' the president said, 'a year or two after independence, I addressed a meeting of about a thousand people at Citibank. Nobody knew anything about Kaza-khstan, so I was telling them the basics – geographical location, population, that we had oil and gas and minerals, cattle breeding and so on. There was a question-and-answer period and somebody said, "Mr President, you say you have oil in Kazakhstan. Do you transport the barrels by camel?" I answered that we transport oil in the usual way, by tanker and pipeline, but continue to breed camels for foreigners to protect them from the wild wolves of the steppe. So I am not so shocked by people's ignorance of my country, but I would like them to know a little more.'

The conversation took a writerly turn. The president said that his own books had been written 'by chance'. He lacked time but picked odd moments to write and dictate – one fact reminded him of another, until he found himself unearthing long buried memories. Trawling through the past was a process both surprising and revelatory, so that when he set out to write about one thing, he ended up on another track. We discovered we both wrote first drafts in longhand and had Balzac in common as a favourite writer

... and I might have launched into a rant about secondary rights and the coded nature of royalty statements, followed by hilarious anecdotes about publishers and agents, but I realized my time was limited.

I brought up the subject I thought might be closest to the president's heart – the creation of the new capital. 'I have taken a lot of risks in my life, but Astana was the biggest gamble of all,' the president said. 'I put everything on it. Critics said I would come up here to Astana and soon hurry back to Almaty. The decision was to expand the idea of private property in a place where *everything* was owned by the State. And I knew that if I got it wrong, and it proved a terrible mistake, it would be the end of my political career as leader of the country. You have to take risks in politics.'

It was the choice of a pyramid as the centrepiece of the big gamble that led to charges of megalomania. 'Critics said I thought I was Pharaoh,' the president said. 'It's true I chose the shape of the pyramid, but as a call to energy, not as a tomb for another pharaoh. The pyramid of Giza is 18,000 years old, while the pharaohs lived only 5,000 years ago. Nobody knows who built the pyramids or why, but for some reason it is a symbolic shape that has great meaning for human beings. It seemed to me the perfect shape for a temple of peace and harmony.

'Akbar the Great had a dream of building one big temple for everyone,' he continued, referring to the medieval Mogul emperor of India. 'He was Muslim himself but was tolerant of all religions. His vision was that everyone would enter the great temple through one big gate, and once inside they would have their own temples in which to pray – Christian, Jewish, Hindu, Muslim. So everybody entered and prayed to their own God, but they arrived and departed through the gate shoulder to shoulder. I'm building that temple now.

'All the major religions insist there is but one God. Well, in my opinion that is so – but we all approach him in our own way. The Koran states that if you kill one person you have killed everyone in the world, and the prophet Mohammed has said it is the duty of Muslims to spread love among people. I want to disprove the Huntington theory which says that the clash of civilizations is inevitable because we are all different. Yes, you can prophesy disaster and apocalypse, or you can think that humans are smarter than that and will not push themselves to that confrontation.

'We have forty-six different religions in Kazakhstan operating in peaceful co-existence. No one is restricted from building his own house of prayer. No one is afraid to pray to his own God. And there is not a hint of one group deliberately offending another. The Kazakhs of the twenty-first century should be tolerant, modern people. I tell young people here that they should be citizens of the world and that for them there should be only one nationality – humankind.'

Propaganda or not, this was stirring stuff. But when I asked the president if he was an idealist, the idea put him on the defensive. Perhaps the word made him think I was suggesting he was Utopian, or a dreamer, or naïve. 'It would be good if the world's religious leaders talked to one another more often, so I have created a place to do that in a forum every three years,' he said. 'If politicians cannot solve certain problems, maybe people will listen to religious leaders. Countries lack trust in one another so I have made Kazakhstan a place where this can be built up. I do not think this is idealism. I think this is practical politics. There is, of course, an alternative. Just start the war!'

The president repositioned the blotter in front of him, and I realized the meeting was coming to an end. 'So ...' he concluded. 'How can we help you?'

Taken by surprise, I asked for assistance in getting to the more remote parts of the country, and wondered if he would talk to me again informally about his early life, and the birth of the nation. The president put his fingers together in a spire and looked thoughtful. 'I will soon be visiting the southern parts of the country where most of the ethnic Kazakh population lives,' he said. 'Taraz, a city on the Silk Road ... the Cosmodrome at Baikonur – a restricted area where I'm certain not many of your countrymen have ever set foot ... and the Aral Sea. If you would like to join me you would be welcome. And we'll find time to talk.'

•

During the flight from Almaty to Baikonur, the president stayed sequestered with his staff in a special section at the front of the plane, but he had come back before take-off to greet his guests. Casually dressed in an unbuttoned, burgundy-coloured waistcoat, he made small talk and cracked jokes with his entourage, which included the chief of presidential staff, the head of protocol, the ministers of agriculture and the arts, and the press secretary – a man of ferocious energy, sinister in wraparound dark glasses, with an attitude of permanent hostility formed by daily proximity to the media. Journalists, photographers and other riff-raff had been confined to the rear of the plane and I was regarded with the deepest suspicion when I told the press secretary I was writing a book on the country. On the journey we were served a collation of cold meats that included, as it always did in Kazakhstan, horse sausage. A sachet of Heinz mayonnaise came with it: 'Globalization,' the man next to me said.

The invitation to join the president on a three-day journey through the country was an unexpected bonus, opening doors otherwise closed tight. Baikonur, for instance, was once one of the most secret places on earth, the launch site for all Soviet space flight since Yuri Gagarin became the first human to go into space in 1961. It is now the only place in this part of the country with a landing-strip long enough to take the presidential Boeing 757 – a four-kilometre runway built to receive the Russian equivalent of the space shuttle.

When the Soviet Union collapsed, Kazakhstan not only inherited a deadly arsenal of nuclear weapons, it was also bequeathed a bankrupt space programme. No one had the money to launch anything, and living standards around the base fell so far during the early days of independence that local Kazakh troops rioted in 1993 and 1994. Since then Kazakhstan has leased the site to Russia for 120 million dollars a year for fifty years. Although the countries have launched joint space projects, Baikonur is a tightly controlled and restricted area administered by the Russians, who are prohibited from using it for military purposes.

Over the years the Cosmodrome has had its triumphs and its disasters. In 1994 the Kazakh cosmonaut Talgat Musabayev and his Russian counterpart, Yuri Malenchenko, flew a joint mission to the Mir space station, numerous communication satellites have been successfully launched, and even wealthy Americans have been sent into space as citizen astronauts. But in 1999 two Proton rockets exploded in separate accidents.

An aviation buff had told me of a cosmonaut tradition: just before Gagarin was sent into space, he is supposed to have stopped to pee on the back tyre of the military bus used to transport him to Site No. 1 – the pad from which the first sputnik and the first intercontinental ballistic missile were launched. The terrestrial, pre-space whizz became a good-luck tradition among Soviet cosmonauts that has persisted ever since. I related the story to one of our party, but it must have become horribly mangled in translation. 'You wish for good luck to urinate against the back tyre of a bus?'

It was exciting to visit Baikonur, but also a disappointment. Without the drama of a rocket launch there was not much to see. In the far distance the towers of the launch pad could be glimpsed, with low buildings to one side and the steppe all around. It was like visiting an airport without any planes.

We boarded a fleet of three portly Russian helicopters, with

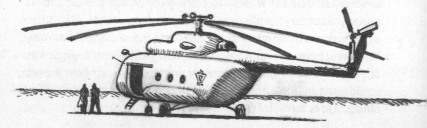

their long, floppy rotor blades, that were to be our transport for the next three days. The president's was very smart and painted cream, and it was flown by a veteran of the Afghan war, a pilot said to be so good he could land a chopper upside down in a cave. The VIPs, the press and I travelled in a grey helicopter that was roomy and serviceable, but hardly comfortable, while the security detail crowded into their chopper of olive green. Our destination was Aral City – previously known as Aralsk – a fishing port on the northern shore of the Aral Sea.

•

At least, Aral City used to be on the shore. Today it is seventy kilometres from the water.

For connoisseurs of desolation and despair, Kazakhstan offers a world-class monument to human folly and unconsidered consequences – the Aral Sea. This great body of water that is the fourth largest lake in the world, has been shrinking ever since cotton was introduced into the region in 1960. It has been reduced by an area the size of Ireland and its salinity has increased threefold, making it the world's saltiest lake. The result is an ecological disaster on the magnitude of the destruction of the Amazon rain forest. The Aral Sea has drained away as if the plug had been pulled in a bath.

We flew towards it on a day of ferocious heat. The portholes in the helicopter were opened for cross ventilation and I wore earplugs to deaden the roar of the rotor blades as we made our way across an eternal emptiness. Occasionally, I saw trails below that came from nowhere and went nowhere. They were a mystery. Who used them? And for what? After flying for an age I looked down and saw a solitary shepherd crouched in a depression with a dozen or so goats. The survival of the man and his beasts was another mystery. There was no village or anything else – not a single tree anywhere to be seen. And certainly no water. I asked how anyone could exist in such hostile terrain. My question was met with a shrug: 'He is Kazakh.'

The helicopters roared over a pair of grubby white camels grazing on grit and sand among a stand of electric pylons, and landed in a storm of dust. 'Somebody in Moscow came up with the idea that you could grow cotton here,' the president told me. 'Nobody thought to calculate what would happen to the Aral Sea. Nobody thought about such a minor detail. So the sea began to disappear.' Before King Cotton, the lake had been home since time immemorial to thriving fishing communities living along its banks. The sea yielded hundreds of thousand of tonnes of fish a year, and fleets of trawlers were kept berthed in its ports. But all that had now gone.

President Nazarbayev had come to this desperate, impoverished place to open a freshwater plant, the first time in history the town had ever had unpolluted drinking water on tap. Previously, it was brought in by truck. The potable water still only runs to a central pump in the main square but it is slowly being piped into individual houses. The owner of one of the first of these had been designated to receive the presidential party.

The man was not an official or a politician but a local who happened to live in a modest blue-and-white cottage close to the pump. A single cow was tethered in a stall in a small, enclosed courtyard, and discs made of dried dung and straw were piled in a shed opposite, to be used as fuel in the winter. 'We had a cow like this for milk when I was a boy,' the president said cheerfully, giving the cow a critical glance. 'But ours was not as skinny as this one. This is a very skinny cow.'

Inside, the cottage was immaculate. A new, gleaming white basin and tap stood proudly in the front hallway, and the president was invited to wash his hands before being led into the family dining-room where tea and food were offered. I remarked to one of our company that the little cottage struck me as much more charming than the modern apartments being built all over the country. It was a view dismissed as old-fashioned and patronizing. 'In Kazakhstan,' my companion said, 'people want modern apartments.'

We were shown through the four sparsely furnished rooms of the house. It all seemed very cosy, ship-shape and Bristol fashion. I was told the family laid thick camelhair carpets on the wooden floors at night to sleep on. The room of the teenage daughter, a bright-eyed girl about to go to university, demonstrated that the psychology of a teenager living beside the Aral Sea is much like that of her counterpart in London or anywhere else. On one wall there were posters of Britney Spears and Linkin Park, and the rest of the room was dedicated to a worshipful montage of dozens of photos of the white American rapper, Eminem. 'You seem to like Eminem?' I said.

'I like him very, *very* much.'

On the way out the president said, 'We noticed how that girl seemed very interested in you.'

'I have this effect on women, Mr President.'

'In Aral City there are 30 per cent less men than women,' the president said. 'According to our tradition a girl cannot leave her parents if there is no one else to look after them, so she stays and does not marry. So I have asked three of my ministers to stay an extra month to help these young ladies out. But they fear there is a chance I will not call them back to Astana, because they know we have too many high officials in the capital.'

Later, the president said seriously: 'When we enrolled 18-year-olds into the Kazakh Army we found the boys from this region do not pass the physical, not because they are sick but because they are weak and have the weight of a child. For some inexplicable reason this environmental disaster has had a greater effect on males than on females, and we still cannot explain why.'

It was a peculiar experience driving around Aral City, a place now as thoroughly out of its natural element as a beached whale. Everything felt wrong. The town has the architecture of a port, with docks, concrete quays, numerous sheds and cranes – but no sea. The water was last here in 1973 when the town processed 20,000 tonnes of fish a year to be sent all over the Soviet Union. Now the fisheries are closed, the canning and freezing plants abandoned, and the reduced population tries to make a living from agriculture. This provides slim pickings because of the quantity of salt in the soil. The one business that does thrive is the salt factory – Aral City could probably provide the world with salt.

'One million tons of salt are blown away by the wind every year from this area,' the president said. 'You can find this salt as far away as the mountain tops of Europe. It gets into glaciers and makes them melt more quickly. It even reaches the Arctic Circle. Some of it probably gets to England, so we are adding a little salt to your life.'

For sheer scale, even the Soviet Union surpassed itself in its plans for the Aral Sea. Moscow found the lake's trillion cubic metres of water irresistible, and with a wave of the central planning wand turned a great expanse of desert into an area dedicated to hydropower and the intensive cultivation of rice and cotton. Both crops require massive amounts of water, a resource that the Aral Sea seemed able to provide without limit. Monster bulldozers in their thousands were imported from all over the Soviet Union to gouge out a great network of irrigation canals.

At first everything went according to plan. Cotton production boomed, particularly to the south in Uzbekistan, which has half the Aral Sea within its borders. Encouraged by the early success of the scheme, Moscow demanded greater and greater production. Every field, orchard and garden was requisitioned for the cultivation of cotton, and the entire workforce – including children and the old – was involved in planting and picking. 'If you do not plant cotton, they will plant you in prison,' the locals joked grimly. 'If you do not collect cotton, they will collect you.' Driven by fear, cotton pickers worked in temperatures of 40 degrees centigrade, bending their backs 10,000 times a day to fill their quota, and they were paid a pittance. Conditions were little better than those of black slaves in the American South a century earlier.

In time enough cotton was being produced to supply the whole of the communist world – Eastern Europe, Cuba, North

Korea and every republic of the Soviet Union. Thanks to the Aral Sea, the USSR became the world's second largest cotton exporter after China. The harvests were always good, not least because the statistics were always inflated, while a corrupt cotton mafia of local communist bosses siphoned off money.

As production continued to grow, propelled by Moscow's insatiable demand, people living close to the Aral Sea began to notice a drop in the water level. It was slow at first, but as the network of irrigation canals expanded and cotton production climbed, the lake shrank at an ever-accelerating rate. Over the next twenty years the flow of one of the rivers that feed the Aral Sea, the Syr Darya (Jaxartes), was reduced by 90 per cent, and the level of the lake dropped an incredible sixteen metres. The surface area of the Aral Sea shrank by almost half, and the volume of water fell by three-quarters. The landlocked sea divided into two in the late 1980s as the water drained away and the lake began to die.

The concentration of salt killed the fish, and an industry that once supported 60,000 people was destroyed. Processing plants were only kept going by the lunatic stopgap of importing fish from Russia's Pacific coast thousands of kilometres to the east. By the 1990s, the Aral Sea had retreated in some places by as much as 150 kilometres from its original shoreline, stranding ocean-going trawlers among sand dunes, and revealing sunken hulks. Camels now roam where ships once sailed.

But the slow death of the lake was only part of the problem, for the cultivation of cotton had created another ecological disaster. Two hundred and sixty kilograms of fertilizers, pesticides and other chemicals were required for each hectare cultivated. These did not just pollute the two great rivers feeding the lake – the Syr Darya in Kazakhstan and the Amu Darya (Oxus) from the south in Uzbekistan – they also leached into the underground water table and contaminated the region's drinking water. The land became saturated with poison.

Every year millions of tonnes of contaminated dust were whipped by the wind into toxic blizzards and carried as far away as the Tien Shan mountains, and into their glaciers which are the source of drinking water for much of the rest of Kazakhstan. The health of people living in the area of the sea's basin deteriorated dramatically: infant mortality and cancer rates soared, while life expectancy plunged. For every thousand children born, a hundred immediately died. Half the population contracted jaundice at one time or another, and death was almost inevitable if the disease was accompanied by dysentery. Even now it is estimated that as many as 80 per cent of women and children in the region suffer from anaemia.

Faced with such a monumental problem, Moscow's central planners came up with a monumental solution: a plan to divert water from the great rivers of Siberia, calling for the construction of a canal 2,500 kilometres long. Ecological movements, which had come into being within the USSR during the Gorbachev years, attacked the scheme. The solution engendered risks as great as the problem, it was argued, and might affect the ecosystem of the entire planet. But cost alone scuppered the project, and when the Soviet Union collapsed in 1991 the plan went into oblivion.

'Look, the land around the Aral Sea is already so contaminated that the most rational solution would simply be to move all the people and abandon the area as a wasteland,' the president explained. 'Kazakhstan is so vast and sparsely populated there is certainly no shortage of land elsewhere. But we do not have the resources to build enough houses for everybody. And even if we did, many people would simply refuse to go. The Kazakhs are very conscious of tradition. They want to die in the place where they were born.'

We drove back to the helicopters and headed south, skimming across the desert landscape at the bottom of a vanished sea. From time to time sunken ships and stranded buoys could be seen beside camels. The combined image of ship and camel was disorienting – like coming across the hulk of the Titanic in the middle of the Sahara. It seemed an age, and Aral City was far behind us, before we actually crossed over water, deep turquoise in colour and so still it looked as if it were painted. And despite everything, the diminished Aral Sea still resembled an ocean rather than a lake. We droned on and on. Most of the helicopter's passengers dozed in the heat. Only the press secretary scribbled furiously.

Halfway along the shore of the lake we dropped down to visit work in progress on an eleven-kilometre dam being built by the Chinese with money from the Kazakh government and the World Bank. In previous years the local population and regional government had experimented with sand dykes which had been washed away in storms. The dykes, however, had proved that both the level and the quality of the water could be improved significantly by damming.

'This dam is the eighth wonder of the world,' an excited engineer told me. 'No one has done something like this before. It's working! In a year the water has been raised four metres. It might not be possible to raise the lake to its previous level, but we should be able to get another five metres – enough to bring key harbours back to life and revive the fishing industry. Where else in the former Soviet Union has there been such success in cleaning up an ecological disaster?'

Certainly not to the south, in Uzbekistan, where the larger part of the Aral Sea lies and where the water is too salty to sustain even ocean fish. There the level continues to fall inexorably, and the Uzbek government has adopted the defeatist, short-term policy of making the most of a bad thing by exploring the dry seabed for oil and gas deposits.

Our next stop was a fish farm struggling to replenish the lake. It seemed odd to see human beings working so hard to put fish back into the sea. The enterprise was a joint Israeli, Dutch and Kazakh one – Jewish, Christian and Muslim, I thought. Nobody else considered the fact worth remarking upon, which is part of the charm of Kazakhstan. The farm is a high-tech establishment where fish are bred and nurtured in test tubes and tanks, and attempts are being made to reintroduce the Aral and Syr Darya shovelhead sturgeon to the lake. New technology has also been developed to suck caviar from the live fish rather than kill them. 'Thirty per cent of all the fish in the Soviet Union once came from here,' the president said with a flash of anger. 'You know what the percentage is now?' He put thumb and forefinger together. 'Zero!'

Three yurts had been erected at the edge of the lake to entertain the presidential party. The water stretched away to the horizon – a sea in a desert and utterly silent – and the brightly coloured yurts were cool and welcoming. We went inside one that had been prepared for lunch. A section of the side had been rolled up to give a view of the lake, and the yurt had been upgraded from traditional to presidential by the introduction of a chandelier and air-conditioning. The president called me over to a table where there were glasses and a bottle of whisky. 'We must drink a glass of Scotch,' he said, pouring a generous measure into a tumbler. 'It is a thirst-quencher, a disinfectant and an antiseptic.' We downed the glass in one, Russian style. He poured a second glass. 'Better have another to be safe.

'Lunch will be fish *besbarmak*. But there will surely also be meat if you prefer. In Kazakhstan meat is destiny. It will always come after you – you cannot avoid it.'

Besbarmak is the national dish, usually of boiled beef or mutton, but traditionally of horse, cooked with onions and served on large, flat squares of pasta laid out on a massive ceramic dish. As we ate a trio of Kazakh girls dressed in traditional costume entered the yurt to dance and sing. A young man of extraordinary talent then played the *dombra*, an elegant, two-stringed instrument of great antiquity, with a long, slender neck and teardrop body. Terracotta figurines fashioned by Sak nomads 2,000 years ago and unearthed in Kazakhstan show men playing a form of the *dombra*.

Eager to demonstrate my wide knowledge of Kazakh music, I said that I had heard that even though the *dombra* had only two strings, an accomplished musician could play Western classical music upon it – even Mozart. The president said something in Kazakh and I realized the musician had been asked to play a classical piece. I instantly regretted my words, fearing I had set the young man up for humiliation. The musician hesitated for a moment, bent over his *dombra*, and then played a strange but seamless medley of Vivaldi, Bach and Mozart.

The president himself now took up the *dombra*. I steeled myself, prepared for a performance along the lines of the frat-boy saxophone playing of Bill Clinton, or the embarrassing air guitar of Tony Blair. Again, I need not have been alarmed. The president proved to have a sure touch, and the music was soft and delicate. In fact, it is rare to find any Kazakh who is not musical in some way.

On our way out of the yurt the president handed me the *dombra* as a gift. The moment his back was turned, and he was making his way to the car, an aide unceremoniously snatched it from me, explaining it was supposed to be a gift for the president. Although I did not engage the aide in a wrestling match, I have an uncomfortable memory of holding on to the *dombra* for just an ungracious moment too long before relinquishing my grasp – I wanted to keep my souvenir of a president playing a folk song in a yurt on the edge of the Aral Sea.

Once again, we climbed into the choppers and prepared to fly for another long stretch. Everyone was drained by the heat, even though it was only spring and far from the scorching temperatures of midsummer. The portholes were opened, earplugs put in place, and we fell into a dreamlike state. It was an ordeal to cross this inhospitable terrain even by helicopter, but while the heat was a trial, I was grateful it was not winter when only those who have experienced the fierce cold can appreciate its extreme nature. I dozed and meditated upon a fellow countryman who had crossed the whole of eastern Kazakhstan from north to south in the depths of winter, skirting the Aral Sea, more than a hundred years earlier.

CHAPTER 5

•

THE EXPLORER, THE BEATLE
AND NEW MONEY

In the nineteenth century there had come to the Kazakh steppe – as come there must, certain as death and taxes – a gentleman English explorer. Captain Frederick Gustavus Burnaby was an officer in the Royal Horse Guards, the Blues of the Household Cavalry, the Queen's ceremonial bodyguard. Large of limb, tall in stature, fearless and stoic, he stood six feet four inches tall, weighed sixteen stone, and had the reputation of being the strongest man in the British Army. In 1875, on a whim, Burnaby decided to cross the most inhospitable region of Kazakhstan on horseback in midwinter. The journey took him through the same empty terrain I was passing over in a helicopter – although Burnaby travelled ten times further on pony and camel.

A portrait of Burnaby hangs in the National Portrait Gallery, a delicate, finely painted work executed in 1870 by the Frenchman James Tissot, who knew him as a fellow man-about-town. It is a study in insouciance and exudes that effortless assumption of superiority guaranteed to irritate. Burnaby wears the 'blue patrols' of his regiment, and his long legs encased in red-striped trousers dissect the canvas in a bold diagonal. A pile of books and a blue-and-red cap are spread beside him on a sofa, and the plumed ceremonial helmet and shining cuirass of the Blues are to one side. The moustache is waxed and twirled, a cigarette is held aloft in his left hand, and the subject relaxes in front of a map of the world, a place his manner suggests might be his own. The viewer can almost hear the aristocratic cavalry drawl.

Fred Burnaby ached for the danger and glory of combat – as he saw it – and regretted that he had become a soldier at a time that did not 'synchronise with a piping time of war'. Life in the Household Cavalry in those days was languorous rather than piping. There were five months of leave a year and military duties were almost entirely ceremonial. The officers were the richest in the British Army and needed a hefty private income to pay mess bills, maintain a fashionable central London residence, and be seen at the opera and society balls. But as a lowly young cornet-of-horse, ceremonial soldiering bored Burnaby, who sought adventure and challenge.

The decision to penetrate Central Asia had been made on the basis that the whole area had recently been closed to foreigners by the Russians, and an Englishman had been turned back. This was a severe provocation to a British imperialist of Burnaby's stamp. He prepared for the legendary winter cold by scouring the gentlemen's stores of London's West End for warm clothes. Two pairs of boots lined with fur were purchased, four pairs of the thickest Scottish fishing stockings, thick jerseys and flannel shirts of a rough texture, and a specially constructed windproof suit that his tailor assured him would keep out any cold: 'Lord love you, sir! No cold can get through them trousers anyhow.' He bought a money belt for his gold, a supply of quinine, and a large quantity of Cockle's Pills as a remedy for chronic liver trouble. 'A most invaluable medicine,' he enthused. The magic boluses not only eased the liver, but also worked on any number of other complaints. On his previous travels he had handed them out generously to suffering natives: 'The marvellous effects produced on one patient in Africa when administered with five Cockle's Pills will never fade from my memory.'

Burnaby was also among the first to avail himself of a new and as yet cumbersome invention – the sleeping bag. This monstrosity took the form of a huge waterproof construct of heavily oiled sailcloth, seven and a half feet long and ten feet round, with a large aperture along one side. 'I found it of great convenience for every purpose save the one for which it was originally intended. The manufacturer, not calculating the enormous dimensions an individual assumed when enveloped in furs, had not made the aperture large enough.'

In St Petersburg, Burnaby cannily used his society connections to collect letters of introduction and travel permits from various Russian generals and dignitaries, and cheerfully set off on his travels in a sleigh drawn by three horses, the middle one sporting a huge wooden collar decorated with brightly coloured ribbons. The cold was terrible. Burnaby discovered almost immediately that his tailor's confident assurances dissolved in the reality of the Russian winter. As the thermometer dropped to minus 20 degrees centigrade, the slightest wind cut through even fur, and penetrated to the bone.

Burnaby was certainly dressed for the cold. He wore long johns, thick trousers, a heavy flannel vest, a shirt covered by a padded waistcoat, three pairs of woollen socks drawn high above the knee, and leather galoshes over fur-lined snow shoes, inserted in turn into a pair of enormous cloth thigh boots. A huge fur pelisse reached to his heels, and on his head he wore a fur hat covered by a cloth cap tied around the throat. He was wearing so many clothes he was unable to buckle on his revolver, which he had been advised to carry as a precaution against the large number of wolves in the area, and he had to strap the weapon to his saddle bags. Despite everything, he found that 'The first thing to get cold were the feet.'

It was an exceptionally cold winter. The snow fell so rapidly and piled itself against the sleigh in such quantities that Burnaby worried at times he would be buried alive. The wind blew the snow into fantastic drifts and hillocks, so that the motion in the sleigh became like that of a Channel crossing, and brought on a feeling of seasickness. Travel in such cold temperatures was hungry work, but when he stopped to eat he found all the provisions frozen solid.

Finally, at the Ural mountains, he crossed from Russia into Asia. His destination was to be Khiva (today in Uzbekistan), chosen because it was under direct and immediate threat of annexation by imperial Russia, which had already annexed Samarkand and had troops quartered within a few miles of the city.

Burnaby refers to the Kazakhs as 'Kirghiz', a misnomer that came into being to differentiate the population from Russian Cossacks, a very different breed. The Russian Cossacks took their name from the Turkic word 'Kazak', meaning free man or wanderer, and thus creating lasting confusion. Cossacks were confederations of Slavic stock first formed in the Middle Ages. Made up mostly of Russian and Ukrainian outlaws and fugitives – serfs who had escaped their masters, bandits and common criminals on the run, and a variety of others in conflict with authority – they were nevertheless devout followers of Russian Orthodox Christianity. Anyone who believed in Christ and followed the Cossack code could join. They roamed the steppe as nomad horsemen, intermarried with native women, and eventually became the fabled cavalry of Russia. Warrior training began at birth when a baby had an arrow touched to his lips and a bow placed in his hand; at the age of 3 he would be taught to ride. The Cossacks acted as the ruthless advance guard of empire, and became a byword for merciless cruelty, the first embodiment of Russian terror.

The Russians had been advancing across Central Asia for over a century. Peter the Great had been the first to see the potential of the Kazakhs and their steppeland: 'This horde is the key and gate to all Asian lands. For this reason this horde must be placed under Russian protection.' In 1694 he proposed a treaty of protection and trade, and while the desire to trade was genuine enough, the price of protection was control. 'If this horde does not wish to come under the Russian shield, try everything whatever the expense, be it a million roubles or more. For they must be under Russian protection.'

A million roubles was an enormous sum, and while protection might have been a euphemism for colonization, it was fast becoming a necessity for the Kazakhs in the face of sustained attack by Jungars from the east, a Mongol tribe inhabiting an empire in what is today north-west China. By 1720 the Russians had built fortresses at Omsk, Zhelezinka, Semipalatinsk and Ust-Kamenogorsk, and although Peter's death slowed the process, in 1731 the Kazakhs were once again offered bribes and protection. Under threat of total defeat by the Jungars, the Lesser Horde agreed to become subject to Russian rule in exchange for territorial protection. The other hordes also accepted Russian protection, but without formal submission as vassals.

The first official act of colonization came in 1760 when Catherine the Great ordered Cossack troops to man a line of ten garrisons and fifty-three outposts in the north. The official reason was that the troops were there to protect the indigenous Kazakhs, but in reality large areas of land were expropriated by Cossacks and their families, and the Russian government actively encouraged settlers to clear land traditionally grazed by Kazakh herds. Resistance, in the form of various levels of armed insurrection, flared for twenty years, but Russia was relentless and laid an increasingly heavy hand on the country. More and more fortresses were built and manned by Cossacks – in 1854 Fort Verny (Almaty) was constructed, and in 1862 Akmolinsk (Astana). By the end of the century Russian colonization was complete. Throughout their wars of expansion in Central Asia, the Russians claimed to have lost only 400 dead, while nomad casualties were counted in their tens of thousands.

Burnaby saw Russia's relentless progress across Central Asia as a potential and inevitable threat to British India, and an eventual cause for war. This was the era of the Great Game, a form of imperial chess played between agents of Victorian Britain and Tsarist Russia on a board stretching from the Caucasus, across the steppe, deserts and mountains of Central Asia, to the roof of the world in Tibet. When the game began the borders between the two empires lay 3,200 kilometres apart; at the end there were, in places, only thirty kilometres between them.

The Russians had established commercial contact with the Central Asian khanates of the steppe 600 years earlier, although it was not until the end of the sixteenth century that trade was properly developed. Englishmen soon appeared on the commercial scene. Anthony Jackson, an envoy for Queen Elizabeth I, reported from the region of the Aral Sea in 1558, and a captain named Elton was later to reconnoitre the lake with a view to establishing a naval flotilla upon it. In the mid-eighteenth century there were further reports of English merchants trading with the natives, including 'the handsome Englishman' Jonas Hanway, who travelled there in 1745 and on his return to England established a mixed reputation as a philanthropist, a lifelong opponent of tea-drinking, and the first man to carry an umbrella. Two years before Burnaby set off, Major Herbert Wood, of the Royal Engineers and the Royal Geographical Society, travelled widely in what is today western Kazakhstan. He found the Kazakhs 'well-fed and good-looking' but already yielding to the softening influences of luxury in the form of English stout and Russian vodka. All these men reported their journeys as hard, difficult and dangerous, but only Burnaby chose to travel in winter.

An appalled local listened to his travel plans and strongly advised him to turn back, explaining that the hardships experienced so far were as nothing to the ones he would face. In the circumstances it was not easy to find anyone prepared to accompany him. The only volunteer was an ugly and thoroughly unprepossessing dwarf. At first, Burnaby found the little Kazakh Nazar repellent, but he soon grew to admire the stoicism and guts of a man who proved to be both loyal and tough.

The moment Burnaby had entered what is today Kazakhstan, his Russophobia came to the fore. Mistrust of Russian intentions, and disdain for their methods, were fed by all he saw and heard. He identified a specific type of Russian officer peculiar to Central Asia: 'Taken from the most part from well-born families, having no inheritance but the sword, no prospect save promotion, they thirst for war as the only means at hand for rapidly rising in the service ... The lust for conquest is cloaked in a garb called Christianity. The sword and the Bible go forth together. Thousands of natives are mown down by that evangelical weapon, the breechloader; and one day we read in our morning newspaper that a territory larger than France and England together has been added to the Tsar's dominions. The Russians shoot down the steppe nomads without any mercy whenever they catch them.'

After renting horses, Burnaby and Nazar crossed into the great flat emptiness of the Kazakh steppe. 'Here, there, everywhere was a dazzling sheet of white, as seen under the influence of the midday sun; then gradually softening down as it sank into the west, it faded into a vast melancholy-looking colourless ocean ... A picture of desolation which wearied by its utter loneliness, and at the same time appalled by its immensity; a circle of which the centre was everywhere, and circumference nowhere.'

The experience of the Russian winter had been an education, but it proved little more than a primer for the brute cold of Kazakhstan. Burnaby was exposed for the first time to the full fury of the east wind, unchecked by any ocean, trees, hills, mountains or even rising land. 'It blows on uninterrupted over a vast snow and salt-covered tract. It absorbs saline matter, and cuts the faces of those exposed to its gusts. The sensation is like the application of the edge of a razor.'

Determined to protect himself from this assault, Burnaby reorganized his winter ensemble. The long fur pelisse was abandoned, and sheepskin adopted as the warmest clothing, despite its appalling smell. His new wardrobe consisted of a riding coat and trousers of sheepskin, high stockings – or 'buckets' – of sheepskin worn over four pairs of thick fishing socks, all encased in high cloth boots. 'When my new clothes were put on over those which had been made for me in London, I thought myself proof against any amount of frost.'

Wishful thinking, as it turned out. In one particularly savage snowstorm, Burnaby took refuge in a small fort built by the Russians and manned by Cossacks, and waited for the weather to improve. The snow slowed and he set off again, although the wind remained high, and the cold was more intense than anything yet experienced. On leaving the fort he forgot to put on his thick gloves, and used instead the fur pelisse as a muff. The road was comparatively smooth, and the landscape uniform and monotonous, and he fell asleep.

As the sleigh bumped along, Burnaby's hands slipped from their fur muff and were exposed to the biting east wind. He awoke to a feeling of severe pain in both hands, 'as if they had been plunged into some corrosive acid which was gradually eating the flesh from the bones'. He looked down to see that his fingernails, fingers and the backs of his hands had turned blue, while his wrists and lower arms were the colour of wax. Frostbite.

The sleigh stopped. Nazar massaged the skin of Burnaby's hands and lower arms in an attempt to bring back circulation, but it was useless. Burnaby felt the burning pain originally experienced in his hands gradually move up his arms, while all sensation in the lower arms was lost. 'Dead to pain – dead to every sense of feeling – they hung quite listlessly by my side.'

The only hope was to travel as fast as possible to the next Russian fort, seven miles away. As Burnaby sat in the speeding sleigh, the most acute pain he had ever suffered climbed to the glands under his arms. Extreme cold acts in two ways on the nervous system, either inducing deep sleep from which the victim never wakes up, or creating a state that makes him feel as if he is being burned alive. Collapsed in the sleigh, with perspiration pouring down his forehead, Burnaby fell into the second category and felt as if his whole body were being roasted over hot coals.

On arrival at the fort, three Cossack soldiers inspected Burnaby's hands. They instantly understood from long experience the danger he was in, and took him under their care. The men prepared a tub of ice and water and plunged his bare arms into the freezing mixture. He felt nothing, and watched in horror as his lifeless blue limbs floated painlessly in the water as if belonging to someone else. 'Brother, it is a bad job,' the eldest of the Cossacks said, shaking his head. 'You will lose your hands.'

'They will drop off if we cannot get back the circulation,' another of the Cossacks said dolefully. The soldiers asked for white spirit, and Nazar ran to the sleigh to retrieve a canister of naphtha used for cooking. The Cossacks then took Burnaby's arms out of the icy water and began to massage them ruthlessly with the strong spirit until the skin peeled raw. He flinched.

'Does it hurt?' the eldest Cossack asked.

'A little.' Burnaby had felt a faint sensation like tickling in the joints of his elbows.

'Capital!' The Cossack spoke urgently to his companions: 'Brothers – rub as hard as you can!'

The powerful Cossacks continued their brutal massage until the skin on both arms was almost flayed, and then plunged them into the tub of melting ice and water. Now Burnaby felt real, searing pain. 'Good,' the Cossacks said. 'The more it hurts the better chance you have of saving your hands.'

After a while they allowed Burnaby to take his arms out of the water. 'You are fortunate, little father,' the eldest Cossack said. 'If it had not been for the spirit your hands would have dropped off, if you had not lost your arms as well.' The physical shock had left Burnaby exhausted, and it would be weeks before the raw flesh of his hands and arms fully recovered. When he forced a present on the Cossacks, the eldest soldier said, 'Are we not all brothers when in misfortune? Would you not have helped me if I had been in a like predicament?'

Although Burnaby was a solid scion of the English upper classes, with all the ties and prejudices that suggests, he genuinely seems to have been more comfortable among straightforward soldiers, and he greatly preferred the Kazakhs to their Russian counterparts. He observed that they put little faith in doctors or vets – although he did occasionally persuade a sickly native to swallow a Cockle's Pill or two. The Kazakhs were intensely suspicious of vaccination, which meant they were often ravaged by smallpox. 'Putting this epidemic out of the question, the nomads are a peculiarly healthy race. The absence of medical men does not seem to have affected their longevity. The disease they most suffer from is ophthalmia, which is brought on by the glare of the snow in winter, and by the dust and heat in summer months.'

As his journey progressed, and he studied the Kazakhs, his admiration for them grew and he also came to understand and value the talents of his servant. As a guide, Nazar could discern distant objects that Burnaby could barely distinguish with his field glasses. The Kazakh's local knowledge was remarkable, and when there was no track or they had strayed, he would dismount and search for flowers and grass beneath the snow to orientate himself.

On one occasion Burnaby saw a party of men and women digging up wads of perfectly preserved grass from a deep cutting in the ground. 'This grass had been mown the previous autumn, and was thus preserved until such time as the owner required it; the extreme cold, or perhaps dryness of the air, keeping the grass as fresh as the day it was cut.'

As a cavalry officer, Burnaby had initially formed a poor impression of Kazakh horses, which struck him as skinny, stunted creatures. He soon changed his mind. The first Kazakh pony he mounted was little more than a skeleton, but it made twenty-kilometre marches in appalling conditions without the least sign of fatigue, and carried its twenty-stone burden for 500 kilometres without trouble. The little animals ploughed their way steadily through snow half a metre deep, while their riders had to dismount frequently to clean out the horses' nostrils which became blocked with icicles. 'If it came to endurance, I much doubt whether our large and well fed horses could compete with the little, half-starved nomad animals.'

The Kazakhs loved their horses dearly, and Burnaby was asked in all seriousness, 'Which do you like best, your horse or your wife?'

The journey had come to seem interminable. Twenty miles or so to Burnaby's right lay the Aral Sea, frozen for several miles from the shore, making navigation impossible. A salt wind blew into his face, parching and drying the skin, and producing a state akin to fever. The tea he drank failed to quench the thirst because the whole area was impregnated with salt, and the only water available was saline and brackish.

Incredibly, and almost impossibly, the cold grew worse. Burnaby had chosen one of the worst winters on record to make his journey, and all along the route he heard stories of people frozen to death. The butter was hard as a billiard ball; bread had to be chopped with an axe. They were now in territory unmarked on English maps. Only Kazakhs and Cossacks used the route on their way to and from Khiva. No Englishman had ever travelled it.

The cold on New Year's Day, 1876, as Burnaby loaded his three camels and two horses at a Russian fort for the final leg of the journey, was the worst he had ever experienced. Sentries posted outside the governor's house wore thick galoshes stuffed with hay, and ran backwards and forwards the whole time they were on duty to prevent their feet from freezing. When a man left the house his moustache was instantly frozen into a block of ice, while an exposed nose turned first blue and then white in a minute.

The journey had its compensations, however, which moved Burnaby to pen prose of imperial purple: 'It was a glorious evening, the stars as seen from the snow-covered desert were brighter and more dazzling than any I had hitherto witnessed. From time to time some glittering meteor would shoot across the heaven. A momentary track of vivid flame traced out its course through space. Showers of orbs of falling fire flashed for one moment and then disappeared from view. Myriads of constellations and worlds above sparkled like gems in a priceless diadem. It was a magnificent pyrotechnic display, a strange, wild scene – the vast snow-covered steppe, lit up brightly as if it were midday by a thousand constellations, which reflected themselves in the cold white sheet below. Not a cloud dimmed the majesty of the heavens. Silence. It was well worth a journey even as far as Central Asia.'

Burnaby drew close to his destination of the fabled city of Khiva. The temperament of its despotic khan had received a bad press in the West, and the eyewitness account of a Hungarian philologist who had visited the secret city disguised as a dervish was not encouraging. He reported human heads rolling out of sacks 'like potatoes', and old men lying eight in a row having their eyes gouged out.

The khan, however, proved to be a man of charm in his late twenties with an easy, welcoming smile, and a twinkle in his eye. He received Burnaby reclining on cushions beneath a canopy. 'He is *muy simpatico*,' Burnaby wrote. 'I must say I was greatly surprised, after all that has been written in Russian newspapers about the cruelties and other iniquities perpetrated by this Khivan potentate, to find the original such a cheery sort of fellow.' When Burnaby left, the khan gave him a dressing-gown as a present.

Burnaby's original plan, after Khiva, was to travel on to British India via Afghanistan. This was now abruptly curtailed by a telegram from no less a person than the Duke of Cambridge, Commander of the British Army, ordering his immediate return to European Russia by retracing his route across the steppe. The journey home was to prove as difficult as the outward one, an endless tedium of cold and hardship made doubly monotonous by the removal of the unknown.

On his return to Britain, Burnaby wrote an entertaining and colourful account of his travels, which became a bestseller and made him a celebrity. His lumbering nature might have had an element of both buffoon and brute, but the English public adopted him as a favoured son. He was seen as an amusing eccentric, not altogether taken seriously, but admired nonetheless. Although Burnaby never claimed to be an intellectual – 'I always think better standing up and better out of doors than in' – the bluff cavalryman was not nearly as stupid as his critics suggested. He had a great gift for languages, and was fluent in at least seven, including Russian, Turkish and Arabic.

Burnaby's adventures seemed the very stuff of empire, as was his death. He met his end at the Battle of Abu Klea Wells, in the Sudan, fighting against an army 15,000 strong. Speared and brought down from his horse, he then received a terrible blow to the skull from a two-handed sword. A young private was the first to reach him, and the boy tried to support the dying man's head on his knee. He turned with tears running down his cheeks to an officer: 'Oh sir – here is the bravest man in England dying and no one to help him.'

◆

Just thinking about Burnaby's midwinter travels cooled me off as I sat in the clattering helicopter. Beneath us, always, was the endless steppe, now turned into inhospitable desert.

Suddenly, after an hour and a half, the helicopter set down in what seemed to be the absolute middle of nowhere. For a moment I thought there might have been a mechanical problem with one of the other choppers, for I had seen no town or even settlement. In the far distance I glimpsed a tiny figure on horseback, and 200 metres to his left I saw another – and so on, forming a great square of horsemen out in the deserted steppe. This was special presidential security, which meant our stop was scheduled. And then I heard a curious whistling.

A bone-white sculpture designed to catch the wind stood in the arid steppe. Beside it was a small white pyramid, and beyond that a collection of low buildings. We had arrived at an ancient holy site pre-dating Islam, the place where legend has it that the shaman Korkut died.

'Korkut was a holy man and great musician who roamed the steppe trying to cheat death,' the president explained. 'He lived to be 101, but crossing the Syr Darya with his fifty women one night he was bitten by death disguised as a snake and died.'

'He travelled with fifty women?'

'That part is a joke. But Korkut is one of our oldest legends.'

The legend goes that Korkut roamed the world in search of the secret of immortality. Failing in his quest, he returned to the steppe and the banks of the Syr Darya. Determined to cheat death, he moved every day to a new resting-place. According to the story, Korkut fashioned the world's first stringed instrument – the kobyz, a kind of primitive violin – after stretching the skin of his beloved camel Jelmai over the lower part of a shape he had hollowed from a single piece of juniper wood. The instrument and bow were strung with camel hair, and the sound – part human song, part swan's cry – was as wonderful as life itself. One day, wearied from playing, he fell asleep on the site where we landed, and death disguised as a snake found him.

The Kazakhs believe that the sweet music of the kobyz drives bad spirits from a yurt and evil from a man's soul. Originally, only shamans were allowed to play the instrument. Storytellers, who were always gifted singers and musicians in Kazakhstan, later took it up, passing the oral history of the steppe from generation to generation. Improvised folk music among the Kazakhs was such a feature of life that the steppe has been described as a 'sea of music'. Today the kobyz is played as a folk instrument.

It was the sound of the kobyz that the wind in the sculpture was supposed to emulate. Despite pre-dating Islam, the monument to Korkut in this desolate spot is a Muslim holy place. The entire presidential party, which so far had not exhibited any outward religious enthusiasm, suddenly became quite pious. The men knelt before the monument, Muslim and Christian alike, and were blessed by an imam, after which they descended one by one into the vault beneath the small white pyramid to make a wish.

We then made our way beyond a low wall where two shepherds

waited with a live sheep, trussed and silent. It was to be a sacrifice. The president raised his arms and said a short prayer in Kazakh, begging the animal's forgiveness for taking its life. One of the shepherds moved quickly and pulled a knife across the sheep's throat in a swift sawing motion. The sheep scarcely struggled, grunted a couple of times, and coughed. The shepherd held it firmly as the blood ran on to the steppe. The act had been skilful and quick, not in the least cruel, and did not seem such a bad way for an animal to die.

The party was served *shubat*, camel's milk, as a thirst-quencher. Everyone was in high spirits as we left the monument and made our way towards the helicopters across steppe that had become rough scrub in sandy soil. As we walked, we bruised the spring growth and a wonderful scent filled the air. The press secretary crushed a small fistful of greenery and held it under my nose. It was not a grass or flower, but a woody shrub that gave off the strong aroma, and we searched for its name. He made tippling gestures and said, 'absinthe'. It was wormwood – *Artemisia absinthium* – one of eighty varieties found on the steppe. Horses are drawn to its root like cats to catnip. It must have been the smell that nomads and warriors welcomed for thousands of years as their horses trampled it underfoot in spring after the winter snows had melted.

·

We flew on to Kyzylorda, a town on the edge of the desert not much visited by foreigners. The name is Kazakh for 'Red Capital', for in 1925–7, before the railway reached Almaty, the town was briefly the capital of Soviet Kazakhstan. Today it is the rundown provincial capital of the region with the highest ethnic Kazakh population.

There is not a lot to do of an evening in Kyzylorda. Back in London I had heard that the town was home to a band known as the Kazakh Beatles, an eccentric attraction I was confident I could give a miss. But I grew bored in my hotel room and eventually decided to seek them out. My motive, I must admit, was a base one. I thought the band might be worth a laugh, and I arranged to meet them in the back room of a gloomy bar.

Alas, the glory days of the Kazakh Beatles had long gone. Like the Beatles themselves, the group had split up and its various members had gone their separate ways, so that only a single Beatle showed up for our meeting. To a man hoping to be tickled pink by the antics of a mop-haired Kazakh Fab Four in the wilds of the steppe, this was a disappointment. The surviving Beatle, Gabit Sagatov, turned out to be a smiling, round-faced, middle-aged man who was not merely a Beatles fan and enthusiast, but a fanatic to the bone. He turned sideways to show off his profile. I made confused noises of appreciation. He looked pleased. 'I have John Lennon's nose,' he said. 'A man who came here from Liverpool told me that.' He spoke no English – only Russian – which did not bode well, for he carried a guitar case with him and clearly intended to sing a tune or two. I wondered if I could sit through a mangled Kazakh version of 'Yellow Submarine' without screaming. He also carried a battered file containing press cuttings and correspondence. I ordered a drink.

But the Beatle was a genial man, and his undiminished enthusiasm for the music, fresh as the day he first heard 'Please, Please Me', was infectious. It was fascinating to hear how profoundly rock music had affected the young back in the bad old days of the USSR when Gabit was a teenager. 'I was studying in music school playing accordion. In those days students were taken to the collective farms in the summer to get in the rice harvest. The older guys who were studying in St Petersburg and Moscow brought tapes and discs and introduced us to all this fantastic music coming out of the West. It was so good it could penetrate any border or frontier, even an Iron Curtain.

'So when I first heard the music everything turned upside down for me. I listened to the songs one after another and came under a spell. I was not alone. Everybody was going crazy, making handmade guitars – global Beatlemania had hit the steppes of Kazakhstan. Everybody's dream was to go to Liverpool to see the Beatles. But it was impossible.

'Officially, the music was disapproved of strongly. Strongly! You know – "Decadent, Western, bourgeois rubbish." Although the government condemned the Beatles officially, to make money they produced a pirate version of their songs under the state's Melodia label. There was no name on the record, just the Beatles music, but the moment those records appeared on the shelves they flew off.'

Gabit played his Beatles records until the grooves disappeared, and the tapes until they broke, and he watched Beatles films in love-struck incomprehension. He copied the music note for note on the guitar, and repeated the words. 'I couldn't understand the words, but I felt the emotion – something good. And then when I had the words translated and did understand it was even better.' And the dream grew and grew – to go to Liverpool, city of the Beatles.

'But it was impossible, of course. To travel in the days of the Soviet Union was not allowed. No way. Then when we got independence I thought, "Big changes are happening. Maybe my dream could become real one day." '

It was after independence that Gabit met up with some younger musicians and founded the Kazakh Beatles. They dressed in dark suits with no collars and developed a repertoire of 120 songs, mostly Beatles material, but with a solid section of Rolling Stones numbers, and an eclectic mix of everything they liked including Engelbert Humperdinck. Gabit wrote to every one of the hundreds of Beatles fan clubs in the West, all of which failed to reply – except one. 'I came home one day and my father was holding up an envelope with his eyes shining. He knew what the Beatles meant to me. It had the queen's head on the stamp and was postmarked Liverpool, where the club's patron is Cynthia Lennon. I was so happy!'

Gabit had brought the treasured document along to show me.

It was a gracious letter that waived the fee to join the club – 'Do not worry too much about getting money to join. We know how difficult it is getting money and sending it to us' – and suggested he might like to think about entering the group in the annual Beatles Festival in Liverpool. 'And I thought, "Wow! My God! What people!"'

Since independence, life in Kyzylorda had loosened up, and there were even a few foreigners who came to work. The Americans built a hotel to accommodate oil men passing through, and in one of those random happy events that Gabit considers a small miracle, he discovered that the chef was not only an Englishman, but also a Liverpudlian. 'The moment I found out I went round to the hotel before breakfast to see him. He was called Peter and was very nice to me. He offered me tea or coffee, and naturally I took tea in the English manner.'

Gabit explained that he was a Beatles fan with a band and wanted somewhere to perform. They sang 'Norwegian Wood' together, taking alternate lines. At the end the chef – perhaps overwhelmed by homesickness and nostalgia – declared: 'This is the place you guys are going to play!'

Gabit was a schoolteacher by day and played at the hotel four nights a week. 'Every kopek I could save was invested in electronic equipment so I had quite good stuff. And we got an immediate audience of expats. One night thirty Englishmen were staying in the hotel, and there was a lot of energy – an unforgettable evening.' I said I could imagine it. 'One of the Englishmen was a Liverpudlian who said he had been to school with Paul McCartney, the same gentleman who told me I had John Lennon's nose.'

The fame of the Kazakh Beatles spread across desert and steppe, reaching Astana and Almaty. 'We played in a bar in Astana called Jamaica and someone who heard us was a speech writer for the president who happened to be a serious Beatles fan. He asked us to play another five songs after our set, and then he went home to get his son so he could hear us. We were amazed to have somebody from the presidential office as a fan. And there was another person from the tax office in Almaty who invited us to play at his birthday party, and I took along one of the travel brochures I had of Liverpool and the man kissed it. And I thought, "If we have people like this in the government – Beatles fans – we will go far in this country." '

Over the years a number of expatriates from Europe and America promised to find sponsors to send the group to Liverpool but nothing came of it. 'At first I got very excited and stayed awake at night. But after a while I realized it was people being nice – promises, promises. But I got a passport, and told the other guys to get them. "One day we will go!" '

But the group's luck seemed to run out. First, Peter the Liverpudlian chef went home, and then the hotel burned down. 'All our equipment was there – speakers, keyboard, drums ... everything. All burned!' His dream was salvaged from the ashes by a BBC team that showed up to interview and film the group. The producer promised to show the footage to the organizers of the annual Beatles Festival in Liverpool. Pointedly, the song the group chose to record was 'Don't Let Me Down'. Four years passed. 'Then in 2003 I got another call from the BBC, and they wanted to send another team to film us. The interviewer called me Mr John Lennon and told me I was going to Liverpool. I didn't believe it because there had been so many promises.'

Then a phonecall came from London to say that the festival organizers had seen the footage and were impressed. Three concerts were organized, and a further seven spots for the Kazakh Beatles. Were they interested? As Gabit told this part of the story his eyes shone and his smile lit up the room. A lump came to my throat.

'This was serious! Suddenly, because of our independence, I had this real chance to fulfil the dream I'd cherished for thirty years.' Gabit shook his head, unable even now to believe his great good fortune. 'Next I got this United Kingdom visa in my passport and I looked at it and looked at it, opening the passport a hundred times a day. I had sworn that the first country I would visit abroad would be the United Kingdom. I had been invited to India but said no, the first foreign country I'm going to put my feet on is the United Kingdom. I had met many expats in the hotel as a Beatle – Americans, Japanese, Germans – but I felt more towards Englishmen. They were more sympathetic. I liked them.'

The great day arrived on 21 August 2003. Gabit boarded the British Airways flight from Almaty, bound for the United Kingdom, and sat in a trance – eyes shining, heart thumping. 'I was flying towards my dream. And then I saw the English Channel beneath me ... and at Heathrow I actually stepped on to the land of the Beatles. The feelings I had are impossible to describe.'

He was to be in the United Kingdom for a week but he now entered some magical zone of time suspended. To say that Gabit was on a permanent, twenty-four-hour, natural high would be an understatement. He was close to a state of religious ecstasy. 'We took a train and went to Liverpool, and when I got there I fell to my knees and kissed the ground.'

Liverpool is not everyone's idea of paradise and I asked gently if the reality had been something of an anti-climax. Had the dream lost just a little of its lustre in the damp, grey reality of the unlovely port city? 'For me going to Liverpool was like going to Mecca,' Gabit said. 'I was breathing that air. Walking on that soil. Surrounded by that atmosphere. The people were responsive and I felt I had come to a place that was a second home. No, I was not disappointed.'

As many as 350,000 people had descended on the city to hear the various groups play. There were no prizes, and little money for the musicians involved, who gathered solely out of love for the music. The Kazakh Beatles played the Adelphi and the back room of the Cavern Club. 'I was out on the streets at dawn every day because I thought it would be stupid to waste any time in that city. I went to the place where Paul McCartney grew up ... Strawberry Fields, Penny Lane. You cannot know how deep these feelings went. It was a wonderful, perfect trip.'

On the way back to London from Liverpool, Gabit received a

casual Beatle blessing. The group had just changed trains, and he was standing at the window of his compartment as the train pulled out when an old lady on the platform who had been to the festival caught sight of him. She ran up to the train and banged happily on the window. 'John Lennon,' she called out, blowing him a kiss. 'John Lennon!'

It was at this emotional juncture that I decided to bite the bullet and ask the enthusiastic Gabit to sing me a song. He was happy and eager to oblige. I closed my eyes, a ploy I hoped would suggest respect and concentration, while minimizing embarrassment. Gabit took his guitar from its case, tuned it briefly, and began to sing. And something uncanny happened. I heard the unmistakeable and absolutely distinct nasal tones of John Lennon; and then I heard what was without doubt the voice of Paul McCartney; then George, then Ringo. I opened and closed my eyes to see if this made any difference, but whatever the song it seemed truly to be a *Beatle* singing it.

I asked for more, and tried to catch Gabit out by requesting obscure numbers. There was not a song he did not know, and he was word perfect in them all. This man, who could not speak a word of English, was singing as if he were a Liverpudlian born and bred. I spoke about the Liverpool accent – Gabit did not know what I was talking about. How many thousands of hours had he dedicated to reproducing this flawless facsimile? It was genius of a sort – crazy, pointless, obsessed, but a genuine talent. The ultimate flattery – or rather, an innocent and perfect form of worship. Once in a while a word came out vaguely flattened, or minimally mispronounced, but thanks to my new friend I had the undivided musical attention of the Fab Four for a couple of hours. An evening that was as enchanting as it was unexpected, in an unpromising desert city on the edge of the steppe.

The following morning I needed to pay my hotel bill (no credit cards accepted) and set off to find an ATM. What I imagined might be something of an expedition proved to be a five-minute mission. Cash machines were everywhere. I stopped at an ATM at the corner of a street where a camel stood nonchalantly snacking on a small tree. I punched buttons, marvelling that in a dusty street in a backwoods town I could place my English Visa card in a hole in the wall in expectation of a delivery of Kazakh cash.

As I waited, the camel turned and looked in my direction as if it had read my mind. The eyes took me in with a haughty mixture of contempt and disbelief that seemed to suggest I was a bit of a hayseed, hopelessly old-fashioned and out of touch, a man who had failed to move with the times. The camel held my gaze for a moment, turned away, made a final tug at the indigestible tree, and moved on. In the meantime there was the familiar whirring sound of the ATM's electronic count, and out popped exotic, crisp *tenge* notes, a currency made unique in that it was introduced by stealth in a top-secret operation.

At the World Economic Conference in Davos, in Switzerland, in January 1993, President Nazarbayev and the recently appointed Russian prime minister, Victor Chernomyrdin, went for a walk together. The prime minister said that Russia was planning to introduce new rouble notes in the spring, when the old ones still carrying the portrait of Lenin would be recalled. 'Bear in mind no one should know. But don't worry. We'll print money for Kazakhstan as well.'

No other republic of the former Soviet Union was more integrated into the rouble economy than Kazakhstan. This was partly because of its size and wealth in terms of raw materials, and partly because of its long border with Russia. Most Kazakh enterprises and almost all the country's industrial production were controlled by Moscow and every one of Kazakhstan's existing gas and oil pipes ran north into Russia, where all of its crude oil was refined.

Despite immense oil reserves, Kazakhstan was faced with constant fuel shortages, and had little choice after independence but to accept the situation – at least in the short term. During the early days of independence it was already clear to Nazarbayev that any breaking of existing economic ties binding the republics would have meant disaster.

But Kazakhstan was about to receive a hard lesson in realpolitik. The men who controlled the money had power not only over the economy, but over everything. Kazakhstan needed to be within the new rouble zone to survive, and the Russian government now made it clear that the price would be control of the country's budget and money supply. The president believed that the price was worth paying if it meant Kazakh factories would not lose ties with traditional business partners, and if people's standard of living would not be hit so hard. The stark alternative was economic collapse.

A solemn personal pledge was given by Boris Yeltsin to President Nazarbayev that Kazakhstan would be warned well in advance about the introduction of the new currency, and that the country would automatically be included in the zone. But a lifetime of dealing with Moscow had made Nazarbayev wary, and he issued a secret decree to create a separate national currency as a contingency against economic betrayal. A posse of financial experts met secretly every month to plan the enormous undertaking of introducing a new national currency. High-level, covert discussions were opened with the International Monetary Fund and the World Bank on the practicalities of such a move. Engravers and designers were hired to make the prototype banknotes, and Thomas de la Rue, of London, was contracted to print and store the amount needed.

The new rouble notes were not actually introduced in Russia until July, when the Russian Central Bank announced it was putting them into circulation. A declaration was signed at the beginning of August in Moscow to the effect that Kazakhstan would remain in the rouble zone. But a week later the banknotes had still not arrived. The period of uncertainty, deliberately planned by Moscow, was a disaster for Kazakhstan. Once Russia had announced its new currency, millions of old, invalid Soviet roubles were dumped in the country, helped on their way by gangsters from Moscow. The value of the old rouble collapsed, while inflation climbed to 3,000 per cent.

Moscow's intentions were clear. Faced with ruin, Kazakhstan would have to accept any conditions. The original price was high, but the one demanded now, with the country on the ropes, was brutal – unification of Kazakhstan's budget, tax, customs and banking policies with those of Russia, after handing over control of the country's money supply to the Russian Central Bank. It made a mockery of Kazakhstan's newfound independence and was seen as a national humiliation. In reality, the country was being stripped of its sovereignty.

In response the Kazakh government sent four empty giant Russian Ilyushin-76 transport planes from Almaty to London on a covert mission. A string of armoured bullion trucks drove out to meet them and, under cover of night, millions of freshly printed *tenge* notes of all denominations were packed into the vast maws of the aircraft. The money-heavy planes lifted off and flew back to Almaty.

An even more hush-hush operation was now launched in which the banknotes were distributed throughout the country, even to the most remote *aul*. Run by the security services, it was completed in total secrecy in a week. On a Friday evening, a stunned population was told through an announcement by the president on television that the *tenge* would be introduced on Monday morning. The rouble in Kazakhstan was history.

The new currency had a rocky beginning. It was backed by a paltry 700 million dollars in gold and foreign exchange, and it immediately became apparent that the exchange rate had been fixed much too high, a serious error. Instant devaluation partially corrected the situation but won the *tenge* few friends. Its value continued to sink for a long time before it eventually stabilized. The risk and the price had been high, but Kazakhstan had retained its sovereignty.

◆

As the presidential party continued to travel in the west of the country, I became increasingly aware of what the Kazakhs called the oilers – men doing well out of the oil business. They come in various categories, from the burly Brits and Americans who spend months on the rigs in the Caspian Sea, to the head of Tengizchevroil, one of Kazakhstan's half-dozen new billionaires. But the breed that stands out, or rather screams for attention, is that of the easily spotted *nouveau riche* oil executive. Loudly but expensively dressed in Armani suits and Italian alligator loafers, they smoke Davidoff cigars, wear massive gold watches and are forever talking on the latest model of mobile phone. At the provincial airports they pay to sit in VIP lounges, holding themselves aloof from the hoi polloi, and they have limousines pull across the tarmac to meet them off domestic flights. The ostentation amuses rather than angers their fellow Kazakhs. 'The older guys probably don't speak English and are a bit of a joke,' a young executive in the oil business told me. 'But our attitude is, "These guys are one of us and they made it!" The younger guys don't show off, and many of them hang out with expats. It's all changing very fast.' Less than ten years after the initial exploitation of vast oil reserves, flashy vulgarity is already out of fashion.

The country has gone through a similar process of sophistication in the way it handles its valuable asset. The early cowboys of the Wild East have been replaced by sober-suited businessmen of multinational corporations. Oil has not only changed Kazakhstan, it has also come to its rescue and made it rich. The wells are already pumping 1.3 million barrels a day, and it is planned to make that 3 million barrels within five years. Oil revenues have made it possible for the country to pay off its loan to the IMF eight years ahead of schedule, maintain a negligible state debt, and achieve an annual 10 per cent growth in GDP since 2000. Oil has greatly added to the country's strategic importance and made it increasingly courted by the world's major powers.

Atyrau is the capital of the Kazakh oil boom, a shabby town going through a transformation as the money pours in, and new shimmering glass buildings are replacing crumbling apartment blocks. The Wall Street Journal has dubbed Atyrau the new Houston – or Houstan as the local wits have it. The Ural river, the boundary between Europe and Asia, dissects the city as it flows into the Caspian Sea. The place is rough and violent, with a frontier atmosphere, and the expat communities are surrounded by fences patrolled by armed guards who stop cars and check documents.

In the days before the oil boom, most of the city's economy relied on fishing and shipping. There was a time when the caviar catch alone in the Caspian was measured in tens of thousands of tons a year. Today a combination of poaching and oil exploitation has reduced it to a mere 500 tons, and a ban on sturgeon fishing has done little to deter poachers. The biggest victim of the oil bonanza has been the Caspian seal, the smallest member of the seal family and the only mammal in the Caspian Sea. Its current population of half a million is stable but vulnerable.

Back in 1978 the Soviets discovered the Tengiz field, nearly fifty kilometres east of Atyrau and the sixth largest oil bubble in the world, containing 25 billion barrels. The oil was more than 4,000 metres below the surface and the Russians did not have the technology to extract the volatile gas-filled crude from such a depth. When they drilled deep the wells blew. In 1985 a blow-out killed many oil workers and burned for a year, shooting flames 200 metres into the sky. One of the Kazakh engineers then working in the field was Boris Cherdabaev, a graduate of the Soviet Institute for Oil and Gas. Frustrated at the inability to extract the black gold at the time, after independence he was at the forefront of efforts to attract foreign investment and knowhow. Today, as head of Teng-izchevroil, Cherdabaev is a billionaire.

In 1993, the American oil giant Chevron bought a drilling concession for Tengiz, investing billions in what soon became its largest international project. More money poured into the country in 1996 when Mobil – Chevron's competitor – bought government shares in the field, giving it a quarter holding. A Californian lawyer called James Giffen, a flamboyant oiler, acted as middleman between the Kazakh government and Western companies. Giffen genuinely opened up the country to foreign investment, but he also became entangled in a corruption scandal when it was alleged that he had paid millions of dollars in bribes.

Giffen had developed a business relationship with the Soviets during the Cold War when he sold them drilling technology, and after Kazakh independence he became an adviser to the government. He set up a New York bank called Mercator and negotiated a deal with Chevron that secured him a commission of seven cents a barrel. The widely held view inside Kazakhstan is that many of the agreements signed with Western oil companies in the early 1990s were unfair, and took advantage of the government's lack of business experience and the country's desperate need for investment.

Giffen's partner, a Jordanian businessman, certainly thought so. He filed a lawsuit in London against Giffen, the Kazakh oil minister and a Mobil sub-contractor, accusing the men of cheating him out of millions of dollars in commission. The suit prompted the US government to launch an investigation into Giffen for corruption, fraud and money-laundering. President Nazarbayev was named in court documents as receiving millions of dollars in a Swiss bank account, a charge he has consistently denied, challenging investigators to find any such accounts. Mobil has also denied any wrongdoing. The case against Giffen has become bogged down in the American courts for the last decade, not least because he claims he was in the pay of the CIA all along.

There is no doubt that many in the ruling élite, including

Nazarbayev and his family, became rich during the 1990s. 'If you had any connection to power then,' a Kazakh journalist explained, 'you had to be either incompetent or stupid *not* to get rich. The whole country was being privatized. Everything! And there were no rules or checks and balances governing anything, so how could people break the law? Kazakhstan continues to be corrupt, but every year there are more and more laws going through, and a move to transparency so Kazakh companies can be floated on the London Stock Exchange. Yes, maybe it should all be moving faster – but look where we've come from. Nowhere. In the 1990s it was the Wild East here. At the time of independence we were fifteen years behind Russia. Uzbekistan was supposed to be the country that would be the most successful in the region. Well, today we're three years ahead of Russia – and Uzbekistan is nowhere.'

The US might have been the initial investor and provided the technology, but everybody wanted the oil. By 1997 Chinese foreign policy was driven by an ever-increasing appetite for oil, and the Chinese National Petroleum Company bought 60 per cent of Kazakhstan's third largest oil field in Aktubinsk. Money seemed no object. The Chinese willingly paid over the odds, soon bought two more fields, and also agreed to pay to build a pipeline across the country into Xinjiang province. Meanwhile most of Kazakhstan's gas, and a large proportion of its oil, goes north to Russia. A further pipeline that runs under the Caspian Sea, across the Caucasus and into Turkey, is up and running. And Iran in the south is keen to receive a pipeline – a project so far stymied by the Americans.

In 2000, as a new millennium dawned, yet another vast oil reserve was discovered. The Kashagan field beneath the Kazakh section of the Caspian Sea is the biggest find in the world for thirty years. Deep below an ancient coral atoll geologists struck a giant oil bubble estimated to hold 30 billion barrels of highly concentrated brown crude, one of the largest fields on earth. (Reserves in the North Sea, in comparison, are estimated to be around 17 billion barrels.) Not since Alaska's Prudhoe Bay has so much oil been found in one place.

The Kazakhs' efforts to attract foreign investment and negotiate deals may have been clumsy and naïve in the early days, but they have been quick to understand the economic dangers of a sudden oil boom. It is not for nothing that oil has been called the devil's tears: the sudden infusion of billions of petro-dollars into a nation's economy can prove more of a curse than a windfall. Economists refer to this syndrome as the Dutch disease, when an economy is simply unable to cope with the influx of so much cash, leading to inflation, the drying-up of exports, and the collapse of local industries. Kazakhstan has studied the Norwegian experience – another country with a small population and a lot of oil – where a rainy day oil fund has been set up into which 15 per cent of all revenues are paid, to be used as a long-term mechanism to diversify the economy. In Kazakhstan oil has helped to create an overall economy that is doubling every seven years. The domestic economy is booming, capital markets are being fed by ever-growing savings and pension funds are expanding. 'Now everybody in the international business world is interested in Kazakhstan,' the journalist said. 'And not so long ago nobody had heard of us!'

•

The presidential party stopped in Taraz, a nondescript town on the Silk Road with an ancient history, and over dinner I met a man who shot wolves from helicopters. The local hunter was a large, jowly Kazakh who looked prosperous, as I suppose a man would need to be to indulge in such a pastime. The hunting of wolves in winter was a passion of his, he explained. Foolishly, I tried to make the case for the wolf.

Some years earlier I had seen a documentary in which an eccentric Canadian naturalist attempted to demonstrate that wolves were harmless old things that ate little more than mice all winter, and that their savage reputation was undeserved. My dinner companion listened politely to my account of Canadian mice-eating wolves, while two friends accompanying him stared at their plates. It was clear they thought I was most peculiar.

'Canadian wolves eat mice, do they?' the Kazakh hunter said. 'Maybe those Canadian wolves have gone soft.' His friends tried not to laugh. 'Our wolves eat sheep and cattle and horses, and sometimes children. They attack men. Last May alone seven people around here were attacked and savaged by wolves. Hunting them isn't just sport, it's a civic duty.'

A little research on my part confirmed that Kazakh wolves certainly do not limit their diet to mice. The current estimated population of wolves all over the country is around 40,000 – Kazakh zoologists say the number should not exceed 10,000 to maintain an ideal balance with other animals. The overpopulation accounts for the loss of 180,000 cattle, sheep and goats each year. The rural Kazakhs hate wolves because they seriously threaten their livelihood, and they fear them because they are dangerous.

The Kazakh wolf – *Canis lupus lupus*, also known as the Eurasian wolf – has thrived since the collapse of the Soviet Union to a point beyond its own good. Overpopulation has led to disease and winter starvation, and an imbalance with its usual quarry, the saiga. This ancient steppe antelope has an elongated snout that lends it an endearingly comical look, while the pink, lyre-shaped horns of the saiga buck suggest a mythical creature. A cheerful-looking animal, it is a living fossil that was wandering the steppes of Eurasia in the Ice Age at the same time as the mammoth. In Kazakhstan the saiga has lived a life similar to the nomads, moving great distances to new pastures in summer and winter. Older Kazakhs remember thundering herds moving across the steppe in great clouds of dust, like the American buffalo on the prairie. And like the buffalo, the saiga has been pushed to the edge of extinction by predatory man.

The collapse of the Soviet Union, and the subsequent lack of control, led to poaching of the saiga on a massive scale as impoverished Kazakh peasants looked for ways to survive in the hard times following independence. The slaughter of the bucks has created a dangerous disparity between males and females. At the beginning of the 1990s there were close to a million head in the country – today there are less than 40,000. Although the antelope's meat was once a staple of every Kazakh market, it is not the saiga's flesh that has led to its demise, but its horns. These are ground into powder and used in traditional Chinese medicine to reduce fever.

'It's a catastrophe,' a zoologist later told me in Almaty. 'The saiga population – the main source of food for wolves – has been destroyed over the past few years by poachers. A wolf kills between fifteen and twenty saiga each year but the disaster is that wolves now outnumber them. So naturally the wolves are going after sheep and cattle, and moving into more populated areas. And a wolf eats four or five kilos of meat every day, so a pack can cost a farmer an awful lot of money. The rural population see them as a deadly competitor.'

Scientific surveys using satellites that track the route of the saiga migrations across the steppe show how wolves follow them. Wolves were controlled in Soviet times by permanent brigades that hunted and shot around 2,000 a year. Wolf-hunting was both a profitable and a respected profession, and for decades every region had its own official squad paid by results. After independence, and the introduction of policed borders with Russia, the wolf population soared. Kazakhstan now has the highest density of wolves in the world.

Villagers resort to desperate measures to deter them, and I heard one story of awful vengeance. Some peasant shepherds believe that if a wolf is captured and skinned alive, leaving only the skin on its head and paws, its grisly fate scares other wolves from the district for several years. I asked the zoologist if this had really happened. 'Let us hope it is a folk myth,' he said. 'But I have heard similar stories, I must admit. Even as a fable this shows the deep hatred of the shepherd for the wolf. It is now permitted to hunt them in any number and by all available means – yes, even from helicopters. Today anyone with a hunter's ticket can shoot wolves without a licence and without limit. Only national parks are exempted.'

The government outlawed the hunting of saiga completely in 1999, and has since provided money to fund rangers and mobile units to track poachers, a big job in a big country. There are plans to set up a 60,000-square-kilometre sanctuary in the steppe under the auspices of the World Wildlife Fund. In the meantime, the wolf population continues to climb. In summer, the wolves go far away from human habitation to breed, but in the autumn when the packs form they approach villages. 'We need to develop a long-term programme to regulate the wolf population,' the zoologist said. 'It should be tailored to suit the needs of different regions. It's essential to distinguish clearly between those wolves that live where there is little human habitation, and there is a natural balance, and those that prey on domestic animals. If you exterminate wolves entirely they are likely to be replaced by wild dogs and mestizos [half-breeds of wolf and dog], and that's the biggest threat of all because those beasts are not afraid of humans.'

I asked my Taraz dinner companion how hunters went about the business of shooting wolves from helicopters. 'We do it through the autumn and winter,' he explained. Two or three hunters fly out into the steppe until a pack of wolves is spotted in the snow. The helicopter drops down low, and as the pack scatters, the most likely prey is picked. The hunters fire from the open door of the helicopter using special long-range cartridges. 'Wolves are savage. I've seen them jump many feet in the air to attack the helicopters. And they're clever. As you go down the rotors throw up a small snowstorm, and the wolves will back into it and disappear. It's not easy. Come and try it some time. Bring some mice.'

•

The local vodka in Taraz is called Parliament, and the label on each bottle bears a picture of the British Houses of Parliament. It is exceptionally popular and not bad stuff. The name of the vodka is a coded dig against Soviet authoritarianism from its makers, who were the first entrepreneurs in Kazakhstan. The Makhmadov brothers are descendants of Chechen deportees, and I met one of them, Zelikhan, at a trade fair in the city. A lean man in a black suit, his manner suggested all work and no play. 'We had the first enterprise working with capitalist rules in Soviet times in Kazakhstan,' he told me. 'You could say we ran up against problems, yes.'

At first the brothers produced fruit juices and spirits extracted from herbs for companies that made shampoo. Then they began to make, package and sell products themselves. There was a local market hungry for quality goods, so the company grew fast, and even before independence it employed seventy people. But it was continually harassed and hampered by the Soviet authorities.

'We were not unusual – we were unique. When the president heard about us he came and visited our factory. He was impressed and it was he who called us Kazakhstan's first entrepreneurs. He sought our advice on what should be done to promote private business in the country, and what our problems were with the system and the bureaucracy, and how to tackle them. We had a lot to say.' The business boomed after independence and, when it became possible to buy land, diversified into agriculture. 'We grow wheat. The best wheat in the world is grown in this region, accepted internationally as better even than Canadian wheat.'

The Makhmadov brothers blazed the way for other entrepreneurs. I visited the farm of a local shepherd who had become the area's most successful farmer. He was a big, bulky Kazakh dressed like General Noriega, and all his farm workers were also dressed as soldiers. Ten years ago he went into business with three partners to set up a farm of forty hectares with 500 horses. Today he has 5,000 hectares – 2,000 of which grow wheat – 8,000 sheep, more than 2,000 cows and 3,000 horses. One hundred people work for him – all kitted out with numbered military uniforms – and an extra fifty are employed each summer. The farmer has built himself a mansion from his profits, with vast rooms, pink walls and pink blinds, and he served me delicious soft balls of salty cheese and *zhent*, grain mashed and fried in butter with raisins – high-calorific nomad food. When I told him that if he lived in England he would be one of its biggest landowners, he displayed not a flicker of interest.

The Makhmadov brothers have had similar success. Their workforce is now 3,000 strong, drawn from thirty ethnic groups. 'The Chechens are the smallest ethnic group employed,' Zelikhan said. 'That's just the way it happened. The relationship between ethnic groups is good, although Kazakhs predominate in this part of the country. You must remember Chechens first arrived here in 1944, deported en masse by Stalin. The Kazakhs supported us and prevented us from dying of starvation. We also share similar customs and traditions. So we have become close to the Kazakhs.'

I told Zelikhan that I had been in Chechnya between the wars, and stayed in the bombed-out capital, Grozny. I had also visited what had been the mountain fastness of the nineteenth-century Chechen hero, Imam Shamil, who had fought the Russians for thirty years. And visited the grave of his namesake, Zelikhan – the Robin Hood of Chechnya – and met the then president, later denounced as a terrorist by the Russians and murdered.

Makhmadov seemed almost reluctant to ask the obvious question, 'What was it like when you were there?'

'Grozny had been flattened,' I said. 'Like Hiroshima. I have never seen anything like it. I don't know what they have found to bomb since. Driving up to Shamil's mountain hideout was surreal – magnificent countryside with the occasional shot-down MIG jet and burned-out tank at the side of the road. The local Chechens were very gracious and hospitable – and amazed to see a foreigner.' I did not add that the man who took me there had subsequently been murdered by a car bomb in Qatar, supposedly planted by the FSB, the Russian Federal Security Service. Or that practically everyone I had met in the country had since been killed. Chechens have had more than their share of misery, and have since dealt it out in kind.

Today, 50,000 Chechens live in Central Asia, children of the survivors of appalling genocide. In the middle of the Second World War Stalin decided that the Chechens – and other small Caucasian nations – should be 'liquidated'. He accused them of mass collaboration with the enemy, a flimsy charge that was made two years after deportation and never substantiated. In reality, 30,000 Chechens fought in the Red Army during the war, and several were decorated as Heroes of the Soviet Union. The soldier who placed the flag on the roof of the Reichstag, as the Red Army stormed Berlin, has been identified as Chechen.

Nevertheless, Stalin decreed that every Chechen man, woman and child should be deported to Kazakhstan. His security chief, Lavrenty Beria, moved to Chechnya to oversee the operation, accompanied by 100,000 NKVD agents and soldiers. The troops were billeted upon their potential victims who fed them for more than a month. The deportation began at 5 a.m. on 23 February 1944 – Red Army Day, a national holiday.

Flares were fired into the sky as a signal for the troops to move into action. American Lend-Lease Studebaker trucks in their hundreds took up position in town and village squares throughout the country, while troop trains stood ready at Grozny station. The troops, many of whom were roaring drunk by the end of the day, set about their work. People were given between thirty minutes and two hours to gather enough food and clothes for a week, and then loaded at gunpoint into trucks.

Men, women and children were shipped out to Kazakhstan at a rate of 80,000 a day, and within a week the job was done. Beria reported back to Stalin that almost half a million people had been loaded on to trains and sent east. The effort had required huge deployments from the front – 100,000 men, thousands of trucks, 12,000 railway carriages, all at a cost of 150 million roubles.

The action was irrational and made no sense – 4,000 skilled oil personnel had been included among the deportees, crippling production of the important Grozny oil fields for the remainder of the war. Even by Stalin's standards, the mass deportation of entire nations on ethnic grounds in the midst of a war for national survival was a massive escalation of terror. The first to be deported to Kazakhstan had been the Pontic Greeks, in 1939, followed by more than a million Volga Germans in 1941. The entire Chechen, Ingush, Kalmyk, Karachai and Balkar peoples followed. Later deportations to Kazakhstan included Meskhetian Turks from Georgia, Tatars from Crimea and Koreans from the Far East, and deportations continued until 1949.

In the case of the Chechens, the old, the sick and the pregnant were declared 'non-deportable' and simply murdered. At one hospital in a provincial town sixty-two people were summarily executed. At the remote mountain village of Khaibakh, 700 people were herded inside a stable block, its windows boarded up, its doors locked, and the building set on fire. In the ensuing panic, people broke down the door, only to be machine-gunned. The colonel in charge of the massacre reported baldly to Beria: 'In view of the impossibility of transportation and the necessity of fulfilling on schedule the goals of Operation Mountaineer, it was necessary to liquidate more than seven hundred inhabitants of the village of Khaibakh.' Beria wrote to the officer announcing a decoration and promotion, and left to oversee the next deportation of Balkars, described as 'bandits who attacked the Red Army'.

Many thousands of the Chechen deportees died on the three-week journey to Kazakhstan. An official memorandum noted approvingly that fewer railway carriages were needed than originally planned as so many of those transported were children. When the trains stopped, passengers who strayed more than five metres from their carriages were shot. The dead were left behind unburied in the snow.

'In my cattle truck, half of us died on the journey,' one Chechen remembered. 'There was no toilet – we had to cut a hole in the floor, and that was also how we got rid of the corpses.' Some people refused to dispose of their dead, hoping for a decent burial at their destination. Conditions on board became so unhygienic that a typhoid epidemic broke out. 'When we arrived in Kazakhstan, the ground was frozen hard, and we thought we would all die. It was the German exiles who helped us survive – they had already been there several years.'

A quarter of those who survived the actual deportation died of hunger and cold within five years. The living were obliged to report to the police once a week, and the punishment for leaving their designated area was twenty years' hard labour. After the disastrous harvests of 1946 and 1947 people were reduced to eating grass, leaving them sick and enfeebled, and reducing their value even as cheap labour. The head of the Department of Special Deportees sent a report to Moscow on the lack of shoes and warm clothing: 'The absence of clothes and footwear in winter could have a fatal effect on their ability to work.'

After the Khrushchev 'thaw', the Chechens decided to try to go home. Thirteen railway carriages full of families, acting as guinea pigs, set off in 1957 for the Caucasus after collecting money from the entire Chechen community in Kazakhstan to pay huge bribes to local police, KGB and railway officials. They were held at the Chechen border for three weeks but were then released on orders from Khrushchev. There were half-hearted attempts to prevent more Chechens returning to their homeland, but they were determined and they left in their tens of thousands, many disinterring the bones of their dead to take with them for burial in Chechnya.

No discussion of the deportations was ever allowed within the Soviet Union, and the names of the deported nations were removed from the *Great Soviet Encyclopaedia* and struck from all official documents as if they had never existed.

For many years it remained a secret shared only between deportees and Kazakhs. Today the descendants of this crime against humanity are among those who make up the thirty ethnic groups of the Makhmadov brothers' workforce. 'The deportation was the past,' Makhmadov said. 'Now we live in the present and can enjoy life. The Kazakhs are a hospitable people. Enjoy yourself in our country!'

•

We flew on across the most beautiful countryside – rolling green meadows cut through with steep-banked streams against a mountain backdrop – and set down on a stud farm. And in a yurt looking across to the mountains my Kazakh destiny caught up with me, as the president had said it would. Meat. Half a horse, to be precise. And a whole sheep's head.

A feast had been prepared in honour of the president, who sat alone at a long table, while the rest of us were seated at two tables set at right angles to it. We were to be served a traditional *besbarmak*, and four waiters carried in two giant ceramic platters loaded with steaming horsemeat and sausages. One of these was placed before the president, the other in front of me. As the only foreigner in the group, I was the guest of honour, and as such was presented with a cold boiled sheep's head. It sat on a plate to my left and eyed me dolefully. I eyed it dolefully back.

'Am I actually supposed to *eat* that?' I whispered discreetly to the man seated beside me. 'Or is it just for show?'

'It is offered to you as the height of hospitality. It would give grave offence if you were to ignore it. It is customary to scoop out the brains with a spoon first. I do not care for the eyeballs myself – but remember, they are just muscle. Crush them with your tongue against the roof of your mouth and swallow. There will be ample drink to wash them down.'

I looked again at the unfortunate sheep with mounting panic. And then I caught a mischievous glint in my companion's eye. I was having my leg pulled hard. He smiled. 'Seriously – just make a gesture of eating it. That will suffice.'

Relieved at not having to swallow cold brains and eyeballs – quite apart from what, to my Eurocentric palate, were a lot of other unappetizing bits – I showily brandished my knife and fork and cut a slice of meat from the sheep's cheek. The meat seemed rubbery in texture and quite difficult to carve. I sliced off a piece, put it into my mouth, and began to chew. The more I chewed the bigger it got. I imagined everyone in the yurt was watching as I chewed and chewed and chewed. Eventually, I swallowed the most masticated sliver of mutton ever to pass human lips.

Although not generally an eater of horsemeat, I had no qualms after the starter and followed the president's lead in sawing off a chunk and putting it on my plate, together with a couple of large squares of pasta. To my relief, the platter was then carried to the other guests. There had been a moment when I thought that politesse might dictate eating half a horse all by myself.

'Would you like something to drink?' the president asked. 'A little red wine?'

Bottles of good French claret appeared. My spirits began to lift, and I even thought of having another whack at the sheep's head. The president chatted knowingly about wine for a while, saying he had recently discovered the qualities of Chilean and South African wines – although First Growth Bordeaux seemed to be his tipple of choice. Wine talk triggered an anecdote about Gorbachev and his ill-starred effort to impose prohibition upon the Soviet Union – an act of such self-destructive political folly, when perpetrated by a Russian upon his fellow countrymen, that it seemed unhinged.

For the president, the policy merely demonstrated Gorbachev's personal hypocrisy, his distance from the reality of the Russian people, and the dishonesty of the old-style Soviet government. 'The order went out to chop down vines throughout the Soviet Union. I managed to have it modified here so that mostly the vineyards were closed down, without actually chopping down the vines. I know how long it takes to grow decent vines. But in Georgia and Moldova they chopped everything down.'

At the height of the anti-alcohol campaign, Gorbachev made a visit to Astana. He was accompanied by an enormous entourage, the most prominent member of which was his wife Raisa. The leading figures of Kazakhstan were in attendance, including the First Secretary, Dinmukhamed Kunayev. The group suffered through long and dreary official meetings with the region's grain farmers, visited a number of collectives in icy weather, and then gratefully went for lunch at the Communist Party leader's residence.

'It was only September but already extremely cold. Everyone was frozen. Ludicrous "sobriety zones" had already been established throughout the Soviet Union, aimed at wiping out drunkenness. However, I made sure a couple of cases of wine and some bottles of vodka and cognac were on hand. Raisa quickly began to dominate the conversation. She had an opinion on every subject under the sun, and her husband always took them very seriously.

We sat listening in silence as she expressed her categorical and often downright absurd views.

'Raisa made the statement that although Kazakhstan was an agricultural republic, it did not produce its own wine. I dared to contradict her. What's more, I said, although the leadership had declared war on alcoholism, perhaps everyone would like to taste a small glass of it? Kunayev kicked me under the table as a warning not to stir things up. But I knew Gorbachev well. I knew he wanted a drink.

'Gorbachev was silent for a bit, then he asked if I really had wine available – he knew everybody else wanted a drink too. He announced that the restriction did not apply to wine, and told the waiters to bring in some bottles. Everyone was delighted. I knew Gorbachev didn't much care for wine but preferred cognac. After a bit, he said, "I'm still cold – don't you have other stuff?" I said we actually had everything – ready to go! He asked for cognac, and lunch became a party and we had fun – even Gorbachev, the leading "abstainer".

'The anti-alcohol campaign highlighted the kind of dual morality that existed among government officials and Party bosses. One set of rules applied when they were among "the people", another when they were among their own kind. The campaign, by the way, was a total failure. People were so desperate to get high that they started using eau de cologne, toothpaste and shoe polish to make moonshine, and problems grew with drug addiction.'

•

One man who would have no truck with 'sobriety zones' was Boris Yeltsin. History might have turned out differently if he had not delayed his departure from a feast of Kazakh *besbarmak*, similar to the one I was enjoying, by staying on for a couple more shots of vodka.

In August 1991, Yeltsin made an official visit to Almaty. At the end of the first day an informal concert had been organized at the

National Museum of Musical Instruments. As the musicians were about to begin, Yeltsin called out to one of his aides, 'Bring me my spoons!' Long-handled spoons were duly brought and he rattled out rhythms on his thighs and elbows, as adept as any old-time West End busker.

The weather was good, and Yeltsin seemed to be enjoying himself so much that President Nazarbayev suggested he stay a little longer. The following day there was a visit to the same stud where we were enjoying our feast. Yeltsin was given a beautiful black stallion, which he sat upon to have photos taken, joking that he had never been on a horse in his life. Stable boys struggled to hold him in place and prevent him falling off.

Then the party moved on to the Talgarsi Gorge, a wild and beautiful spot in the mountains near the capital, where the water flows in a foaming white torrent over boulders and jagged rocks. Three yurts had been set up on the bank where the group could eat and rest. At the sight of the rushing water, Yeltsin declared he wanted to go swimming – a dangerous undertaking and a cold one, for the fast-running glacial waters were like ice even in midsummer. But he was not to be dissuaded. He insisted he was a strong swimmer and said that he liked to swim in the Moscow river when the temperature was a bracing four or five degrees.

'So we let him swim,' the president said. 'And then we sat down and drank a little vodka.' Refreshed and energized by the icy water, Yeltsin did not spare himself on the vodka. It was a balmy afternoon, and although he was scheduled to fly back to Moscow at five, the hour came and went. Six o'clock passed, and then seven. 'We Kazakhs take our hospitality very seriously.'

Finally, at eight o'clock, Yeltsin took off from Almaty in his plane and headed back to Moscow. Exhausted by the rigours of traditional Kazakh hospitality, Nazarbayev went home and straight to bed. But while the men had been enjoying a Sunday summer afternoon at the Talgarsi Gorge, plotters in Moscow were finalizing their plans to topple Gorbachev in a coup. 'The three-hour delay caused by our celebrations may have saved Yeltsin's life,' the president said. 'According to one of his aides, an order had been given by the coup plotters to shoot down his plane as it flew past a military base near Aktyubinsk, in western Kazakhstan. Soldiers were waiting to carry out their orders, oblivious of the identity of their intended victim. But the set time came and went and when the plane did not appear, and as there were no further orders, the later flight made its way safely to Moscow.'

At nine o'clock the following morning, a Monday, the president's wife woke her husband with alarming news. She had just heard a radio report announcing that Gorbachev was ill and had temporarily stepped down in favour of his vice-president, Gennady Yanayev. Nazarbayev turned on the radio to hear a series of statements issued by a newly created State of Emergency Committee: the Soviet Union was on the verge of breaking up and drastic measures were needed to hold it together. Gorbachev was too ill to control the situation, the radio announcer said, so the vice-president had stepped in to deputize. 'But as soon as I heard the name Yanayev – one of the most hardline members of the leadership – I knew something was wrong.'

It was imperative that Nazarbayev go immediately to his office to maintain control within Kazakhstan. He understood Yeltsin was in great danger – and that he might be as well. It was just after six in Moscow, and he tried to use the special government telephone circuit to call the Kremlin, but he was unable to get through. Nazarbayev left the residence to take the official car that waited for him each morning, but for the first time it was not there.

'The thoughts that went through my head would not surprise anyone brought up in the Soviet Union. I thought of Stalin's purges of 1937 and of the events after his death in 1953. Even the smallest thing out of the ordinary could be a sign. Shaken, I went back inside the house and picked up the special hotline that links me with my head of security. "Who's there?" came the reply. And that was the special line which only I had the right to use! "It's all over!" I thought.'

Nazarbayev discussed with his wife whether they had any

compromising material in the house. 'I had enough experience of working in the Soviet system to know how this kind of thing was arranged. They would search my home and produce documents and that would be it.'

In the meantime, the official car drew up at the residence but with an unknown driver. The chauffeur apologized for the delay, saying there had been a mechanical problem, and explained that the usual driver was ill. Nazarbayev was obliged to accept the explanation but suffered a tense drive to the office. 'As we drove along I thought of the possible scenarios. Where would they stop the car? At one of the fixed police posts, perhaps? Or as I got out to go into my office?'

The journey into town passed without incident. On arrival, Nazarbayev walked from the car to his office and at every step thought he might be arrested. Nothing happened. Inside the office, people were at their desks as usual. The first call of the day was from Yeltsin, who was still at his dacha outside of Moscow. 'I intend to go to the White House,' Yeltsin said over the phone. 'The main thing is that we stand together.'

Yeltsin might easily have been arrested by the secret police on his way to the White House, where the Russian parliament had its headquarters, but the plotters made the mistake of not stopping him. The result was seen on television across the world. He climbed on to a tank in front of the parliament building to address the crowd, and instantly became the symbol of resistance against the illegal regime. Boris Yeltsin has since squandered his reputation, and been justly reviled, but on the day of the coup he was heroic.

In Kazakhstan, Nazarbayev appeared on television and announced that he was tearing up his Communist Party member-ship card and leaving the Politburo in protest at the coup. Not a word of the broadcast was carried in Moscow. That evening he called Vladimir Kryuchkov, overall head of the Soviet KGB, and one of the principal architects of the coup. Nazarbayev attempted to persuade the KGB chief not to launch a military attack on the

White House. 'No, there won't be an attack,' Kryuchkov said. 'But there are people killing one another and we have to restore order.' Nazarbayev was blunt: if there *was* an attack and the KGB did intervene and kill innocent people, then all the Soviet republics – including Kazakhstan – would rise up against him.

Later, in the early hours of the morning the following day, Nazarbayev spoke to Dmitry Yazov, the Soviet Defence Minister, another of the coup plotters whom he felt to be essentially decent. 'What are you doing getting involved in this, Dmitry Timofey-vitch?' he asked. 'And what are you going to do now?'

'I don't know,' the Defence Minister replied. 'I have got myself caught up with these fools. What do you suggest?'

'Pull your tanks out of Moscow!'

Nazarbayev wished he had suggested that the tanks swivel their turrets to point their guns at the Kremlin, where the coup plotters were holed up. He now proposed to Yanayev, who had established himself as acting head of the Soviet Union, that he (Nazarbayev) travel to Moscow and act as mediator. Yanayev agreed, but when Yeltsin heard of it he warned against such a move: 'They will arrest you when you arrive at the airport.'

A strange unreality settled over Almaty, as all contact with Moscow was cut off. The special government telephone lines were silent. A looped recording of the Bolshoi Ballet performing Tchaikovsky's *Swan Lake* played throughout the day on the government television channel. But by the afternoon of the third day it became clear that the coup had failed.

Nothing was known of the fate of Gorbachev, and it was feared he might even have been killed. Nazarbayev learned that the three coup plotters, Yanayev, Kryuchkov and Yazov, had left Moscow by plane, but no one knew where they had gone. CNN reported rumours that some of the coup members were on their way to Kazakhstan to seek political asylum. 'The theory was completely absurd,' Nazarbayev said. 'Even so, I ordered my civil aviation chiefs to check for any unusual air traffic.'

The uncertainty over the fate of Gorbachev was particularly

worrying for Nazarbayev, who was convinced that the plotters would stop at nothing to save their crumbling coup. 'Honestly, when the long-awaited telephone call came from Faros, in the Crimea, where Mikhail Sergeyevitch was being held, I was overjoyed. I find it difficult to reconstruct in detail my conversation, so powerful were my emotions at that moment. I will never forget the unusually intimate tone of his agitated voice which made it impossible not to appreciate the enormous shock which the man had suffered.'

The tension of the three-day coup had also taken its toll on Nazarbayev. The conversation with Gorbachev had lasted less than ten minutes, but afterwards he found himself as moved and disturbed as the man himself. CNN continued to play on the television in the office, and aides came in to try to talk to him. 'But I just sat there motionless, seeing and hearing nothing.'

•

The story of the coup had been a first-hand account of one of the most important events in twentieth-century history. The party listened attentively and then fell silent. The president changed the mood. As I was tucking into a slice of surprisingly delicate and tasty horse sausage – known as kazy – he asked, 'Do you like sushi?'

I said I did but presumed there was not much taste for it in a landlocked country. 'In recent years many Kazakhs have developed a taste for sushi,' the president said.

At that moment waiters carried two miniature wooden Viking longships into the yurt, each packed with every type of sushi. It was a vision as surreal in its way as the sheep's head. Waiters placed bottles of Japanese beer on the tables, and carafes of hot and chilled saké. I looked about me: the sheep's head remained on my left, while up and down the table was a mountain of horsemeat besbarmak, bowls of steaming broth and boatloads of sushi. Scattered among the food were bottles of French claret, Japanese beer and saké, Kazakh and Russian vodka, and Armenian cognac. As my companion on the plane had remarked: 'Globalization.'

The president had mentioned that he was currently reading an anthology of Franklin D. Roosevelt's radio broadcasts, *Fireside Chats*, made between 1933 and 1944, and I asked if he was an admirer. 'I was in a similar position to Roosevelt in 1994. Enterprises had collapsed and there were no jobs. It was worse than the Depression. I saw the solution in rapid privatization – to take the initiative away from the State and give it to ordinary men and women. I studied the theories of the German economist Friedrich Hayek, who had advised Adenauer, and what Thatcher had done in Britain, and the experiences of the tiger economies of Singapore and South Korea, which were particularly interesting for us as successful Asian models. And, of course, I studied what China was doing. No other country has had a nation state for 5,000 years – China sees a hundred years as a day and takes the long view. We would be wise, perhaps, to think like this.

'The situation in Kazakhstan is different now from the early days. We have accumulated financial resources and can use that to pay teachers more, build houses, roads and hospitals. And prosperity and growth among the whole population will call for more demand and create another surge of economic development.'

It seemed to me, I said, that the president was a free-market socialist. 'I will tell you something that is seen as politically incorrect these days,' he replied. 'If Adam Smith was the greatest economist of the eighteenth century, then the nineteenth belongs to Karl Marx. He understood how the capitalist system worked. He foresaw how monopolies would come out of it, and that the unjust exploitation of workers would lead to revolution. And clever capitalists paid attention to these things and adapted. In many ways the most socialist countries today are Germany and the United States, because they pay enormous sums to improve the social conditions of the people. So you can call these countries socialist – although Americans don't like the word. My point is that the quest for the best model is still going on around the world. Here in Kazakhstan I'm trying to adopt the good experiences of other countries and get rid of the bad practices of the past.'

•

After the feast, the president took me by the elbow and turned back to look at the tables loaded with leftovers. 'Do not think any of this will be wasted,' he said. 'The moment we leave there will be a party and only white bones will be left. The locals will be surprised and delighted you did not finish the sheep's head.'

The party was shown around the stud and led through immaculate stables which contained a hundred magnificent horses. The president began to tease one of his team, a man apparently considered a hopeless urbanite, long divorced from the ways of the nomads. 'Do you know what happens on a stud?'

'Of course, Mr President.'

'We don't have to get a couple of horses out here to show you?'

'No, Mr President, thank you.'

The president turned to someone nearby. 'He's such a townee. Can't ride a horse, speaks lousy Kazakh – it's a wonder we keep him around.'

At the end of the tour the president was presented with a finely worked leather riding crop, and he swished the air with it. 'I need this badly,' he said – adding quickly for my sake, 'Not to use on the people – but on the bureaucrats.'

'Bureaucrats are people too, Mr President,' the head of protocol said gently.

The president saddled up and went for a ride on a challenging black stallion. I wandered towards the security troops who were standing in the shade and who seemed to be in sleepy good spirits. They had been cautious about me at first, but by now I had been around long enough to be accepted. I pointed to a group of what looked like brick houses in the far distance, and asked if there was a village there.

'It's a cemetery,' I was told. 'We do not point at a cemetery.' My apology was waved aside lightly. 'You could not know, but *we* do not point at cemeteries.' It was the most gentle rebuke, and I was not sure if I had committed an offence against Islam or Kazakh custom. The Kazakhs do not point at the moon and stars, which are holy, or spit near a well, or talk disrespectfully of women or the old. When I asked whether all Kazakhs were Sunni, or if there were Shia among them, I was told, 'We are Sunni. But if you ask anyone in a village, or even in the towns, they will just tell you they are Muslim. They will not know or care much.'

I enthused about the extraordinary beauty of the place we were in, and the soldiers' own pleasure came out in a rush: they talked of the glorious setting, and of drinking spring koumiss from the best horses in the world at the best time of the year – could anything be more blessed?

There was a shocked murmur when I said that I had never tasted koumiss, and one of the detail went off to fetch me a wooden bowl of the stuff. This was brought to me by the president's taster – a qualified doctor, armed with a Glock pistol in a shoulder-holster. When I wondered aloud whether there really were potential presidential poisoners about, he laughed. 'Nothing so paranoid. But when we travel to remote and wild parts in the country my job is to make sure the food and water aren't contaminated. You'll never taste better koumiss than this.'

The fermented mare's milk, which is mildly alcoholic, tasted smoky and rich, and though it struck me as being an acquired taste, I drank it gratefully. The place was magical, the mood mellow, and I waxed poetic. Perhaps it didn't sound so good in Russian, but the guards smiled happily enough:

'For he on honey-dew hath fed,
And drunk the milk of Paradise.'

CHAPTER SIX

•

LOVE AND DEATH IN OLD
SEMIPALATINSK

I had become weary of the steppe. I had flown over steppe for hour after hour in jet and helicopter, travelled through steppe by car and train, surrounded forever by the Sea of Grass. After a while the steppe's featureless enormity bred the sort of negative thoughts and moments of loneliness that a castaway might feel adrift on an ocean flat as a millpond. No wonder the Kazakh nomadic tradition contains so much music and song to fill the emptiness.

So when I told my friend Umbetov that I was going to the edge of southern Siberia to visit the town of Semey – known previously to the Russians as Semipalatinsk – he shrugged. There was not much to see, he said, not much at all. Or rather, a lot more of the same. 'You have seen the steppe – the empty steppe?' I nodded. 'Then you will see more empty steppe.'

It's true, there's not much to see in Semey. The town's moment of glory came in 1917 when it was the capital of the short-lived Alash Orda government of briefly independent Kazakhstan. Today it is a city of 300,000 people, slowly coming back to economic life, with a new suspension bridge crossing the River Irtysh. Strangely, the decent hotels were full when I visited, forcing me to spend the night in an ancient Soviet firetrap where everything clanked but nothing worked. The lift was terrifying, there was no hot water and, while there was no disco in the basement, there was one in the backyard.

But this region of the country is the land of the Middle Horde, known for their intellectual and artistic prowess. Kazakhstan's greatest writer, Abay Kunabaev – the founder of Kazakh literature who died in 1904 – was born in a village close by, and a large museum in the town pays lavish tribute to his memory. Abay recorded Kazakh traditions and legends, and also translated Russian and European classics into Kazakh – making Alexander Dumas' The Three Musketeers every Kazakh's favourite foreign book. Abay also recognized the Russian contribution to Kazakh life: 'Study Russian culture and art – it is the key to life.' (This did not, however, protect him from a period of Soviet disapproval for his 'feudal' politics.)

By mid-morning of the first day in Semey I felt I had seen the town, but I had not come for the sights. There were two things from the past that had brought me to this part of Kazakhstan, a story of doomed love, and a history of doom itself.

◆

Although modern Semey is a scruffy place unlikely to stir the casual visitor with ecstatic feelings of freedom and rebirth, or suggest itself as the site of a grand passion, old Semipalatinsk was all of these things for Fyodor Dostoyevsky, who lived here for five years. He had been exiled to Kazakhstan in the spring of 1854, and the wooden house where he lived for part of the time is now incorporated into yet another writer's museum, where his rooms have been preserved in the simple style of nineteenth-century provincial Russia. For the most part the museum consists of a multitude of photos of Fyodor, forever deadpan, and drawings and etchings of old Semipalatinsk.

At the time, the town was just another Russian military garrison, founded by Peter the Great in 1718 to suppress the local Kazakhs and hold the line of empire. Built upon the ruins of an ancient Mongol settlement on the steep right bank of the Irtysh, it was half-city, half-village, with a mixed Russian and Kazakh population of a few thousand. The Russians lived in one-storey wooden houses in the town, while the Kazakhs mostly inhabited yurts across the river. The minarets of seven mosques pricked the skyline, but the only stone building was the Russian Orthodox church. Caravans of camels, mules and horses, trading between Russia and Central Asia, carried goods to and from the large covered market place. Mail was delivered once a week and took at least a month to arrive from Moscow. The unpaved streets were clouded with dust in summer, deep with mud in spring, and buried in snow in winter. The limitations of the town's cultural life can best be illustrated by the fact that it possessed but a single piano.

An American newspaperman who passed through the place in the late nineteenth century described it as having the air of a 'Mohammedan town built in the middle of a North African desert. It presents a peculiar grey, dreary appearance, owing partly to the complete absence of trees and grass, partly to the ashy, weather-beaten aspect of its unpainted log-houses, and partly to the loose, drifting sand with which its streets are filled.' Semipalatinsk in the mid-nineteenth century was colourless, impoverished and unimaginably dull, but to Dostoyevsky it was very heaven.

He arrived in the town after serving four years in a Russian prison, sentenced to indefinite exile as a private in the Siberian Seventh Line Battalion. This ragged regiment was composed almost entirely of released prisoners and exiles, apart from its officers, and was little more than a punishment corps. The journey from the prison in Omsk across the steppe had taken three days through monotonous landscape, broken only by the occasional Kazakh yurt on the horizon or a passing caravan of camels. But Dostoyevsky travelled in the best of spirits, and at the end of his life told friends that he had never been happier than when he drove beside the banks of the Irtysh 'with the clean air around me and freedom in my heart'.

The writer's journey to this place of exile had been long and hard both physically and psychologically. Like so many Russian writers and intellectuals before and after him, Dostoyevsky had fallen foul of the implacable and merciless Russian state. As a member of the minor nobility, and a precociously successful young writer, it was a fate that had moved him from the centre of the St Petersburg intelligentsia and placed him before a firing squad.

At the age of 24, Dostoyevsky had earned a *succès d'estime* with his novel *Poor Folk*, which was praised by the most austere critics and became the talk of literary St Petersburg. But writers inflate grotesquely with praise, and the plaudits went horribly to his head. He metamorphosed almost instantly from a youth of chronic timidity to one of unbridled vanity, pitching up at literary salons in white tie, top hat and tails. 'If I began to recount all my triumphs,' he wrote to his brother, 'I would soon run out of paper.'

In the meantime, Dostoyevsky had fallen in with a group of Utopian Socialists and *soi-disant* revolutionaries known as the Petrashevsky Society, a group of young firebrands who met each week to drink hot punch and discuss the political issues of the time, such as the emancipation of the serfs, the struggle against censorship, and judicial reform. The society was essentially revolutionary in voice only, and was otherwise orderly even in argument – a little bronze bell was rung if tempers frayed, and when it sounded members were required to lower their voices and calm down.

But the talk was strong stuff. Tsar Nicholas I was declared the Antichrist, the existing social order condemned to death, and revolution plotted. When a report on the meetings reached the Tsar he issued a secret order to have its members arrested, Dostoyevsky among them. They were incarcerated in the Peter-Paul Fortress while a four-month investigation into the society's 'crimes' was launched. A military court subsequently found fifteen of the accused, including Dostoyevsky, guilty of 'a conspiracy of ideas'. The men were taken from their cells on a cold December morning and driven in black carriages with frosted windowpanes to a city square where they saw a scaffold draped in black cloth. Behind it stood a line of carts loaded with empty coffins. To one side three platoons of sixteen men leaned on their muskets, while in front three stakes had been driven into the frozen ground. As Dostoyevsky took in the scene he exclaimed, 'It's not possible they mean to execute us!'

An official took a paper from his pocket, hurriedly read out a list of names, and proclaimed sentence: 'Condemned to death before a firing squad.' The men were to be shot in groups of three – and Dostoyevsky was designated to the second batch. The first trio were tied to the stakes and a platoon of soldiers took up position in front of each of the condemned. An order was shouted for the soldiers to load their weapons and there was a rattle of ramrods in muskets. Another order was shouted: 'Take aim!'

The soldiers levelled their muskets, the drum roll intensified, and the entire square waited for the final order to fire. And waited. On the scaffold, Dostoyevsky calculated he had only minutes to live. The condemned men waited in an agony of tension for the death volley. The crowd waited. And Dostoyevsky waited. It seemed like an eternity but was probably as little as thirty seconds, during which he felt 'cold, terribly cold', and was overcome with a 'mystic terror' of the unknown.

Suddenly, one of the Tsar's aides-de-camp galloped across the square, dismounted and handed the general a sealed letter. It was a last-minute reprieve – the death sentences had been commuted to hard labour and exile. There had never been any intention of shooting the men, but the Tsar had commanded that the death sentence be acted out until the very last moment, a despot's dark joke to show his absolute power over his subjects.

Dostoyevsky's sentence was reduced to four years' hard labour, followed by an indefinite period as a private soldier in exile – a lenient term for an enemy of the Tsar. After the mock execution he was returned to his cell in the Peter-Paul Fortress, and at midnight taken to a blacksmith. As the bells of the fortress chimed 'Glory to the Tsar', he was put into the ten-pound leg irons that he would wear day and night for the next four years. He was placed in an open, horse-drawn sledge with a guard and sent 3,000 kilometres to his punishment. Beyond the Urals the temperature dropped to minus 40 degrees centigrade. After weeks of rough travel he reached Tobolsk, a transit centre for convicts from all over Russia. Three hundred men, women and children were chained to the walls of their cells, awaiting dispersal to various prisons, work camps and slave-labour mines.

Dostoyevsky now travelled another 600 kilometres in open sledge to Omsk, an eighteenth-century fortress that had been turned into a military prison, on the edge of western Siberia, bordering the lands of the Kazakhs. As someone greatly moved by song, he listened with despondent pleasure to the plaintive Kazakh melodies that wafted across from the far bank of the river.

The convicts were never released from their chains: they worked in them, slept in them, went to the bath-house in them, and to the hospital – and for those able to bribe the guards for a woman, fornicated in them. Political prisoners were treated no better than common criminals, the worst of whom had their faces branded. Dostoyevsky had one side of his head shaved and was given a grey uniform with a diamond-shaped yellow patch on the back. He had been condemned to live among men who had committed the most appalling crimes: 'A world in itself that resembled no other. It had its own laws, its own dress, codes and customs – it was a house of the living dead, and life here resembled no other place on earth.'

As a writer, Dostoyevsky had no useful trade and was classed as a labourer. He waded knee-deep through the icy waters of the Irtysh, unloading the wooden state-owned barges. He also fired bricks and carried them in hods to construction sites as Alexander Solzhenitsyn would do a hundred years later. After he had served four years, and the first half of the sentence was completed, he was able to present himself to the blacksmith to have the irons struck from his legs: 'Freedom, a new life, resurrection.'

•

Indefinite exile in a punishment corps, even in such a remote spot as Semipalatinsk, was a featherbed experience after the miseries the novelist had suffered in prison. At first, Dostoyevsky was required to live in barracks, but he had few duties except to attend parades. His status denied him the company of the dubious local gentry, but he found his fellow soldiers a great improvement on the criminals. 'Those of us who have lived among soldiers know how far removed they are from fanaticism,' he wrote in a letter to his brother. 'If you only knew what nice, likeable, dear fellows they are.'

For their part, the soldiers found Dostoyevsky an acceptable but glum companion. 'With his shaven, emaciated cheeks, his face looked ill and made him appear old,' one remembered. 'He had grey eyes and a serious, morose expression. In the barracks, none of us soldiers ever saw him smile. Mostly he sat, lost in thought.'

The 'secret surveillance' that Dostoyevsky was supposed to be under seems to have been a casual business, and he was soon given permission to live in the Russian section of the town where he rented a small cottage. Cockroaches swarmed over the table, bed and walls. He was looked after by the landlady's barefoot daughters, who in summer wore only shifts tied with red scarves – which after four years in prison must have been an uplifting sight. (The youngest, a 16-year-old, earned pocket money through occasional prostitution with the local soldiery.)

Previously denied books – except for his beloved New Testament – he now devoured the latest literature sent to him by his brother from Moscow. One story, entitled *Boyhood* and signed L. T., attracted his attention. He wrote to his brother asking who the author might be, and wondered whether the obvious talent was just a flash in the pan. 'I believe that he will write very little, but perhaps I am mistaken.' Very mistaken, as things turned out. L. T. was Count Leo Tolstoy.

Early on Dostoyevsky made the acquaintance of one of the town's officials, a petty customs officer named Alexander Ivanovich Isayev. The man drank so heavily he was incapable of regular work, and Dostoyevsky observed that he had already 'gone terribly to seed ... lived a very disorderly life, and his nature too was disorderly, passionate, obstinate and rather coarse. He was irresponsible as a gipsy, vain and proud, and had no self-control whatever.' (He was to become, in part, the prototype for the character Marmeladov in *Crime and Punishment*.) When Isayev embarked on his drunken binges he mixed with the dregs of the town with the result that the doors of polite society – such as it was in Semipalatinsk – were firmly closed to him. But Dostoyevsky developed a generous and tolerant view of the drunken customs officer's character because he had fallen in love with the man's pretty, blonde wife.

Maria Dmitrievna was 27 years old, slender, of medium height, with a high forehead and sensuous lips. She was well read, vivacious and impressionable. Her married life was a catastrophe. Isayev became so violent when drunk that she had to protect their 7-year-old son from his rages, but she suffered her fate with dignity and without complaint.

Dostoyevsky was smitten the first time he saw her, and within six months he was besotted. 'She is beautiful, educated, very wise, good, sweet, gracious, and has a fine and noble heart,' he wrote to his brother. 'A knight in woman's clothing.' She reminded him of their mother.

Maria was also fickle, manipulative, excessively jealous, paranoid, neurotic to the point of hysteria – and absolutely not in love with Dostoyevsky. Over the next ten years this deadly emotional cocktail slowly poisoned him, but Maria was the first true love of his life.

In the meantime, he had made a male friend in Semipalatinsk. Baron Alexander Wrangel, a 21-year-old Russian-German aristocrat of Baltic origin, had chosen to take up the position of public prosecutor in the town because he had a passion for travel and hunting. As a teenager he had read and admired Dostoyevsky's first novel, and he had later witnessed the mock execution in St Petersburg and been greatly disturbed by it.

On arrival in town, Wrangel immediately sought out the writer, whom he found reticent in the extreme. At the men's first meeting Dostoyevsky wore a grey soldier's greatcoat with a high red collar and epaulettes, and appeared sickly and morose. 'As he examined me attentively with his intelligent grey-blue eyes he seemed to be trying to penetrate into my very soul,' Wrangel remembered, 'to discover what kind of person I was.' It was the beginning of a long and deep friendship.

Dostoyevsky's lowly social position was changed at once by his relationship with the young baron, who not only introduced him to local worthies as an equal, but also made it possible for him to meet the town's handful of intellectuals who treated the exiled writer with great respect. One was the Kazakh scholar Chokan Valikhanov, ethnographer, folklorist and historian. Valikhanov was a descendant of a family of khans of the Middle Horde and a sultan in his own right. An officer in the army, he was the first Kazakh to receive a Russian higher education, and he became the first ethnographer of his people. He mapped the unknown mountain wilds between Russia and China, and was the first historian to record the oral folk legends, epics and sayings of the steppe. His work provided the foundation for all that is known today of old Kazakh culture.

Through his friendship with Valikhanov, Dostoyevsky developed an interest in cultural archaeology and began to collect early Kazakh objects – rugs, coins, bracelets, beads and spear heads. The scholar loved Arabic poetry, which he recited to his friend; Dostoyevsky for his part urged the Kazakh to make the Russians 'understand the steppe' and foster rapprochement between the races. (Valikhanov did his best, but by the time he died he had become completely disillusioned by Russian attitudes and the mistreatment of his people.) The men became close, affectionate friends.

Dostoyevsky also renewed his acquaintanceship with a man who had attended meetings of the Petrashevsky Society in St Petersburg. Peter Semenov, the eminent geographer whose book would later be taken into exile by Trotsky, had grown so famous for his mountain exploration in Kazakhstan – together with Valikhanov – that he was already known as 'Tien Shan' Semenov. It was to his friend Semenov that Dostoyevsky read the first studies of *Notes from the House of the Dead*, the book of his prison experiences prepared in exile that would later make him internationally famous. The men had not known each other well in St Petersburg, but they became close friends in Semipalatinsk.

Wrangel and Dostoyevsky found a dacha, named Cossack Garden, on a high bank of the Irtysh and moved in together. They read endlessly and went swimming and fishing. In the garden they grew dahlias, sweet williams and varieties of stock in the sandy soil that had previously only yielded sunflowers. Dostoyevsky, wearing a rose-coloured calico waistcoat faded from washing, found great satisfaction in watering the young seedlings.

The friends went on long rides through the surrounding pine groves and lakes, but Dostoyevsky proved indifferent to the natural beauty of the region, unimpressed even by the mirror-like Lake Kolyvan, considered by the great nineteenth-century traveller Humboldt to be the most beautiful lake in the world. Only the vast, starlit night sky, stretching over the endless steppe like a canopy, moved him.

The close friendship extracted a price from Wrangel in that he became the confidant of Dostoyevsky's love affair with Maria Dmitrievna. Wrangel understood the grand passion was founded on a misconception that could only torture both lovers. 'I don't think she really appreciated him, rather took pity on an unhappy man, whom fate had treated so harshly,' he wrote. 'It is possible that she even became fond of him, but she was never the least in love with him. She knew that he suffered from a nervous disease and that he was extremely short of money – he was a man without a future, she used to say. But Fyodor Mikhailovich mistook her feelings of pity and compassion for reciprocated love, and he loved her with all the ardour of a young man.'

Doubt over whether the object of his passion loved him led Dostoyevsky into fits of debilitating jealousy. In the meantime, Maria's married life tumbled into absolute misery. Her husband's alcoholism resulted in the loss of his modest post, and for two years the family survived in Semipalatinsk without an income, practically reduced to beggary. Finally, Isayev accepted the humiliating and – for him – fatal position of innkeeper in Kuznetsk, a Siberian wilderness town of hunters, trappers and prospectors 600 kilometres to the north. He was obliged to sell the last of his possessions and borrow money for the trip, and even then he could only afford an open wagon.

The prospect of Maria's departure plunged Dostoyevsky into new levels of despair. When the family set off across the steppe on a beautiful, moonlit night in May, he accompanied them for the first part of the journey as was the Russian custom, together with Wrangel. Isayev got drunk in Wrangel's carriage and fell asleep, leaving the lovers alone in the open wagon. When it came time to part, Dostoyevsky sobbed like a child. 'As the cart pulled away,' Wrangel remembered, 'he stood there as if rooted to the spot, speechless, his head bowed, tears rolling down his cheeks.'

The misery of absence fed Dostoyevsky's passion. He told Wrangel: 'God preserve us from this terrible, frightening emotion. The joys of love are great, but the suffering is so horrible that it is better never to have loved at all.' And to his brother he wrote: 'I am so unhappy, so unhappy! I am tortured, killed! My soul quakes.'

Maria's letters complained of poverty and illness, which were real enough, but they also contained provocative phrases suggesting rival male admirers, calculated to feed Dostoyevsky's jealousy. On one occasion he set off for a clandestine rendezvous with his love half way between Kuznetsk and Semipalatinsk, but then he received a note saying Maria had been unable to leave her sick husband. Later, news arrived that Isayev, denied proper medical treatment in the Siberian wilderness, had died an agonizing death from the stone.

Maria was now utterly penniless, without money even for her husband's funeral. Dostoyevsky borrowed cash from Wrangel and sent it to her as a gift. Sometime later a letter arrived requesting advice – what should Maria do if 'an older man of good character, a well-situated government official' asked for her hand? The sly, heartless manipulation unhinged Dostoyevsky. 'I am like a madman! It is already too late now! Things are horribly bad and I am practically desperate. It is hard to suffer as I have suffered. I tremble lest she get married, God help me, I'd drown myself or take to drink.'

Another letter arrived. Maria revealed that in reality there was no wealthy official, and she had only wanted to test her lover's devotion. She seems to have played her helpless admirer ruthlessly, tamping down his jealousy in one letter only to stoke it in the next. She now wrote describing encounters with a 'young, sympathetic teacher with a noble soul'.

Once again, Dostoyevsky sank into depression. He took the considerable risk of an illegal journey to Kuznetsk to woo his love and confront his rival. The teacher with the noble soul turned out to be a hard-up, dreary, lachrymose youth five years younger than Maria, who was also a victim of her emotional drubbing. She now mercilessly played the men off against one another, telling Dostoyevsky that she thought she loved the younger man, but did not wish to deny Dostoyevsky hope. Days later she told the hapless writer, 'Do not weep, do not be sad, all is not yet decided. It is you and I and no one else.' A blizzard of letters followed in which Maria vacillated between the two men, while Dostoyevsky wallowed in an ecstasy of misery. 'Oh those days I spent with her – the bliss, the unbearable agony! My heart is breaking.'

The unhappy but encouraged lover made the long uncomfortable journey back to Semipalatinsk, only to receive a letter from Maria saying she loved the young teacher after all, and the emotional flaying continued. Maria seems to have been an emotional sadomasochist who took pleasure in torturing her suitors, while suffering genuine guilt, uncertainty and jealousy herself. But she had a practical as well as a hysterical side and she now suggested that while she might have certain feelings for Dostoyevsky, he remained an ex-criminal and a lowly private soldier, 'a man without a future'. If she were to marry, it would be to an officer. Dostoyevsky was a man of his times and saw the logic of this: 'After all, she cannot marry a common soldier, can she?'

Wrangel, who by this time had returned to St Petersburg, began to make representations on his friend's behalf to obtain a commission and have his status as a hereditary nobleman restored. The old Tsar had died, and although it took considerable energy and effort on Wrangel's part, within a year Dostoyevsky was granted a commission, and the restoration of his nobility followed.

Donning the uniform of an officer, Dostoyevsky returned to Kuznetsk to convince his love that at last he was a man with a future. He vowed to educate her son, find a position for his rival, and provide for her as a husband. She agreed to marry him. Dostoyevsky had paid a high price for his prize during an exhausting and emotionally draining seven-year courtship. Triumphant in love at long last, he was suddenly overcome with indifference. The tone of his letters changes, and instead of the expressions of a tortured lover on the perpetual edge of nervous breakdown, there are dry calculations on how much everything is going to cost and how he is going to pay for it all. The writer might have been elevated to the rank of officer and noble, but he remained a man whose worldly wealth consisted of a mattress and a pillow.

A variety of people were petitioned for gifts and loans, including the faithful Wrangel, and enough was raised to satisfy the immediate ambitions of his future wife. Maria needed costly material for her dress, Dutch linen handkerchiefs, and a pretty blue bonnet with ribbons. The wedding service was a quiet affair with few people present. One of the witnesses was the young rival, a situation that allowed Dostoyevsky to indulge in a few final moments of hysteria: Maria might suddenly change her mind; the spurned suitor might kill her in a fit of passion – or kill the groom ... or Dostoyevsky might go out of his mind.

But no such thing happened, and the wedding went off without incident. The honeymoon on the other hand was a disaster. The newlyweds had journeyed south towards Semipalatinsk, stopping at the town of Barnaul to stay with Peter 'Tien Shan' Semenov, and it was at his friend's house that calamity struck. 'Here misfortune overtook me. I had a completely unexpected attack of epilepsy, which frightened my wife to death and filled me with sadness and despair.'

Dostoyevsky had suffered seizures before – dating from the time of the mock execution – but this was a particularly bad and ugly attack. He screamed, suffered spasms, wet himself and foamed at the mouth until he lost consciousness. A doctor was summoned who found the writer weak with a rapid pulse rate, and breathing with difficulty.

Maria had witnessed the attack in terror and instantly regretted the marriage, reproaching herself for not choosing the young teacher over the epileptic ex-convict. For his part, Dostoyevsky felt guilty for marrying when suffering from such a serious condition. From now on he no longer wrote of his wife as a noble soul and heavenly angel, but complained instead: 'My life is hard and bitter.'

Back at Semipalatinsk, the couple's home life was miserable. Emotional roles seemed to have been reversed, and it was now Maria who was jealous, resulting in a perpetual cycle of tearful and angry scenes. Dostoyevsky's epileptic seizures became more frequent and resulted in exhaustion, amnesia and deep depression. As a result, he was eventually discharged from the military as unfit for service.

Then, after eighteen months of domestic hell, good news arrived. Dostoyevsky was to be allowed to leave Kazakhstan and return to European Russia. His exile was over.

Dostoyevsky and Maria travelled westwards to the foothills of the Urals. There, in a forest, on a fine afternoon, they reached the boundary between Europe and Asia. The couple stepped from the carriage and Dostoyevsky crossed himself. It was an emotional moment. 'We took out our bottle of orange liqueur and raised our glasses in a farewell toast to Asia and went into the woods and picked heaps of wild strawberries.'

The picture of Fyodor Mikhailovich, home at last, picking wild strawberries with his bad-tempered beloved in the woods of Mother Russia, presents an uncommon moment of calm in a troubled life.

Little reliable information exists about Maria's subsequent life in Russia, mostly because the majority of it has been handed down from Dostoyevsky's family who loathed her, but it is certain she was deeply unhappy. Her relationship with her husband continued its volatile course, there were constant scenes of break-up and reconciliation, and her health went into decline. She was diagnosed with malignant consumption, and as her tuberculosis advanced so her mental health deteriorated and she began to experience terrifying hallucinations. Finally, she haemorrhaged. Blood flooded her throat, choking her, and she died soon afterwards. It had been a dismal marriage, yet Dostoyevsky had genuinely loved his wife and her death was a tragedy for him. His requiem for her would eventually take the form of the portrait of the ferocious and tragic Katerina Ivanovna Marmeladova, one of the characters of *Crime and Punishment*.

The importance of imprisonment in Dostoyevsky's development as a writer is incalculable. At the end of his life he said: 'Fate came to my rescue. Prison saved me ... It was a good school. It strengthened my faith and awakened my love for those who bear all their sufferings with patience.' Exile, too, in Kazakhstan had provided him with experiences that would feed his imagination as a writer for the rest of his life, and it was there that he had experienced his first great passion, the doomed, unhappy love for Maria.

Two Kazakh images of the writer at peace remain with me: Dostoyevsky in awe beneath the vast canopy of a starlit night sky, the like of which can only be seen at sea, in the desert or out on the steppe; and watering the seedlings in the garden of the cottage on the bank of the River Irtysh, dressed in his faded, rose-coloured calico waistcoat.

◆

But images of peace were not destined to be the lot of provincial Semipalatinsk. Its very remoteness had marked it out not merely as a place of exile for enemies of the Tsar, but also as the site for one of the most cynical experiments ever conducted by man upon man. This was the second reason for coming to Semey, for I wanted to visit the super-secret Polygon, a place shrouded in mystery.

I called my friend Umbetov in Astana to see if he could help. 'Is it possible to visit the Polygon?'

'Why would you want to go there?'

'To see it first hand.'

'You want to be a tourist in Hell?'

'A day trip, maybe. For a glimpse.'

'No one will take you to the Polygon. It's impossible. There's nothing to see.'

Actually, it is possible – but it's true, there's nothing to see. The Polygon, 160 kilometres to the east of Semey, was the principal test site for Soviet nuclear weapons. A total of 18,500 square kilometres – a territory the size of a small country – were set aside for five nuclear testing sites, the largest of which was the Semipalatinsk Polygon. The first atomic explosion occurred there in 1949, and over the next forty-one years there would be a further 752 nuclear explosions in Kazakhstan – 26 in the atmosphere, 78 at ground level, and the rest underground. Back in Moscow, Kazakhstan was perceived as a remote, isolated and empty region, an underpopulated and faraway place capable of absorbing any amount of pollution.

Visitors are still turned back at checkpoints on the borders of the Polygon site, and all agriculture in the area is banned. Inside, the site is a desolate moonscape, cratered and blasted by the most powerful weapons on earth. A permit, however, is no longer required to visit the city of Kurchatov – named after Igor Kurchatov, the physicist who led the team that developed the Soviet atom bomb. Kurchatov was one of the Soviet Union's sinister 'closed cities' – meaning off-limits to all unauthorized personnel because of military activity. In the Cold War it was the headquarters of the Soviet nuclear weapons programme and home to 40,000 scientists and military men. Today it is a ghost town, with only a fraction of its original population, situated at the end of a depressing stretch of barren road enlivened by the occasional deserted village, abandoned factory, and military base along its route.

When I inquired locally if there was any way to get permission to explore the site itself, I was met with blank looks of utter incomprehension. A little research soon explained why. Radioactive fallout from the tests had contaminated an area of 300,000 square kilometres inhabited by 2 million people. The incidence of cancer in communities close to the test site is three times higher than normal, and the local population continues to suffer from birth defects and mental illness. At the village of Sarjal, inhabited by 2,600 people thirty kilometres from the site, almost everyone suffers from one radiation-related illness or another. In nearby Lake Balapan, a crater created by a 130-kiloton nuclear explosion, radiation levels are 200 times higher than normal. But all data concerning the Polygon was suppressed until the mid-1980s, and the high incidence of cancer was explained away by such ludicrous reasons as the Kazakhs' habit of drinking scalding hot tea.

In the circumstances, I decided to abandon my day-trip to Hell and rely on eyewitness accounts. Summers in this part of Kazakhstan, nicknamed the Devil's Sandbox, are infernally hot. Eggs sizzle and cook when broken on to the ground. Although locals are inured to extremes of temperature – winters are bitter – in the summer of 1949 they witnessed what they described as a *second* sun in the sky. For a brief moment this fiery ball burned brighter and hotter than the sun itself, before mutating into a giant, spiralling cloud. Shock waves from the explosion travelled across the steppe and were felt as far away as Astana and Karaganda. Coal miners working underground felt the earth shake. Later, a strange snow of grey dust fell to earth.

The Soviet Army had exploded its first atmospheric nuclear bomb over the Polygon, and the flakes that fell to earth were radioactive. The authorities – military and medical, as well as nuclear scientists – were eager to learn all they could from the bomb blast. Schoolteachers in Semipalatinsk had been instructed to have their pupils watch the explosion in order to evaluate the effects of fallout and radiation on the human body. In later tests, trains loaded with human beings were sent close to ground zero. 'Almost no one on the trains had any idea that in a week or two they would all become guinea pigs for the testing of nuclear bombs,' a witness later recalled. 'The train was a sort of Noah's Ark. There were not only people but horses and sheep, dogs, snakes and lizards – even specially packed insects.'

Groups of people of all ages were taken to special rural settlements, given cases of vodka and a hundred roubles each, and told, 'Wait here – we'll collect you later.' After the nuclear blast, officials returned to see what effect the radiation had had on the human guinea pigs. A secret hospital was set up in Semipalatinsk to monitor the consequences of nuclear explosions on the local population.

The early explosions proved successful, and in 1953 the Soviets prepared to test their first hydrogen bomb. Among those who witnessed the blast was its creator, Andrei Sakharov. The scientist was destined to become one of the USSR's most outspoken opponents of nuclear weapons, and would later be sentenced to years of internal exile as a dissident. He would eventually be awarded the Nobel Peace Prize, but in the early years of Soviet atomic research Sakharov believed his country needed to develop its own H-bomb to protect itself from the possibility of attack by the USA. And he found the prospect of splitting the atom thrilling: 'A thermonuclear reaction – the mysterious source of the energy of the sun and stars, sustenance of life on earth and potential instrument of its destruction – was within my grasp.'

Sakharov left the top-secret research station known as the Installation, outside Moscow, and travelled by private railcar to Semipalatinsk. He flew the final 100 kilometres to the test site in a small Yak biplane, and had his first view of the Kazakh steppe from the air. As the biplane flew over lakes, ducks rose in clouds. It all seemed so peaceful, idyllic even.

Once on site, the scientists were immediately faced with a human dilemma. The H-bomb was to be detonated on a tower, but the team had failed to take into account the full extent of radioactive fallout from an explosion of the power anticipated. Even though the Polygon was remote, the blast threatened the lives of thousands. A kind of political panic ensued: to postpone the test would anger Moscow, but to go ahead might kill innocent people. Teams of scientists worked around the clock on the problem, using a classified American manual on the effects of nuclear explosions, which the Russians had bleakly named The Black Book. The resulting calculations were not encouraging – the fallout pattern would extend over a vast area, and unless the population was evacuated there would be widespread illness, genetic damage and death.

The scientists predicted serious injury to children and the infirm at 100 roentgens – a unit measuring radiation – while half of all exposed adults would be killed outright at 600 roentgens. And this was limited to a study of the immediate medical damage to living beings – the poisoning of the earth's atmosphere that would cause long-term biological effects was not even considered. The scientists decided it was imperative to evacuate everyone living downwind of ground zero in the zone where radiation fallout was calculated to be above 200 roentgens. This meant moving tens of thousands of people.

The officer in overall charge of the military operation was

Marshal Mitrofan Nedelin, a thickset, softly spoken man with the confidence of absolute authority earned commanding frontline artillery in wartime. He explained to the scientists the reality of evacuation on such a scale. Casualties were inevitable when tens of thousands of people – including the sick, the elderly and the young – were hastily forced to move long distances in a region lacking decent roads. 'There's no need to torture yourselves,' he told the scientists. 'Army manoeuvres always result in casualties – twenty or thirty deaths can be considered normal. And your tests are far more vital to the country, and its defence.'

Sakharov reacted to the pragmatic reality of nuclear testing with horror. 'Catching a glimpse of myself in a mirror, I was struck by a change I looked old and grey.'

'Don't worry, everything will be fine,' a colleague said in an attempt to cheer him up. 'The Kazakh kids will survive. It will all turn out okay.'

The evacuation began immediately, and 700 trucks carried families and their belongings away from ground zero, to the south, east, north and west across the trackless Kazakh steppe. The evacuees were told they would be able to return to their homes in a month. In fact it would be eight months before they were allowed back.

On the day of the test Sakharov was awoken at 4 a.m. by alarm bells. He saw headlights criss-crossing the steppe in every direction as observers were driven by the military to their posts. Two and a half hours later he reached the bunker reserved for VIPs thirty kilometres from ground zero. The tension was palpable among military officers and scientists alike as the countdown began. Two minutes before blast-off, Sakharov lay on the ground facing the tower and put on dark goggles. The final ten seconds seemed endless.

Suddenly, there was a flash. 'A swiftly expanding white ball lit up the whole horizon,' Sakharov wrote. 'I tore off my goggles, and though I was partially blinded by the glare, I could see a stupendous cloud trailing streams of purple dust. The cloud turned grey, quickly separated from the ground and swirled upward, shimmering with gleams of orange. The customary mushroom cloud gradually formed, but the stem connecting it to the ground was much thicker than those shown in photographs of fission explosions. More and more dust was sucked up at the base of the stem, spreading out swiftly. The shock wave blasted my ears and struck a sharp blow to my entire body. Then there was a prolonged, ominous rumble that slowly died away after thirty seconds or so. Within minutes, the cloud, which now filled half the sky, turned a sinister blue-black colour. The wind was pushing it in a southerly direction towards the mountains and the evacuated Kazakh settlements. Half an hour later the cloud disappeared from sight, with planes of the radiation-detection service following it.'

Sakharov went on a tour of the test site dressed in a dustproof jumpsuit and carrying a dosimeter. He was driven in an open car past buildings destroyed by the blast until it braked abruptly beside a steppe eagle whose wings had been badly singed. 'It was trying to fly but couldn't get off the ground.' He watched a soldier put the eagle out of its misery – Russian-style, with a fatal kick. The scientist later learned the obvious but previously unrecognized truth, that thousands of birds were inevitably destroyed in every test. 'They take wing at the flash, but then fall to earth, burned and blinded.'

The scientists were driven beyond yellow warning flags to within sixty metres of ground zero. Most of the team remained in their vehicles, but Sakharov, accompanied by one other colleague, walked over the fused black crust created by the intense heat. The earth crunched underfoot like glass. The men stood looking at the debris of twisted metal and concrete that had been the tower, while all around was a scene of total desolation.

The team remained in Kazakhstan for a further two weeks to

review test results. In his free time, Sakharov took walks along the Irtysh river and picked sweet and tart rosehip berries from the thick bushes growing on its banks. It was a strange period of professional exhilaration clouded by doubt, when the success of the test raised human and moral questions that were to concern him for the rest of his life.

On his return to Moscow, Sakharov was rewarded handsomely. He was paid the enormous sum of half a million roubles, given a dacha in an exclusive suburb of Moscow, elected to the Academy of Science, and awarded the title of Hero of Socialist Labour. But within months he was running a temperature of 106 degrees Fahrenheit and was admitted to the Kremlin hospital suffering from radiation sickness, which took the form of severe nosebleeds and a mysterious blood disorder. (The single colleague who had walked with him over the blackened crust of ground zero died of acute leukaemia the same year.)

The team at the Installation now worked on plans for a bomb of even greater power. In October 1955, three nuclear devices were assembled and loaded into a train headed for Kazakhstan, and Sakharov followed a few days later in a private railcar. This time two male secretaries accompanied him. In reality they were KGB minders, a colonel and a lieutenant, and both carried concealed Makarov pistols that they boasted could be fired from their pockets. The minders' principal mission, which they openly admitted, was to prevent the scientist making 'undesirable contacts'.

Once again, complications arose at the Polygon test site. This time, in order to minimize the fallout pattern, it was planned to drop the bomb from a plane and to detonate the explosion at sufficient height for dust to be drawn up into the radioactive cloud. The problem with this was that heat radiation might destroy the aircraft. As a precaution the plane had been painted with white reflective paint to reduce the danger, and even the military's traditional red stars had been painted over in case the heat melted holes in the wings.

Unable to sleep one night, Sakharov calculated the bomb's trajectory, the plane's exposure to heat in calories per square centimetre, and the likely effect of the heat on the plane's surface. It was clear that the aviation experts had underestimated the power of the bomb, and more distance was needed between the plane and the explosion. The solution was to attach a parachute to the bomb to slow its fall.

As Sakharov awaited the day of the test, he enjoyed the natural wonders of the region. He witnessed the autumn ice rush that comes in mid-November, one of the great sights in Kazakhstan: 'It was a new and spellbinding experience for me, a majestic, amazingly beautiful sight. The dark, turbulent waters of the Irtysh, dotted with a thousand whirlpools, bore the milky-blue ice floes northward, twisting them and crashing them together. I could have watched for hours on end until my eyes ached and my head spun. Nature was displaying its might – compared to it, all man's handiwork seems paltry imitation.'

But the thermo-nuclear explosion of an H-bomb gives Mother Nature a run for her money. For the next test Sakharov and his colleagues were assigned observation places on a low platform built in the grounds of the laboratory, and from there they watched the dazzling white plane carrying the bomb take off: 'With its sweptback wings and slender fuselage extending far forwards, it looked like a sinister predator poised to strike.'

Loudspeakers announced when the plane was over the target, when the bomb was dropped, and when the parachute had opened. The countdown began. This time Sakharov did not wear the dark goggles provided. Instead, he stood with his back to ground zero and turned the moment his surroundings were lit up by the flash.

'I saw a blinding, yellow-white sphere swiftly expand, turn orange in a fraction of a second, then turn bright red and touch the horizon, flattening out at its base. Soon everything was obscured by rising dust which formed an enormous, swirling, grey-blue cloud, its surface streaked with fiery crimson flashes. Between the cloud and the swirling dust grew a mushroom stem, even thicker than the one that had formed during the first thermonuclear test. Shock waves criss-crossed the sky, emitting sporadic milky-white cones and adding to the mushroom image. I felt heat like that from an open furnace on my face – and this was in freezing weather, tens of miles from ground zero. The whole magical spectacle unfolded in complete silence.'

Several minutes passed before the shock wave arrived. It could be seen rippling across the steppe and flattening the plumes of feather grass protruding through a light dusting of snow. Sakharov shouted for his companions to jump from the platform as it hit. The shock wave blasted ears and battered bodies, and there was the noise of breaking glass as it moved on its way. But for the scientists the bedlam of destruction was the sound of success. A colleague rushed over and threw his arms around Sakharov: 'It worked! It worked! Everything worked!'

The successful test was the result of long, hard years of effort, making a whole range of nuclear weapons possible. 'We all understood the military implications of the test. It had essentially solved the problem of creating high-performance thermonuclear weapons.'

The new knowledge came at a cost. The scientists learned hours after the test that the consequences of a nuclear explosion were difficult to predict. Temperature inversion – when the temperature of the air rises with increasing altitude instead of falling – had unexpectedly increased the force of the shock wave beyond the calculated predictions. In a settlement supposed to be far beyond the danger area, a 2-year-old girl had been killed. The shock had also damaged a trench sheltering a platoon of soldiers and killed a young recruit. In Semipalatinsk, 160 kilometres from ground zero, it brought down the ceiling in a women's hospital ward, seriously injuring half a dozen patients. And at a meat-packing plant shards of shattered glass embedded themselves in sides of beef like shrapnel.

The scientific team drove to the site. Many of the special structures erected to determine the effects of the shock wave and heat radiation had been destroyed. Water spouted from ruptured mains, an oil tank blazed, and acrid black smoke filled the air, reminding Sakharov of the worst images of the Second World War. The crew that monitored film and instrument recordings went about its work, part of which was to retrieve the tethered experimental dogs, goats and rabbits. 'I found it painful to watch their suffering, even on film.'

Sakharov's exhilaration at success was checked by a host of conflicting emotions. 'Perhaps chief among them was a fear that this newly released force could slip out of control and lead to unimaginable disasters. The accident reports, and especially the deaths of the little girl and the soldier, heightened my sense of foreboding.'

These were compounded at a celebratory banquet given by Marshal Nedelin. Brandy was poured, and with KGB 'secretaries' lining the wall, the marshal indicated that Sakharov should propose a toast. 'May all our devices explode as successfully as today's,' the scientist said, raising his glass, 'but always over test sites and never over cities.'

There was an awkward silence. The marshal rose, glass in hand. 'Let me tell a story. An old man wearing only a shirt was praying before an icon. "Guide me, harden me. Guide me, harden me." His wife, who was lying on the stove, said: "Just pray to be hard, old man. I can guide it in myself." Let's drink to getting hard.'

Sakharov's whole body tensed and he turned pale. He drank his brandy in silence and didn't speak for the rest of the evening.

Later, he would write that he felt as if he had been lashed by a whip. The marshal's parable was meant to convey the absurdity of pacifist sentiments in relation to the bomb. 'The point of his story – half lewd, half blasphemous, which added to its unpleasant effect – was clear enough. We, the inventors, scientists, engineers and craftsmen, had created a terrible weapon, the most terrible weapon in human history – but its use would be entirely out of our control.'

Sakharov had always known this, of course, but he had never truly *understood* it until the banquet. The evening changed his thinking about his own involvement and moral responsibility. Senior members of the Communist Party hierarchy were on hand to further disabuse Sakharov of his naïvety, and crudely emphasize his complicity. In one of the last meetings before he became a 'renegade', he went to see Leonid Brezhnev over a matter concerning the military budget. Brezhnev was on his way up the power pyramid, and had been summoned by his mentor Khrushchev back to Moscow from Kazakhstan after running the Virgin Lands programme.

'So, the bomb squad is here!' Brezhnev said, as Sakharov and a colleague were ushered into his office. He then quoted his father – 'a thoroughbred proletarian' – who spoke of the creators of lethal weapons as consummate villains. The father had declared that such men should be taken to a high hill and hanged as a warning to others. 'And now I'm involved in that dirty business,' Brezhnev said, 'just as you are.'

•

One night in my hotel room in Semipalatinsk I watched an old Russian black-and-white film from the 1950s about the Great Patriotic War – as the Soviets called the Second World War – in which decent, clean-cut men and women sacrificed their lives for country and Party. (During the war, the USSR moved its entire film production to the comparative safety of Kazakhstan, where

Sergei Eisenstein made the iconic film of Stalin's favourite tsar, *Ivan the Terrible*. After independence the studios were used to film the country's first soap opera, *Crossroads* – a hybrid of *EastEnders* and *The Archers* charged with the didactic mission of rekindling the nation's trading instincts.) Another film I saw showed life on a pristine Volga, where fine-looking girls and strapping young men struggled for the communal good on a collective threatened by flood. They were pure propaganda but well made and rather good, and no doubt as comforting in their way as Hollywood and British films of the same period. Movie worlds. Worlds that never were and can never be, but a distraction for Soviet citizens from the 'dirty business' of the Cold War's superpower policy of Mutually Assured Destruction.

Year after year, the innocuous-sounding Ministry of Medium Machine Building – the body that controlled the whole nuclear programme – sent its KGB-guarded teams of scientists to the secret Polygon testing site for one nuclear test after another. The republic of Kazakhstan seemed to have become little more than a vast testing site for weapons of every description. Ballistic missiles, anti-ballistic missiles and laser weapons were tested there, while on an island in the Aral Sea there was a test site for bacteriological weapons. In all, 15 million hectares were set aside for such tests.

One of those who had actually felt the physical shock waves of nuclear tests, and heard the horrific stories from Semipalatinsk, was the future president, Nursultan Nazarbayev, then working in the steel plant of Temirtau. 'I knew a man from a family of four children who lived near the test site. His sister went mad, one of his brothers suffered from anaemia, and the other committed suicide.'

It was obvious during the various conversations I had with the president which subjects gave him pleasure to talk about and which seemed to cause him pain. Although he showed mild irritation when questioned about charges made by critics ('Nobody likes criticism!') he only showed anger over two topics – the ecological disaster of the Aral Sea, and the damage done to Kazakhstan through nuclear testing. His eyes burned with intensity when he discussed either, but on the nuclear issue he had risked his political career.

Although Kazakhs during Soviet times had few hard facts to go on, anecdotal evidence of the horrific consequences of nuclear testing spread from person to person. At first Nazarbayev had accepted the testing as a necessary evil, but his instinctive opposition had grown over time as more information was revealed. Once Gorbachev's glasnost policy had gained momentum within the Moscow ministries, senior political leaders in Kazakhstan slowly began to penetrate the wall of secrecy surrounding everything to do with the nuclear programme. Previously, only a very small circle of people had been allowed to see the data. The disclosures were shocking – as many as half a million Kazakhs had received damaging doses of radiation from the effects of the tests either directly or indirectly without any form of compensation. Research results suppressed for decades revealed widespread illness from an astonishing variety of virulent cancers. The suicide rate had soared, and there were extensive deformities and birth defects. Many children, both boys and girls, would grow to adulthood to find themselves impotent.

The disclosures had a profound effect on Nazarbayev as politician, family man and Kazakh. Things were much worse than even he had imagined. 'It was only then that I fully understood the extent of the crime committed against us,' he said with disgust. 'Kazakhstan had been turned into a giant rubbish dump.'

He was prime minister when he received a call informing him that a decision had been made to create a new nuclear testing site in the Taldy-Kurgan region, a highly inappropriate choice because of its relative proximity to the capital, Almaty. 'The Central Committee of the Kazakh Communist Party has given its agreement,' Nazarbayev was told over the phone. 'We now urgently need some land. Please arrange for between 10,000 and 12,000 hectares to be allocated. And be ready to receive a delegation of generals and specialists.'

Nazarbayev asked whether there had been a concrete resolution passed by the Central Committee of the Soviet Communist Party and whether anyone had been consulted in Taldy-Kurgan. 'And why am I, the leader of the government in Kazakhstan, only hearing about this now for the first time?'

'What does it matter?' the Moscow official snapped. 'The project has been drawn up and the Central Committee has agreed. Simply sign the document when we send it to you and do as you are told.'

'I am not going to sign such a document,' Nazarbayev replied angrily. 'What's more I am going to formally ask for it to be reconsidered.'

'You just try!' the Moscow official said, hanging up the phone.

Moscow's unpopular man, Gennady Kolbin, had recently been appointed the Kazakh Communist Party leader, and Nazarbayev immediately appealed to him. He asked whether it was true that he had agreed to a new nuclear test site in the republic. 'There was such a conversation,' Kolbin said, unconcerned, 'but as I recall, it was not about building a new site, but rather extending an old one. Why are you interested anyway? Is there some problem?'

To anyone born and bred in Kazakhstan, any new nuclear test site was naturally a problem. Nazarbayev attempted to convince Kolbin that such a project was both undesirable and unwelcome but received no support. 'If you're really opposed to the new site, just try and stop it!'

Nazarbayev knew that a direct, unsupported appeal to Moscow would be futile, so he decided to launch a whispering campaign to have the decision reversed. He recruited a trusted colleague from the threatened region to spread rumours about the new nuclear site. 'Spontaneous' protest meetings of angry locals were not only allowed but encouraged, until both the Kazakh and Moscow KGB began to receive reports of growing unrest caused by the proposal. The popular discontent alarmed Moscow sufficiently to cancel the project.

Nazarbayev's continued opposition to nuclear testing was seen as insubordination, and he was summoned to Moscow and put under pressure to change his mind. Gorbachev argued that if Nazarbayev, a respected Kazakh, agreed to testing it would greatly help to calm public opinion. More bluntly, Gorbachev warned that if he continued to be difficult he might be removed as prime minister.

While Nazarbayev worked behind the scenes to cancel or at least shift nuclear testing from Kazakhstan, a genuine anti-nuclear movement had sprung up. It was known as Nevada-Semipalatinsk, after the USA-Soviet nuclear test sites. Strong feeling had been growing within the country as the full extent of the damage done to both the environment and people became known. The leader of the independent movement was a popular and charismatic figure, Olzhas Suleimenov, a poet, one of the country's best-known and respected cultural figures, and a leading civil rights advocate. The grassroots movement mounted an unheard-of challenge to Soviet authority, organizing non-stop protests in the form of meetings and marches, and linking up with like-minded international organizations. When the Soviet military carried out yet another nuclear test in the face of public opposition – and announced plans for three more – the movement was able to harness public outrage and organize a petition signed by a million people.

Shaken, Gorbachev and leading members of the Soviet military offered to fly to Kazakhstan in an attempt to explain the need for more tests. Nazarbayev held his ground. 'I was determined to stop the destruction once and for all. The authorities had lied and withheld information about what was really going on and about the damage to people's health. Semipalatinsk remained a wretched, poverty-ridden place. The contrast with Las Vegas, close to the American test site in the Nevada desert, could not have been greater. There was no doubt that the Soviet authorities were completely indifferent to the fate of their own people.'

The first thing Nazarbayev did, when appointed president of Kazakhstan in April 1990, was to demand the closure of the

Polygon. A decree was issued forbidding nuclear testing of any sort on Kazakh territory. Moscow continued to attempt to exert pressure, but the leadership no longer had any real power and caved in. The three blasts planned for the Polygon were shifted to the Arctic site of Novaya Zemlya, in Russia, and forty years of unchecked nuclear testing within Kazakhstan had come to an end.

The Polygon was closed, its testing tunnels sealed. Kazakhstan had set an international precedent, and both the USA and Russia later followed its lead with the closure of the Nevada and the Novaya Zemlya test sites. The long and expensive task of environmental clean-up now began, but there was still one massive nuclear problem to be resolved. A significant portion of the Soviets' most deadly intercontinental nuclear arsenal remained in Kazakhstan: 104 SS-18s, each with ten separately targeted nuclear warheads, were scattered throughout the steppe in concrete bunkers forty metres beneath the ground. Kazakhstan reluctantly found itself with the fourth largest nuclear arsenal in the world – bigger than those of China, France or Great Britain. Only America, Russia and the Ukraine had more weapons.

Newly independent, and mostly unknown, a nuclear Kazakhstan presented the world with an alarming imponderable. The universal fear was that nuclear weapons might fall into the hands of unstable Middle Eastern regimes or, most alarming of all, terrorist groups.

Early in 1992, the CIA had picked up reports that Iranian intelligence agents were systematically visiting nuclear installations throughout the former USSR. The agents had been all over Russia, the Ukraine and Belarus, and had particularly focused on Kazakhstan, which not only had warheads, but also a mass of bomb-grade uranium and plutonium. The West feared that newly independent Kazakhstan might be susceptible because it had a predominately Muslim population, was within Iran's sphere of interest, and was desperately poor.

Iranian agents had visited Semey and Kurchatov, the Ulba Metallurgical Zinc Plant at Ust-Kamenogorsk, and the breeder reactor at Aktau, on the Caspian Sea, known to produce a particularly pure form of plutonium known as 'ivory grade'. Rumours circulated around diplomatic circles in Almaty that the Iranians had offered 300 million dollars for bomb-grade uranium 235 or plutonium. The CIA was so alarmed by the reports that its director, Bob Gates, took the unusual step of going public with the information, announcing that the Iranians were 'actively shopping' for fissile material.

Nuclear weapons suddenly put Kazakhstan at the centre of the international map, and the world came calling. The first to visit was Margaret Thatcher. Although no longer prime minister, she remained internationally influential and acted as a kind of independent diplomatic plenipotentiary on behalf of the West. The French and German foreign ministers were quick to follow, but the most active were the Americans.

Superpowers apart, representatives from various Arab and Islamic states also visited the country – the Iranians saw the stockpile as a shortcut to their own ambitions to acquire a nuclear bomb. Some countries came in an official capacity, some in secret. The message from the Islamic states was always the same: how much money would Kazakhstan need in order to keep its missiles? And unofficially, was it possible to buy uranium or plutonium?

'But it was more than just a matter of weaponry,' Nazarbayev explained. 'The West saw us as a Muslim country and were worried that our weapons would find their way to other, more radical Islamic states. We could not leave the world in fear. And we could not allow our young state to find itself isolated because of nuclear weapons. Given my determination to attract Western investment, I had to give special attention to our relations with the United States and its allies.'

The US Secretary of State, James Baker, arrived in Kazakhstan, accompanied by the US ambassador to Moscow, as part of a carefully calibrated American diplomatic mission involving all the post-Soviet 'nuclear' republics – the Ukraine, Belarus and Russia. America was exerting pressure on Kazakhstan to give up its weapons – much more than it had ever brought to bear on Pakistan or India. Baker and Nazarbayev seemed to get on well together, and after a dinner at which they sang Kazakh and American songs, they ended up discussing the bomb in a blisteringly hot *banyā*, a Russian steam bath.

The American Secretary of State opened the negotiations Texas-style with a warning that three American missiles were targeted for every one on Kazakh soil. Nazarbayev shrugged off the crude threat as irrelevant. Kazakh independence and sovereignty did not mean the country was staking a claim to the weapons on their territory, he said. They were realists. But there was the practical problem of expensive maintenance. 'We need to know what Kazakhstan will get in return for dismantling these weapons. In particular, security guarantees.'

Kazakhstan was determined to become nuclear-free, but it needed to protect its borders. There were legitimate concerns after the collapse of the Soviet Union over the intentions of both the Russians and the Chinese, with Yeltsin's own spokesman at the time supporting Russian nationalists who claimed large swathes of northern Kazakhstan, and official Chinese history books claiming other parts of Kazakh territory. The newly independent country had never wanted to become a nuclear power, but its people had paid a high price in personal suffering for the imposed status, and now they needed guarantees to give it up.

In the end Kazakhstan agreed – along with the Ukraine and Belarus – to surrender nuclear weapons on their territory by the year 2000. In exchange, the US committed hundreds of millions of dollars to pay for the transfer of missiles to Russia to be dismantled, and financial compensation for the weapons-grade uranium in the warheads. An aid package of $150 million also came with the deal, and a $15 million fund to help start the rehabilitation of the Aral Sea. Kazakhstan had been in a position to blackmail the world but had chosen not to do so. The rewards were nugatory.

•

One serious piece of nuclear business remained unfinished. Loose batches of uranium and plutonium left over from various military projects had to be accounted for, and the Kazakhs were discovering previously unknown caches of the stuff all over the country. It soon became clear that the Soviet military statisticians had been as creative in their bookkeeping as their counterparts in the old Moscow ministries.

In 1993, Kazakh officials approached the US ambassador in secret and alerted him to the existence of a large cache of weapons-grade uranium of the type sought by both Iraq and Iran. In one location alone there were 600 kilograms, enough for twenty powerful bombs. Processing the material within Kazakhstan was technologically impossible, so in order to avoid the risk of the uranium falling into the wrong hands, and to comply with the Nuclear Non-Proliferation Treaty, the metal needed to be transported either to Russia or the USA. Russia had been offered the uranium but had rejected it. Although the Soviet Union had manufactured the bomb-grade metal, the new authority in charge of nuclear weapons seemed to have no record of it. 'I had the impression from their reaction that they had simply forgotten about it,' Nazarbayev said.

It was an alarming thought and one that rattled the Americans, who offered to buy and process the entire cache. A secret programme was devised by Presidents Clinton and Nazarbayev to transport the uranium to the American nuclear facility at Oak Ridge, Tennessee, where the Manhattan Project had built the first plant to enrich uranium. This was an elaborate and highly classified undertaking involving thirty-one CIA and other American experts, foreign and national security agents, and elements of the government inside Kazakhstan. It was launched under the codename Operation Sapphire.

The principal target for Operation Sapphire was the Ulba Metallurgical Plant, in the 'closed city' of Ust-Kamenogorsk, the largest lead-zinc smelter in the country. Kazakhs had found half a ton of highly enriched uranium in the plant left over from a top-secret Soviet Navy programme in the early 1970s aimed at producing a new type of reactor for submarines. The reactor was supposed to enable the Russian subs to go faster, dive deeper and outmanoeuvre any American submarine in the ocean, and the Ulba plant had been responsible for producing the nuclear fuel pellets. The Soviets lavished so much money on the project that those working on it nicknamed the new submarine 'Goldfish', because it might as well have been made of gold. The reactor failed to perform, the project was eventually abandoned, and a thousand canisters of uranium enriched to 90 per cent were placed in a vault and forgotten for more than twenty years.

The job now fell to the Americans to open the canisters, accurately measure their contents, and transfer the uranium into quart-sized American stainless-steel containers, and ship the whole deadly cargo back to the US. The briefing given to the airforce colonel responsible for flying the nuclear payload to America in huge C5 transport planes had a top-secret classification flagging the mission as one of the highest priorities of national security.

The team sent in to do the job was twenty-five strong – twenty-three men and two women, operating under a cover story that they were members of the International Atomic Energy Authority. Everyone was an expert: there were specialists in packaging nuclear material, nuclear laboratory workers, a three-man Navy team of linguists with a specialized nuclear vocabulary, mechanics, electricians, secret communications personnel, engineers, a doctor and even a 'nuclear accountant'.

Before going to Kazakhstan, the Americans rehearsed for the dangerous task ahead in a guarded building at a classified location. Uranium 235 gives off alpha radiation, which attacks the living cells of the human body, and some of the metal was known to be blended with beryllium, which can induce slow suffocation in berylliosis victims as their lungs close down. (Doctors at Ust-Kamenogorsk knew all about berylliosis – in 1990 there had been an explosion in the beryllium plant that sent a fine dust over the city and caused a rash of cases.) The Americans dressed accordingly: C suits (zip-up, yellow plastic contamination overalls), close-fitting respirators and masks, radiation galoshes worn over shoes, and safety glasses and gloves. They worked in a space identical to the one in Ulba, marked off as a 'hot zone' and rigged with fluorescent lighting and heating.

The 130 tons of equipment earmarked for Kazakhstan constituted a well-equipped mobile nuclear laboratory and included three portable 'hoods' – sealed units enabling technicians to work on radioactive material, using long gloves fitted to holes – forklift trucks, generators, lighting, heaters and two tons of classified satellite communications devices.

Once inside Kazakhstan at the Ulba plant, the team worked for six weeks, twelve hours a day, six days a week, to repack the uranium in stainless steel containers. Records of the bomb-grade metal had been kept on handwritten sheets, and early on the Americans were given a lesson in Soviet nuclear accounting – a significant amount of uranium found in the production line had never been recorded. (They also found a warehouse stacked to the ceiling with money – the zinc coins manufactured at the plant for Kazakhstan's new currency, but which had never been put into circulation as galloping inflation made them worthless.)

Finally, the stainless-steel containers were packed into special fifty-five gallon drums, marked Fissile Radioactive Material, loaded on to a convoy of twelve trucks, and driven to waiting transport planes. The runways were cleared of ice Soviet-style: an ancient military truck with a jet engine mounted on the back lumbered on to the strip and blasted the thick layer with its exhaust. The planes took off for the long haul back to the US, connecting with KC-10 tankers every few hours to refuel, as no country en route would allow them to land with their nuclear cargo.

The successful conclusion of Operation Sapphire, announced at a 1994 press conference, led to a flurry of sensational newspaper reports. Newspapers ran stories that the uranium had been unguarded and was there for the taking. In reality, although the plant where it had been stored was vulnerable, it maintained many of the paranoid security procedures devised by the Soviets. No one could enter the region without security clearance, and the uranium had been kept under guard.

Operation Sapphire provided a model for future operations. The Americans were obliged to return to Semipalatinsk to remove uranium left over from a top-secret Soviet space programme to develop a nuclear-powered rocket, and various joint Kazakh–US decontamination projects continue inside the country to this day. The true significance of Operation Sapphire, however, seemed to have passed unnoticed: relations between the USA and Kazakhstan – previously a communist republic of the Soviet Union, and now an independent country with a Muslim majority opting to be nuclear-free – had become so cosy that the countries had conspired to undertake a highly sensitive covert operation together.

CHAPTER SEVEN

•

PICKLED TOMATOES FROM THE GULAG

On the sideboard of my London kitchen sits a large glass jar containing five kilos of pickled Kazakh tomatoes flavoured with sprigs of fennel, spiced with a single chilli pepper, and preserved in a mixture of water, sugar and vinegar. The tomatoes have a subtle flavour and are delicious, the best pickled tomatoes this side of the Syr Darya. They also look splendid in their glass showcase. Most importantly, they were a gift from the wife of a survivor and victim of the Gulag.

A ten-pound jar of pickled tomatoes is not the easiest souvenir to carry half way around the world from what was once the heart of Kazakhstan's Gulag complex, in Karaganda, but I happily lugged it by car, bus and train, from hotel room to hotel room, and from airport lounge to airport lounge, and parried all the questions from customs and immigration officials that travelling with an enormous jar of pickled tomatoes engenders. As a symbol of the triumph of the human spirit, a jar of tomatoes might seem one of fatuous bathos, but it has that significance for me. It stands for the victory of the quotidian pleasures of ordinary life over the monstrous forces once used to snuff them out. And it reminds me of an emotional afternoon spent in Karaganda with a decent, gentle 78-year-old man named Boris Godunov.

•

It is 240 kilometres from Astana to Karaganda. The route out of town passes through Astana's new, multi-coloured Post-Modernist suburbs that are creeping out into the steppe. Most of the housing is still in various stages of construction – and now sells at around $300,000 a pop. It was minus 19 degrees centigrade the day I set out but there were clear blue skies with no wind, so it was considered mild by the locals. When it gets really cold and there have been blizzards, the road takes on the aspect of a tunnel through the snow.

Once outside the city, we passed through a fairyland of snow-frosted trees and thickly iced telephone and electric cables, until there was nothing but the steppe surrounding us like a frozen sea. The driver took it very slowly, and at first I wondered why he was so cautious. But when I got out of the car to stretch my legs during one of the driver's many cigarette stops, I immediately slid on the ice and had to steady myself against the car. He made a snakelike gesture with his left hand to suggest the danger of skidding. The road was one long stretch of continuous black ice, slick as oil on glass. Few people in Kazakhstan use snow tyres in winter (too expensive for most) so cars shudder and squeal as they move off, and often skid out of control. Concertina'd automobiles, some of which look as if they have been dropped from planes, are mounted on concrete bases alongside old Soviet police roadblocks as a deadly warning of the consequences of veering into oncoming traffic.

The driver took against me early on. It was the ring on his mobile phone that did it – a hysterical, jarring laugh. I remarked on its originality and said that it sounded demented. 'It's my daughter's laugh,' he said, shooting me a sour look.

'Very lively.'

'You said, "Demented!"'

The music playing was a popular CD of Russian prison songs performed by a growling individual who seemed to have trained his voice on a strict regime of cheap black tobacco smoked in newspaper. After an hour or so the songs began to sound alike, and I realized the CD was repeating. I pointed this out to the driver. He said he liked the CD a lot, and played it over and over. Didn't he ever get tired of it? No, he didn't. I asked if he would mind turning the music down. He turned it up.

On arrival in Karaganda, I checked into the Hotel Cosmonaut, which used to be the government guesthouse for cosmonauts. Shot into space at Baikonur, the sputniks came back to earth in the steppe around Karaganda. The hotel has been privatized and is comfortable and efficient in the faceless International Modern style. The young girls on reception chirped cheerful slogans in American English: 'Will you be having breakfast?' and 'Will you be leaving us today?' Sometimes they muddled these up. After I had put my bags in the room and was on my way back to the car, the receptionist trilled 'Will you be having breakfast?' It was two-thirty in the afternoon. My confusion caused a cloud to pass across her face. 'Hello – will you be leaving us today?'

I pointed out that as it was past lunchtime, I would not be having breakfast, and as I had only just checked in I hoped to stay the night. The receptionist studied something on her desk: 'Please enjoy your stay!'

'What is that you have there?' I asked. 'A script?'

'Yes.' She smiled and blushed. 'My English is not so good. I talk like a parrot.'

My contact in Karaganda was Larissa Zorenko, who runs the Artists' Union. The front of her office was a gallery exhibiting the work of local artists, which ranged from the original, through the competent, to the god-awful. The office itself was an old-fashioned Soviet muddle, and only two of a bank of neon lights in the ceiling worked, while a couple of others fizzed and blinked.

Larissa had a sense of humour and an engaging laugh, but like all Kazakh citizens her past was complicated. Her family were Poles, she told me, who in the 1930s had moved to Odessa on the Black Sea. After the war, Soviet officials conspired to bring false charges against her father in order to confiscate the family home, and they were deported to Karaganda. Larissa grew up in the city, married and had children. She shrugged: 'So this city became my life.'

Before my arrival I had heard grim stories about Karaganda. They suggested that the whole city was slowly sinking, and that part of it had collapsed because the ground beneath was honey-combed with mines; it was surrounded by slag heaps the size of mountains; and the legacy of the Gulag was a network of violent criminal gangs that were out of control. I expected hell on earth.

But things have changed since independence and the place has been transformed. The slag heaps have gone, along with half the population – a quarter of whom, in the old days, worked underground. At Karaganda's industrial peak, only 15 per cent of its inhabitants were Kazakh, but after independence many Russians, Ukrainians and Volga Germans left. The population now comprises 60 per cent Russians and 40 per cent Kazakhs – a fact oddly resented by many of the remaining Russians. There has been massive new construction, including a Russian Orthodox church and a mosque built by public subscription, and a smart new Catholic cathedral with marble and tiling imported from Italy, paid for by the Vatican. The old-style criminal gangs have dissolved.

Still, the past weighs heavily on Karaganda. 'In the Russian encyclopaedia before the Revolution, this whole area was described as uninhabitable,' Larissa explained. At first the town was no more than a temporary settlement with only a few buildings. British companies were granted concessions to mine copper and coal in the area but were forced to leave soon after the Revolution. 'Then, beginning in 1926, people began to be sent here. They were put in temporary barracks and ordered to build the city. The mines opened and expanded, steel works were built, and more and more slave labour was sent to keep it all going.'

Many were political prisoners, including scientists and agri-culturalists, who tried to find out what plants would thrive in the region. 'It is difficult to grow trees in the steppe, but they found that properly fertilized poplars grew well. Karaganda became known for its avenues of poplars. And they were certainly well fertilized. The bodies of prisoners were thrown into sewage ditches by the side of the roads and trees were planted. Each poplar had the corpses of five prisoners to feed it.'

Karaganda was also the hub of the Kazakh Gulag. The word Gulag is the Russian acronym for the Chief Administration of Corrective Labour Camps that ran the system. This enormous network of penal institutions, and all the rest of the machinery for oppression and terror, evoked for its most celebrated chronicler, Alexander Solzhenitsyn, the image of a far-flung archipelago of islands, 'some as tiny as a detention cell in a railway station and others vast as nations'.

The Gulag had camps everywhere which metastasized like a malignant cancer through the whole body of the Soviet Union and formed a dark psychological parallel continent. Every hour of the night and day unmarked planes, ships and trains carried their human cargo to this terrible place. 'An almost invisible, almost imperceptible country inhabited by tribes of the *zek* [convict] people,' Solzhenitsyn wrote. 'And this archipelago crisscrossed and patterned that other country within which it was located, like a gigantic patchwork, cutting into its cities, hovering over its streets. Yet there were many who did not even guess at its presence ... And only those who had been there knew the whole truth.'

Karlag – translated as Kazakh Camp – was the name of the Gulag network in Kazakhstan, made up of twenty-nine departments. Each department had its own camps, and each camp had its own purpose and level of security. Some were enormous, others quite small, but all were hellish in their own way. Tens of thousands of *zeks* were crammed into cattle trucks and brought to the region, and the area around Karaganda became notorious for a rash of camps ... Dolinka, Ajir, Ekibastuz, Spassk and many others.

'In Dolinka there were many intellectuals, scientists and artists

– people from the Bolshoi Ballet, actors and musicians,' Larissa said. 'The Kazakhs took these people into their homes and cared for them – they are naturally hospitable people, even when they have nothing. In Dolinka there was a fabulous theatre that put on wonderful shows and the audience was made up of the commissariat and the guards.'

Ajir was a camp fifty kilometres from Astana where the wives of 'public enemies' from all over the USSR were imprisoned. Mostly innocent of anything other than marriage to a declared Enemy of the People, they suffered the same fate as their husbands, worked for no wages and often perished before their sentences had been completed. Ekibastuz, to the north-east, was the camp where Alexander Solzhenitsyn was sent and which inspired the novel *One Day in the Life of Ivan Denisovich*, the book that gave the West its first glimpse into the world of the Gulag.

The worst of them all was Spassk, known as the Camp of Death, because of its high execution rate and large population of the incurably sick. We drove out of the city towards the camp, passing a ramshackle village that had once housed the central administration. As we pushed further into the empty steppe, I asked about the exact location of the camp. 'Everywhere around you,' Larissa replied, 'as far as the eye can see in every direction. It was all part of Spassk.'

We arrived at a section of steppe curiously ribbed, as if the earth had been turned over by a giant plough. Each mound was fifteen metres long and a metre wide, and there were hundreds of them. One section the size of a football pitch had a rough wooden fence around it. 'Mass graves,' Larissa explained. 'They would dig a ditch and put in as many bodies as it would take. No markers. No names. And when it was full they would dig another ditch.'

A bleak memorial has been erected here in memory of those who perished. The light was beginning to go as I walked through the snow to the modest, lonely marker put up during glasnost to commemorate the dead. At the foot of the fenced-off area there were a score of smaller memorials spread out over a hundred metres. I made my way along them, stopping to read the melancholy inscriptions: one was to the memory of the Japanese prisoners-of-war who built half of Karaganda, and there was a cross in memory of German prisoners-of-war (one shuddered to think how foreign enemies might have fared in a system that treated its own so brutally). Every nation seemed to have a memorial: Hungarians, Poles, Romanians, Armenians, Finns, Lithuanians, Italians, Ukrainians, even the French: 'France does not forget her dead children, so far from home.' I wondered aloud how Frenchmen could have ended up in Kazakhstan, to be told they were Vichy French who had formed a volunteer division to fight alongside German troops on the Russian front. A general memorial remembered the unknown number of Russian prisoners who died at Spassk – both political and criminal. 'To the Victims of Repression,' it read, and was signed, 'Weeping Russia.'

I was frozen by the time I returned to the car after just half an hour outside. It was a clear day with no wind, the temperature was only minus 20 degrees centigrade, and I was dressed in a heavy overcoat, fur hat, warm gloves and winter clothes that included thermal socks. The inhabitants of the Gulag lived and worked in rags, their hands and feet bound only in strips of cloth, and they sometimes spent twelve hours a day in temperatures of minus 40 degrees centigrade in fierce winds. (It was said that old hands in the camps could determine the temperature without a thermometer, depending on the degree of difficulty they had in breathing. If their spit froze in mid-air it was below minus 60.)

The visit left me empty. The memorials flanking the ribbed field of mass graves seemed pitifully inadequate markers for the many thousands buried there. Those stiff, official acknowledgements to gross inhumanity neither captured the imagination nor touched the heart. Perhaps nothing could. The graves seemed as emotionally remote and removed as the mausoleums in Victorian graveyards.

Earlier, Larissa had introduced me to Anatoly Belyk, a 76-year-old sculptor who had spent his life in Karaganda. He had made the great sculptures celebrating proletarian achievement that stood in the city – two miners holding up a massive piece of coal; a Kazakh aviator famous for his role in the Great Patriotic War; and, since independence, a naturalistic sculpture of steel workers at Temirtau. All highly accomplished work in the old style.

'I've never met an Englishman before,' he said sweetly when I visited him in his studio. 'I'm honoured to have you here. Welcome.' His work was his life, and he lived, slept and ate in a small room above the shop. As I left, I caught sight of a small maquette quite unlike all the other work. It was of a man in a quilted jacket and fur hat with the flaps down, battling his way through a blizzard, bent against the wind with his right arm held across his face to shield him from the fury of the storm. The model had been made many years before but had never been cast.

'I was caught outside when a blizzard came up suddenly and I had to fight my way home,' the sculptor said. 'A common experience here. You see it often enough. And as soon as I had battled my way back to the studio I began work on the clay model. Man against the elements.'

The sculpture would make a fitting memorial to the nameless zeks who died of work, illness and cold at Spassk. The figure of an ordinary man in fur hat and quilted jacket, cast in bronze, and placed out in the harsh steppe beside the ribbed earth of the mass graves.

◆

The most famous zek to emerge from the Kazakh Gulag was Alexander Solzhenitsyn, who spent years in a camp north of Karaganda before being sentenced to perpetual exile in the country. He had been arrested towards the end of the war in 1945 on the Russian front where he was fighting as a captain of artillery, his crime the expression of scepticism regarding Stalin – unwisely referred to as 'the whiskered one' – in letters to a friend. The correspondence was intercepted by the Soviet counter-espionage agency, SMERSH ('Death to Spies'). He was found guilty of disseminating anti-Soviet propaganda and sentenced to eight years' hard labour – a relatively light sentence. (The arrest probably saved his life: his former artillery battery was wiped out almost to a man in the advance on Berlin.)

Meanwhile, Solzhenitsyn's first wife, Natasha, had fled from the family home in Rostov as the Wehrmacht overran the city. She walked 150 kilometres, carrying her husband's early manuscripts with her, crossed the Caspian by ship, and travelled over 3,000 kilometres across Kazakhstan by train to Almaty. She ended up in Taldy-Kurgan, a further 300 kilometres to the north-east. Although they would never meet in Kazakhstan, and she could not know it, her husband would soon make a similar journey.

The first years of Solzhenitsyn's prison term were served near Moscow, but in the autumn of 1950 he was transported east to Kazakhstan on a journey that took three months. The train stopped from time to time to take on coal, food and water. At one anonymous place Solzhenitsyn was lying on the top bunk of the front car, talking to his friend Dimitri Panin, when they saw a small peasant woman with oriental features standing by the side of the track. Impoverished, in patched, coarse clothing and broken-down boots, she wore a faded coloured scarf tied under her chin. The men regarded her disinterestedly at first, but suddenly both stopped talking and stared. Tears streamed down the anguished woman's small face, as she lifted a calloused hand to make the sign of the cross, again and again. The men watched, hypnotized. As the train moved off the woman continued to make the sign of the cross, as if she hoped her blessing would travel with them. 'Sanya and I carried away in our hearts that beautiful image in ragged clothing,' Panin wrote later. 'The blessings of a tiny, heart-weary woman at a nameless whistle-stop.'

For the final leg of the journey the zeks were taken from the train and packed into lorries for a long ride through water meadows and steppe, until they crossed the Irtysh river: 'The breath of the Irtysh, the freshness of the evening on the steppe, the scent of wormwood, enveloped us whenever we stopped for a few minutes and the swirling clouds of light-grey dust raised by the wheels sank to the ground,' Solzhenitsyn wrote. 'Thickly powdered with this dust, we looked at the road behind us (we were not allowed to turn our heads), kept silent (we were not allowed to talk), and thought about the camp we were heading for with its strange, difficult, unRussian name.'

Their destination was Ekibastuz, a hard-labour camp with extra security, inhabited almost exclusively by political prisoners and run by a handful of criminal trusties who occupied positions of privilege. Solzhenitsyn worked as a bricklayer on a power station, where he was to learn the hard lessons of cruelty, hunger, cold and misery that gave him the material for *Ivan Denisovich*.

Sleep was the only time the zeks considered their own, huddling together in groups of two or three for warmth, lying on lumpy sawdust mattresses on bug-ridden bunks. Everyone had so many lice that their clothes moved when cast off. But cold was the true enemy. Men tried to cover their heads, never removed their padded trousers, put their feet in the sleeves of jackets, and placed their coats on top of the worn blankets they were given. They were always tired, and on Sundays slept all day.

The zeks' working day began at 5 a.m., when they were awakened by blows of a hammer on a length of rail. In winter, the frozen dark outside resembled the middle of the night. The barracks at Ekibastuz were long, windowless oblongs built of brick and permeated inside with the sour smell of wet clothes and sweat. At reveille the cold made the men gasp as they stumbled half-asleep towards the vile latrine buckets. Cobwebs of hoarfrost lined the walls of the barracks where they joined the ceiling. A single stove was lit long enough to melt the ice on the walls, forming pools of dirty black water on the cement floor. Outside, frost two inches thick lay on the ground; the sharpest frost was always at sunrise, the coldest point of the night.

At breakfast the zeks pulled spoons from their boots to eat solid lumps of frozen porridge, savouring each mouthful. Afterwards, the first of a series of roll-calls that punctuated the day was taken. The ritual obsessed the guards, for if a zek escaped they could expect to take his place. Anyone who missed a count was sent to the cells where a ten-day stretch was enough to ruin a man's health for life.

The zeks then trudged to their places of work: 'Half dead men strung along the ice in a grey line.' No chances were taken on the way, and the marching orders had to be strictly obeyed: 'Keep to your ranks. No hurrying, keep a steady pace. No talking. Keep your eyes fixed ahead and your hands behind your back. A step to the right or left is considered an attempt to escape and the escort has orders to shoot without warning.' Guards demanded absolute deference, and prisoners were obliged to take off their caps five paces before reaching one.

In a blizzard, when snow fine as ground glass made it difficult to see, a prisoner could get lost between the barracks and the mess hall, and work would usually be cancelled. The authorities were not concerned whether a prisoner froze to death in these conditions but worried that there might be an attempt at escape. On normal days the men worked from dawn to dusk, an official workday of at least eleven hours. 'The days rolled by in the camp, over before you could say knife,' Solzhenitsyn wrote. 'But the years, they never rolled by: they never moved by a second.'

The zeks followed their own commandments: 'Don't believe, don't fear, don't ask.' Any humour that survived in the camp was black. 'If you live in a graveyard you can't weep for everyone.' If the moon shone in freezing temperatures a zek might suggest a warm-up beneath 'the wolf's sun'. And when a man complained he had been given a twenty-five-year sentence for nothing at all, he would be told, 'You're lying. The sentence for nothing at all is ten years!'

Age differences between zeks became indistinguishable as each man developed the white puffy skin, swollen features and skeletal frame of the malnourished. Cold, hunger and exhaustion made friendship impossible as a man's humanity dissolved along with body fat. Love, honesty, compassion and dignity didn't stand a chance. The last emotion to go was bitterness. Not even envy or vanity survived, only sloth, viciousness and hatred. Zeks hated everything – the State, the Party, the camp, the guards, fellow zeks ... and themselves. Nature was seen to conspire against them, and God for most became a personal enemy. Sooner or later every zek achieved a psychological state of absolute indifference. Fear gave way to fatalism, death became no worse than life and was often welcomed.

A man who was considered to have lost his will to live, and even his soul, was labelled a goner – to be despised rather than pitied. A starving goner was known as a wick. Nothing moved these men, not guards beating an old man unable to walk, or criminals 'dancing' with a political – the word used to describe a kicking (more serious scores were settled by strangulation with a towel). As one survivor of the Gulag wrote, 'No man should see or know the things that I have seen and known.'

Just after Solzhenitsyn was sent to Ekibastuz, a group of 2,000 Ukrainian nationalists arrived. The men had mutinied in a camp to the north, and reprisals were harsh. The authorities devised a punishment regime and relied upon a network of informers to keep the Ukrainians in line. But the rebels quickly developed a method of dealing with these, as masked men made lightning strikes on huts and knifed stool pigeons in their beds. Forty-five informers met their deaths in this way in eight months. In reaction, the authorities separated suspected ringleaders from the main body of prisoners, encouraging criminals and informers to take hideous revenge.

The result was a full-scale war against informers, an unheard-of event in the Gulag where disobedience was suicidal. Zeks pulled up stakes from the camp's outer fence and attacked the cells in which informers had been placed for their own protection. A barrel of cooking oil stolen from the bakery was rolled against the jail's wall, and fuel splashed inside. As the zeks tried to set it alight, guards opened up with machine-guns and mowed down the perpetrators. No one knows the exact number killed.

The following day the entire camp went on spontaneous hunger strike, a defiant and hopeless gesture on the part of men perpetually on the edge of starvation. The zeks remained in their huts and not a soul ventured outside to the mess hall. A deathly quiet descended over everything. After four days, officials attempted to negotiate. They agreed to accept complaints in an attempt to eliminate the causes of internal conflict. The men held out for a week until one hut cracked. Its inmates shamefully made their way to the mess hall. One after another, other huts followed suit.

Senior officials flew in from Moscow and Almaty to set up an inquiry, while the camp authorities temporarily calmed the zeks with double rations and a film show. Punishment came later. Suspected ringleaders were carefully weeded out and sent to Spassk, the Camp of Death, where they were welcomed by graffiti scrawled over lavatory walls: 'Greetings to the heroes of Ekibastuz!'

During the hunger strike, Solzhenitsyn discovered a lump in his groin that caused great pain. He was admitted to the camp infirmary where doctors found a malignant tumour the size of a lemon. Immediate surgery for the cancer was prescribed, and the tumour successfully removed. On leaving hospital, he was ordered to the foundry to work as a smelter's mate, the most physically demanding occupation in the camp.

When Solzhenitsyn's sentence came to an end, he was released into 'perpetual exile' in southern Kazakhstan. He was sent to the region of Kok-Terek, a dusty area bigger than Belgium, on the edge of the Bet-Pak-Dala desert. Taken by train to the small town of Chu, he walked ten kilometres to a hamlet, after which he was driven sixty kilometres into the steppe. To right and left he saw 'Harsh grey inedible grass, and only very occasionally a wretched Kazakh village framed within trees ... At length the tops of a few poplars appeared ahead of us, over the curve of the steppe.' They passed a scattering of adobe huts. A dark girl stood in a doorway ... a group of Kazakh girls in flowery red dresses laughed by the side of the road – wonderful images of the return to humanity. A fellow exile, who had once been a sea captain before becoming the laundryman at Ekibastuz, called out: 'This is okay! We'll find wives for ourselves.'

At the local office of the Ministry of the Interior Solzhenitsyn was given permission to walk unescorted to the District Education Department. 'And off I walk! I wonder if everybody knows the meaning of this great free word. I am walking along by myself!' A middle-aged secretary at the Education Department took him into her confidence. Exiled in perpetuity herself – she was a Cossack accused sixteen years earlier of being a 'terrorist' – the woman admitted there were no mathematics or physics teachers with his qualifications in the whole region. Nonetheless, the director sent him away. It was not worth the risk to employ a released political prisoner who had run foul of Stalin.

That night Solzhenitsyn slept out in the open. He listened to the noises of the night and the braying of donkeys. It was cold and uncomfortable, but he was happy: 'I am free! I am free!'

•

Yekaterina Kuznetsova has made it her life's work to document the Kazakh Gulag and the people who inhabited it, tabulating the numbers shot, unearthing names in hidden archives and chronicling the stories of both the zeks and their jailers. Like everyone in Kazakhstan, Yekaterina has her own convoluted family history. 'I was born in China,' she told me when we met in Karaganda, 'and my father was born in China, because my grandfather had been the Russian General Counsellor there before 1921. When my grandfather died my mother didn't get back to Russia. After the war Stalin invited all those Russians living abroad to return, but my father was not so stupid. Everyone who had lived in a foreign country was considered a public enemy, especially those from the ruling class. They were all arrested and sent to the camps.'

In 1956, after Khrushchev had denounced Stalin, the invitation was renewed and this time the family did go back to Russia. 'When my parents returned they were sent to Karaganda as part of the Virgin Lands programme. They were given no other option.' Yeka-terina was brought up in the city, attended university at Almaty and returned to Karaganda after graduating in journalism in 1961, the year the camps were closed. She began to write for the city's only newspaper. 'Everybody in the city knew about the camps – how could they not?

'I began to socialize with the people who lived here and I found them well read, well educated, sometimes brilliant – and, of course, all ex-convicts. It was obvious that these men were zeks from the camps, although they didn't talk much about their expe-riences at the time. I later found out that one of the conditions of release was that every zek was obliged to sign a confidentiality agreement swearing him to silence for twenty-five years.' The law of silence concerning everything about the camps was strictly enforced within the Soviet Union until 1985.

'There was no intelligentsia in Kazakhstan before these people were released from the camps. They worked as teachers and professors, artists, engineers and scientists, and they created an extremely high cultural standard in the city. The irony is that Karaganda, the city of the Gulag, had a higher level of intelli-gentsia than any other Kazakh city. At the same time Karaganda was famous for having the toughest criminal gangs in all Kazakhstan. You must remember that in the perverted world of the Gulag, the criminals were the ones who were made the trusties.'

Most of the *zeks* released from Karaganda stayed in the city, partly because there were jobs in construction work, but mostly because there was nowhere else for them to go. Yekaterina sought them out, and over the years she interviewed thousands – political prisoners, common criminals, guards and members of the administration. 'Karlag started in 1931, and around 700,000 people went through it over thirty years. The prisoners formed a slave army and the idea was to use these men as slave labour. They were paid in soup and bread and not much of either. The mortality rate was very high. People died from malnutrition, climatic conditions, disease and pure hard work. The scope of the tragedy is enormous.'

Yekaterina began to form the idea that both *zek* and guard were victims of the same appalling system of repression. 'You must understand that both sides were under pressure. Neither group had chosen their fate. Both were victims. The barbed wire between them was almost theoretical, a ribbon put there by the government. I interviewed one of the camp administrators, an official who was really like a Gestapo leader. He talked quite openly about his job and his work. He knew for sure what was going on – the shootings, the terrible mortality rate. He spoke about it all, and admitted everything – not admitted, because he could see nothing wrong in it. Was he cruel? Was he vicious? Was he a monster? No. It was his job, in a regular institution of the Soviet Union – the vast institution of the Gulag. And he did it as well as he could.'

Before Yekaterina, nobody had written about the camps in Kazakhstan, despite glasnost, because the only newspaper in Karaganda was a Communist Party mouthpiece. "Yes, yes, yes, it was very difficult to write about, and yes, yes, yes, there was enormous resistance. The administrators and people who were guards in the camp reacted angrily. As things leaked out little by little, there was a strong reaction. It was not easy. I struggled. I fought. And articles were published.'

Party bosses, Communist Party members and personnel from the Gulag administration claimed that everything Yekaterina wrote was a lie. The widow of a camp commander brought a politically motivated court case against her and the newspaper. 'The widow claimed she was fighting to preserve her husband's good name – this Gestapo leader I had interviewed before he died. And while perestroika had been declared in Moscow, the courts in Karaganda still operated on the level of 1937. In court everything was done to maintain the lie that life in Karlag was routine – there had been no shootings, no high death-rate, no starvation. I had published the figures for those shot in the camps, and described their treatment, and the cause of their deaths. It had all come from official records, but the court found against me. It said I had published incorrect information, and the paper was forced to publish an apology. It was a terrible defeat at the time, but I continued to fight and a few months later the decision was reversed.'

The floodgates opened when Yekaterina wrote an article in the mass-circulation, Moscow-based magazine *Ogonyuk*, which specialized in publishing exposés. Victims from camps all over the Soviet Union began to write to her. 'It was overwhelming. Some sent memoirs and I corresponded with people for ten years. There is a man who comes each year from Moscow because his father was shot here, and he is trying to find where he was buried so he can place flowers on his grave. And, of course, the new authorities can't help him. Nobody knows where the corpses are because they shot so many in the 1930s. They kept a record of the ones they shot but they threw the bodies in unmarked graves. So this man comes here every year searching for his father's grave, and he cannot understand that this is impossible.'

Early in 1991, soon after independence, things changed. 'All the archives were opened and I was given free access,' Yekaterina said. 'You must remember that President Nazarbayev had people in his family who were politically repressed during that time.' A book she wrote based on the hard facts of her research, published in Russian in 1998 under the title *Both Sides of the Barbed Wire*, sold out in days.

◆

There were even a number of British subjects sent to the Kazakh camps. Yekaterina told me about Joe Glazer, who served an eight-year sentence from 1949 to 1957. Born in Johannesburg, Joe had been taken to Soviet Russia when he was 16 by his father, Henry Glazer, an idealistic communist who ran a fish-and-chip shop. Disillusioned by life in South Africa, Henry had decided to respond to Stalin's open invitation to foreign communists to go to Russia to form a truly socialist society.

Father and son travelled to Europe and at first the teenage Joe saw the whole thing as an adventure. They were obliged to wait in Poland for an entire year before being granted a visa to enter Russia. Then, in the winter of 1932, they took a train to Moscow. On the journey Henry enthusiastically questioned travellers about life in Russia. 'No one answered our questions,' Joe remembered. 'The silence was eerie.'

Once in Moscow, father and son were granted Soviet citizenship. Joe attended the Anglo-American school where he began to learn Russian, before the government closed it down as a 'spy centre'. He then found a job in a car factory until the KGB arrested his father, who had been reported for looking at Stalin strangely when the leader was giving a speech at a political rally. Henry disappeared into the Gulag and was never heard of again. Much later, when the KGB archives were opened during perestroika, Joe learned that his father had died two years after his arrest: 'I don't know how or where.'

Joe was now stigmatized as an Enemy of the People and lost his job. Every time he found work, it was the same story – he would last ten days until his reputation caught up with him and he would be fired. Eventually, he found a job driving a trolley-bus after the woman in charge of personnel chose to ignore his past. He drove the bus for ten years, fell in love with an Estonian woman, and married. On several occasions the KGB questioned his wife about her reasons for marrying a foreigner, and suggested it would be wise to leave him. The interviews were disturbing and frightening, but the wife stayed.

In June 1949, when his wife was three months pregnant, Joe picked up his wages on a Friday evening and returned home as usual for the weekend. An evening at the Bolshoi had been planned for Saturday, but in the early hours of the morning the KGB came to the apartment and arrested Joe. He was charged with anti-Soviet rhetoric and sentenced to ten years in the Gulag.

Joe ended up as Prisoner 3566 in Karlag, at Karaganda, where he was forced to do hard labour. 'I was hungry all the time. I was thinking only of one thing. Bread, bread, bread.' One day he received a letter from his wife containing a small, black-and-white photo of his baby daughter, born six months after his arrest. He paid a fellow zek with a precious three-day ration of black bread to draw a coloured portrait of the little girl. The portrait helped to sustain him through the awful time of his internment. Joe Glazer was finally released in 1957, and joined his wife in a small town south of Moscow where he lived until his death.

'And now all the survivors from both sides of the wire are dead?' I asked.

'Almost all, yes,' said Yekaterina. 'But there is a man who was sent to the Gulag as a child with his father. I will take you to him. He will tell you the story of the Green Roof Prison.'

•

Boris Godunov had been sent to the Gulag at the age of 8. Today he lives in the centre of Karaganda with his wife, Aphanasy. He is a quiet, gracious man with a grave manner, and his wife has a sweet, open face. Their one-bedroom apartment is a cosy, compact, well-kept place with a galley kitchen, furnished in heavy Soviet style.

Now 78, Boris told me that he was born in Donetsk, in the Ukraine. His father had been a country boy who had moved to the city to become a miner, a hard, dangerous life of endless work and little money. 'Towards the end of the 1920s the Party showed some propaganda films of Central Asia to Ukrainian miners to try and attract them to go there,' he said. 'My father saw a wonderful film of

Karaganda that showed a city with big beautiful buildings and lots of trees. The film also showed forests and beautiful lakes, and the green grass of the steppe covered in flowers, and the animal life in Kazakhstan. To my father in the Ukraine it seemed like paradise.'

In 1931 his father volunteered to go and work in the mines of this paradise, taking his wife and two sons with him. Boris was 3. 'And he came here and there was nothing. Nothing! The film had shot a brick building – a hospital built by the English – from a hundred different angles to make it look like a city of brick. But there was nothing! Just mines. No housing, no buildings, no trees ... nothing! The miners were put up in miserable barracks beside the mines, and the living area of families was just divided by sheets hanging from clothes lines. My father worked in Mine No. 1 close to the Red Hospital – the single brick building that had tricked him. The men had nowhere to wash and lived in their working clothes.'

Boris was only a toddler and remembers little of this time, but he was told of it later by his elder brother. He seemed to flounder when I asked about childhood memories. 'The circus coming from Moscow, I remember that. And hunger. There was starvation in 1935 when the city was under construction. The Kazakhs were dressed in rags, summer and winter, and came to the barracks begging. Living conditions were incredibly bad for them. At least the miners had soup and a ration of bread – and sometimes tins of beef or caviar.'

'Caviar?' I asked in amazement.

'Vats of the stuff came from the Caspian. It had no value whatsoever in those days. It was the food of the poorest of the poor. People were sick of caviar – they wanted a decent hunk of black bread. They never saw white bread, of course.'

Another childhood memory was the visit to Karaganda of Sergei Kirov, Party boss of Leningrad, Politburo member and close ally of Stalin. 'I was then 6 years old and had never seen such a car as the one that drove Kirov around. It was beautiful. A big black car. But it got stuck in the mud in a swamp that is now one of the main boulevards, and Kirov declared he would build an opera house there. He got his wish. It was built in his memory, for he was assassinated soon after he returned to Leningrad. There was a system of signals on the mine's hooters – calling the men to work, sounding when they changed shifts, and so on. The hooters also sounded in emergencies, or when somebody important died. All the hooters sounded for Kirov. And the city came under severe repression.'

Although the facts have never been fully uncovered, it is highly probable that Stalin ordered the murder. He then used Kirov's assassination as a pretext to arrest hundreds of the most prominent survivors of the Revolution whom he no longer trusted. They were shot for their supposed role in the killing, while a multitude were arrested for their alleged part in the vast conspiracy supposed to be behind Kirov's death. Many were sent to camps around Karaganda.

New two-storey housing had been built in the city by this time, and Boris moved with his family to share a house close to another of the city's new buildings, the notorious Green Roof Prison. 'I was to become closely acquainted with the Green Roof Prison.'

In 1935 there was a serious fire in Mine No. 1, which was run with scant regard for the workers' safety, and many miners were burned to death. Scapegoats were needed. Boris's father had been in charge of the centre where fuel was put into the miners' lamps. 'A woman called Bobroska, a real Party person, was jealous that my father was head of the department, and she saw her chance to remove him. So she denounced him. She claimed he had deliberately not put fuel in the lamps. It was a completely false charge, but he was arrested and blamed for the fire.'

Father and son were sent in a prison train to a nearby camp, while his mother, who now had a baby girl scarcely a year old, was left behind. 'I was 8. I distinctly remember the prison car – the bars and the faces of criminals. So – another childhood memory.' Boris's father was once again sent to work in a mine, but this time as a slave labourer. 'I remember in the barracks how everybody whispered, and how everyone had fear in their eyes. A child could see it and sense it. But I didn't understand what people were talking about, or why they were so frightened.'

Apart from attending a school with a brutal schoolmaster who beat boys across the palms of their hands with a cane, the children were unsupervised. They ran about the camp barefoot in packs, rarely seeing their fathers who were either working or sleeping. 'Childhood memories? I remember the birds along the Chu river, and hunting for sweet beans along the banks. I was always hungry. The gift of destiny for me was bread. Bread was eaten with joy. I remember the cold barracks and the owls at night. And that's all I have in my memory of childhood.'

After two years, his father was released. 'And he was always angry. Always angry.' The family were reunited, but life was so difficult that freedom seemed indistinguishable from the Gulag. One morning agents from the political police forced their way into the house and began ripping up floors, walls and ceilings with crowbars. 'They were making a terrible mess looking for something, I don't know what. My mother had just had an abortion and was lying on the sofa unable to stand. She began to cry as the destruction got worse. "Why are you crying?" one of the policemen shouted at her. "Don't cry," he taunted, using the Stalinist slogan of the time, "Moscow doesn't believe in tears!"'

Terrified neighbours watched as Boris's father was taken away in a police van known as a Black Crow. The agents took everything the family owned, which was little enough – cutlery and plates, Boris's mother's moth-eaten fur coat and her rings. 'They took every photo in the house – all the family photos,' Boris said, faltering. He found it difficult to speak. 'I don't have any pictures of my mother and father.'

Tears ran down his cheeks and he bowed his head. Silence fell over the room. It was terrible to see an old man weep over something that had happened almost seventy years before, and I suggested quietly that we stop. 'No! I want to tell this story,' he said, almost fiercely. 'I want you to know my story!'

His father, Boris continued, had been taken to the Green

Roof Prison, while his mother was forced to leave the wrecked apartment. 'There was a district in the city known as Shanghai, just a collection of poor shacks where the Kazakhs lived. A family took us in and we lived in a corner of their cowshed. They gave us shelter, which was a very dangerous thing to do at that time.'

Boris often went with his mother to the Green Roof Prison to try to see his father. 'A swarm of men moved through that prison. People lived in a kind of shantytown beside the prison in the hope of finding out some information about their relatives. There was a list of names and if your relative was on the list you could visit. My father's name appeared on the list, but at first he was not charged with anything, but just called a Trotskyist. I found a hole in the fence I could struggle through as a little kid, and I used to smuggle in pieces of bread and some oil.'

Finally, his mother received an official letter declaring that her husband had been charged under Item 10 of Article 58 of the Soviet Criminal Code, accused of taking part in counter-revolutionary activity. One day Boris went to the prison with his mother to be told that his father's name was no longer on the list. 'People were on the list and then for no apparent reason they were dropped from the list, and nobody knew why. My mother went round various offices in the city trying to find out where my father had been sent. The bureaucrats began to get angry. Finally, she was told that if she bothered them again she would be arrested as well. Not only were people arrested for nothing in those days, but family members were arrested for being related to them. My mother was so frightened she gave up.'

The mother now entered a paranoid world and imposed it on her children. Boris was told never to say anything to anybody about his father. He must never mention the time in the camp or say anything about the raid by the political police. The lesson was drummed into the 10-year-old child day after day until he understood it as a law of nature. 'We lived in eternal fear. The fear! Always the pressure from the fear! It made people permanently depressed. Everybody lived under this fear all the time. Everybody!

False conversations were held all the time. You never made a statement that was not superficial.'

It was only much later that Boris learned the truth about the fate of his father. Anyone whose name was dropped from the list of the Green Roof Prison had been shot. His father had been executed four months after his arrest. Altogether, 3,500 people from Karaganda were shot during this period.

The son's life was to be blighted for ever by the status of his father as an Enemy of the People. The Party never forgot and never forgave, and the invented sins of the father were duly visited on the wholly innocent son. At school, when other children became Pioneers and were given official ties and pins of membership, Boris was excluded. It was made clear to him at every stage of his education that he was a pariah because of his father, and he found it hard to make friends or even join in sports. Children of Enemies of the People were dangerous company.

Boris left school at 14 and went to work, studying at night school for a diploma to become a skilled worker. 'At college I was offered the position of foreman, but every enterprise had a special political department that kept records on everybody. I was told: "You can never be a foreman. Remember that!" ' Later, he worked in a factory where Bobroska, the woman who had denounced his father, had a position in the political department. She rejected his application to become a member of the Komsomol with the words, 'You will never be a Komsomol member. Remember who your father was!'

After the secret denunciation of Stalin in 1956, a certificate of rehabilitation was issued declaring the father innocent of any wrongdoing. Boris wrote a grateful letter to the authorities and asked where men from the Green Roof Prison who had been executed had been buried, so he could place flowers on his father's grave. 'And, of course, the head of the prison service wrote to say he knew nothing. In truth, nobody knows where the corpses are of the men who were shot.'

As more and more information became available through

glasnost, many victims sought revenge on those who had denounced them, but Boris merely wanted to regain psychological peace through official recognition of what had happened. Victims of repression were invited to register at the Prosecutor's Office to get documentation for reparations. A lawyer advised him to pursue his claim on the grounds that he was a victim three times over – he had been interned in a camp as a child, his father had been unjustly imprisoned and shot, and he had been stigmatized as the son of an Enemy of the People. He wrote down his story, produced proof of his father's internment, provided the certificate of rehabilitation, and the names and addresses of living witnesses, and sent everything to the authorities. Officialdom replied that the guidelines were clear: only children born in the camps, or deported to them, were eligible. No records had been kept of children who had just lived in the camps, so he could not officially be considered a victim.

The decision dealt a terrible psychological blow. Boris felt that the reality of the most painful episode of his life had been denied. Friends advised him simply to claim he had been deported. 'So I lied. And I received official recognition as a victim and compensation – 200 dollars. But having to lie has made everything worse psychologically and I worry now that people will say I was not really a victim, just a liar. The fact that the government never recognized my status has left me in a terrible emotional state – and it is not only me who is suffering.' Boris looked with sad affection towards his wife. 'Today I am still obsessed by the Stalin period and have read a lot of books about it. But still I do not understand. And now the Soviet Union no longer exists, so it can never make amends.'

It had been a painful and draining conversation for Boris. Larissa and Yekaterina had accompanied me to the interview, and we had all been moved and saddened. After a gruelling couple of hours, Boris insisted we move to the table for the food that his wife had quietly been setting out as we talked. The emotional tension lifted. He now enjoyed being a generous and thoughtful host, and opened a bottle of spirits, while his wife brought out more and more food, including pickled tomatoes.

The conversation became general and roamed from subject to subject, until an argument broke out between arts director and journalist. It was one I had heard before and which goes to the root of the new, independent Kazakhstan. Larissa thought the country had tipped too far in favour of ethnic Kazakhs, and that genuine benefits supplied by ethnic Russians were now forgotten; Yekaterina argued that it was not only inevitable that Kazakhs should be at the centre of real power, but also that such a change corrected a historical wrong. Voices were raised and lips pursed.

Boris did not join in the discussion, so I asked him his opinion. He smiled gently, shrugged and answered in a soft voice: 'It is a real debate and everybody talks about this. I am happy enough to hear it over my table knowing that my guests will not be shot, as they would have been in Stalin's time. Or imprisoned as in later years. Or just ignored as before independence. If you want to know what in my opinion is the greatest thing about life now in Kazakhstan I will tell you. It's not the new prosperity, or whether Kazakhs or Russians should be in charge, it's that there is no fear. This is something impossible to understand if you have not lived with fear. It's a big, big thing – the fear has lifted.'

When I said goodbye, Boris clenched his fist and put it over his heart in the Russian gesture of friendship. As we stood at the doorway, his wife gave me the recipe for the tomatoes I had enjoyed so much: a little cranberry juice, a single chilli pepper, salt and pepper, fennel and herbs, and a dash of vinegar added after three weeks. And in a surprise gesture, she went off to fetch a jar from her larder.

The tomatoes were a trivial but suitable coda to a terrible story. The ordinary domestic world had triumphed over the terror apparatus of a murderous state. All Boris Godunov had ever asked from life was to live without fear, and to enjoy the simple pleasures of his family and his table.

CHAPTER EIGHT

◆

THE HOWLING OF WOLVES

My interviews with the president were conducted over a period of two years in which I was able to put together a mosaic of an extraordinary life. Sometimes they were snatched between engagements, often in front of other people, but on occasion they were lengthy sessions one-on-one. At first, an aide conspicuously ran a tape-recorder beside my own, but after a few encounters this stopped, and no restrictions were imposed concerning questions.

It was fascinating to witness a master politician in action up close. The political machine of the presidential staff purred like a Rolls Royce: cars arrived on time, security was always in place, and meetings were prompt. The people around the president were capable and intelligent, and his manner towards them was courteous, tinged with humour. But his authority and power were obvious. Although nobody seemed frightened of him, they were certainly respectful, and everyone referred to him as 'The Boss'. I asked a junior aide what happened when the boss lost his temper. 'He is usually very calm, but when he is angry he lowers his voice and speaks very quietly. And everyone knows, "Look out!" Once, I heard him whisper. It was quite worrying.'

In public Nazarbayev carefully calibrates his behaviour to the occasion, always making his way to the oldest man or woman in a crowd to ask for a blessing, out of respect for Kazakh custom. At any gathering – from small trade fairs to local government meetings – he sits down to talk to people, often removing his jacket. His style is avuncular, and it is clear he is comfortable at every level of government, as he dispenses a mixture of advice and pep talk. To an outsider the performance is impressive and Kazakhs love it. Nazarbayev also has the common touch. In the street one day, in a small town where a crowd had gathered to greet him, the president took an old lady's hand and led her in a stately Kazakh dance.

At every presidential event the indefatigable press secretary bullied the staff photographer and TV cameraman to run this way and that in his efforts to choreograph the evening news. After a rocky start, we became quite friendly. Without his wraparound dark glasses, he looked less of a bruiser and more like the Kazakh intellectual he is, with carefully trimmed beard and fierce, intelligent eyes. He proved not just to be conversant with English literature from the nineteenth century, such as Dickens, Thackeray and Trollope, but also quoted the eighteenth-century writers Fielding and Swift. Other senior officials around the president tended to keep their own counsel, but the press secretary was vocal and unguarded in his opinions. After an anti-American diatribe against the Iraq War, and a homily on the calamity of confrontation with Iran, I interrupted to say that if I were Kazakh I would not be worried about the Americans but about the Chinese. 'That,' he said, 'is clear.'

My favourite image of the energetic press secretary, for ever etched on my mind, comes from a visit by the president to dedicate a newly-built apartment complex for the elderly. Fifty or so Kazakhs waited in an orderly line to greet him. They applauded gently and smiled as he passed in front of them, somewhat overawed by the proximity of their leader in the flesh. It was a decorous and respectful reception, but not nearly enough of a show in the eyes of the press secretary. He wanted a physical display of overflowing gratitude and noisy rapture that could run as a clip on the evening news. It is not in the nature of the reserved and dignified Kazakhs to behave like this.

Out of sight of the president, but in full view of the crowd, the press secretary exhorted everyone to a greater show of enthusiasm. He jumped in the air, flapped his arms wildly and grimaced in a horrible leer that was meant to convey excitement. The crowd failed to respond but continued to smile and applaud politely. Again and again the press secretary jumped, higher and higher, waving his arms like a human windmill. His bemused audience stared at the gesticulating figure in mild alarm. Unaware of the manic performance being enacted silently behind his back, the president disappeared into the apartment building. Defeated, the press secretary followed, muttering and shaking his head.

Evidently, with such an active man around, it was not easy to get to the president unattended. The press secretary always wanted to be in on the act. He tapped his watch if he felt things were going on too long, and made signals indicating how many more questions were allowed. I ignored him as best I could, but he was a pro and difficult to get around. Especially at election time.

I was in the country at the time of the most recent presidential election in the winter of 2005. The opposition had spread stories to the Western media that there would be rioting in the streets, and possible revolution, and that the Interior Ministry had bought 100,000 machine-guns as a precaution. In reality, the election was rather dull. There were no riots, not even a whiff of revolution, and no sign of all those new machine-guns.

A different kind of army, however, was very much in evidence. A horde of officials descended upon Kazakhstan to monitor the election. The West's bureaucratic storm troopers for democracy seemed to be everywhere, packing planes, restaurants and hotels, each armed with a clipboard, a checklist and an expense account. The largest of these bodies, the Organization for Security and Co-operation in Europe – one of the world's fastest growing bureaucracies – seemed to demand a democratic gold standard that Utopia would be hard-pressed to fulfil. Great Britain has historically denied the body access to her own elections, perhaps wisely, but has come under pressure to do so, as developing democracies struggling to meet the gold standard have complained of the hypocrisy of the British refusal to be scrutinized. (The US now has its elections monitored by the OSCE, and at the last presidential election observers included representatives from Kazakhstan.)

The Kazakhs, who are eager to be taken seriously as a democracy by the West, welcomed this army of monitors – close to a thousand, whom Kazakhstan partially funded – with deference and respect. But they brought out the subversive in me. I had become so gung-ho for the country by this time that I verged on hyper-nationalism. I shocked my Kazakh friends by regaling them with stories of dubious practices in American elections by Republicans and Democrats alike, hundreds of thousands of lost postal votes in British elections as well as charges of honours in exchange for party funding, the corrupt shenanigans of French and Italian presidents, and the massive power of the new European tsars, the unelected commissioners in Brussels. 'Maybe we have a long way to go,' one Kazakh said, 'but I don't think we are as bad as what you're describing.'

On Election Day I was in Astana, and decided to go outside the city to visit a couple of villages to see how things were done. The previous evening reporters from London had called people in the hotel probing for news of riot and revolution. One guest was asked in all seriousness to put his head out of the window of his room to check for angry mobs in the street or the sound of gunfire. The report of winter calm – a woman with a pram crossing the road, a man cleaning thick snow from the roof of his car – seemed to disappoint.

Both of the rural polling stations I visited were packed with voters. At the first of them things seemed to be run fairly well, although there were signs of confusion. I saw an old lady go into a booth with her daughter, and an old man ask an official which box he should tick for the president – innocent and understandable behaviour in a young democracy, but serious electoral violations that would have had the international monitors reaching for their clipboards.

On the road to the second polling station there was a lonely signpost in the snow – Yekaterinburg 1,246 kilometres. Bumping

along the track into the village I passed a field containing a dozen Yak bi-planes used in summer as crop dusters, suggesting agriculture on a massive scale. About a kilometre from the polling booth an old lady, bent almost double by osteoporosis, leant on a cane as she made her determined way through the snow to vote.

The polling station was inside a building I took to be the village hall. The place was bustling with voters, and once again on the whole seemed to be well run. But there was no sign of representatives of the opposition parties or the usually ubiquitous international monitors. As I was leaving, the old lady I had passed on the road arrived. At the entrance she asked a prosperous-looking man in a black mink hat, 'Is the president going to win?'

'I'm sure he's going to win comfortably.'

'Thank God,' the old lady said, and she turned to go.

'No, no – you must vote!'

The old lady looked confused as she entered the polling station, mumbling to herself about the mysteries of democracy. The man in the mink hat turned out to be the local farmer who owned 50,000 hectares and the Yak crop dusters. He told me he was of German descent, his farm manager was Kazakh, while most of the villagers were Russian or Ukrainian. He was a staunch

Nazarbayev supporter, as was almost everybody in the village. 'It's like that in the rural areas,' he said. 'We are very traditional and like the strong man. Ten years ago life was hard – now it's good. Like everywhere else in Kazakhstan, agriculture collapsed here along with the Soviet Union. I put together a consortium and bought land. The land was cheap but there was no market, no equipment ... nothing. But everybody worked hard and now this village is doing very well.' So was he rich? He grinned. 'I have a new Mercedes and an apartment in Astana. But I've worked hard for them. We've all worked hard here for what we've got.'

He took me for a walk through the village and showed me a new community centre and school that had been built. I asked why there were no opposition monitors inside the polling station. 'They are concentrating their energies in the cities. There are almost 10,000 voting stations throughout the country and they just don't have the people. Only a handful in the village here vote for any of the opposition parties. Thirty-six in the first election, six last time.'

The election result announced soon afterwards suggested there weren't many voters for the opposition in the cities either. The vote for Nazarbayev was 91 per cent. True, in the villages I had visited, it was probably 98 per cent, but even so to a Westerner the figure seemed ludicrous and highly suspect. I liked the president, and had been impressed and charmed by him, but I began to wonder if I had also been duped.

I attended a victory rally in the sports arena in Astana packed with flag-waving supporters, many of them young. Nazarbayev entered like a conquering hero to a blizzard of tickertape. He looked tired, as if he had been up all night, but charged with adrenaline and happy. Large cannon-like contraptions fired strings of silver paper into the air, a band played patriotic music, and the president made an emotional speech. It was politics as show business, American-style, and the people loved it.

At a press conference afterwards, choreographed by my friend the press secretary, the questions were tame. Only the resident

BBC World Service Central Asian correspondent spoilt the mood by asking about oil and corruption. Unsurprisingly, the president answered that he was not going to respond to slander and lies. But these were among a number of questions I wanted to hear answered myself.

At the airport in Astana, just after the election, I encountered two young Scandinavian women who had been monitors. 'So what do you think?' I asked. 'Free and fair, or fiddled and fixed?'

'Well ...' one began.

Her companion immediately cut her off. 'We are not at liberty to say. There will be a full report expressing the considered opinion of the OSCE in due course. Come along, Ingrid.'

On the flight to Almaty I sat beside another election monitor, a young man from Istanbul. The whole of the rear of the plane was full of his OSCE colleagues of differing nationalities, although the Turk – who spoke Russian badly – seemed to have long since exhausted the patience of his companions. They listened to his endless talk with fixed smiles. Chastened by my brush with his tight-lipped Scandinavian colleagues, I kept to my book.

After the meal, the Turk began to gather from his companions the small plastic containers in which the main course had been served, until he had a haul of about ten. He carefully cleaned each of them with a paper towel, stacked one inside the other, and wrapped the entire cache in newspaper. He then placed them on the floor out of sight. There was confusion when the stewardess later came to collect the trays and discovered that ten plastic containers had disappeared. She giggled in embarrassment, and appealed to us as if we were playing a childish game: 'Where are they please?'

There was silence as an absurd situation developed. Eventually, the Turk confessed. He brought up his newspaper-wrapped booty and the stewardess stared at the bundle with an inane smile of incomprehension. 'I want to take them home,' the Turk said.

'No sir, they are airline property.'

The Turk reluctantly handed them over. He did not seem in the least embarrassed or humiliated. We flew on in silence. It would have been too cruel, but I wanted to ask, 'In your expert professional opinion – was this election free and fair?'

•

In Almaty, I dropped in on the press secretary at the Presidential Residence, a grand building originally designed to house a Lenin museum. (The 'residences' in Almaty and Astana are not homes but administrative buildings. Unlike the incumbents of 10 Downing Street and the White House, the president of Kazakhstan does not live above the shop.)

'Quite a result,' I said, with a note of sarcasm in my voice. 'Ninety-one per cent!'

'Nobody expected it,' the press secretary said, ignoring my tone. 'We would have been satisfied with 75 per cent – a figure that would no doubt be more acceptable to the West.'

'Yes, because 91 per cent seems unbelievable.'

A combative glint appeared in the press secretary's eye, happy to be provoked. 'The American ambassador gave an interview to one of the opposition newspapers and was asked if he believed the results of the election. He replied that the US had financed NGOs that were entirely independent, and had nothing to do with the government, to conduct exit polls. All the results showed the outcome of the voting to be over 83 per cent. The difference between exit polls and real results varies between 5 and 7 per cent. And that's the opinion of the US ambassador.'

Game, set and match, the press secretary's manner suggested, and I was dismissed. The president's wily spin-doctor might have quoted the American ambassador to deflect criticism, but I wanted an entirely independent opinion. I sought out the BBC World Service's Central Asia correspondent who had seemed unafraid of asking difficult questions at the victory press conference. At the time, Ian MacWilliam had been reporting from Kazakhstan for three years, and is as knowledgeable about the country, its politics and its recent history as any foreign journalist alive. (Today he is Eurasian editor of the BBC World Service in London.)

We arranged to meet in a popular bar and shashlyk restaurant in Almaty called the Golden Horde, named after a street gang of the Soviet period which the owner is rumoured to have run with in his youth. The place makes its own very good beer and we talked at length over a couple of pints. I explained that I had been impressed both by Nazarbayev as a man, and by what he had done for the country, and asked whether I was being naïve. Trotsky had described Stalin as 'Genghis Khan with a telephone' – was Nazarbayev an oriental despot with a slick PR machine? 'Well, I would have voted for him if I were Kazakh,' Ian said. These were not the first words I expected to hear from the BBC's man on the spot.

But what about this figure of 91 per cent of the vote? 'I guessed he would get about 85 per cent,' Ian said. The rest, he explained, was made up by local fixers doing things the old way when remote provincial governors told the population how to vote, but this was not controlled or even encouraged by the government or the president's office. There was evidence that they actively worked against such practices. The election had been an improvement on all previous ones when there had been no real debate or opposition campaign. 'This was the first time I saw something different, a big move in the right direction. The biggest in my ten years of experience.'

In that case, I asked, why on the day after the election did the BBC's website lead with OSCE criticisms of the election, namely that there were restrictions on campaigning, interference at polling stations, media bias and multiple voting? 'The OSCE report said good things and bad things,' Ian said. 'But the media only has one minute and forty-five seconds to cover this, so we put out the bad news. My report said things were going in the right direction – and I was irritated to see London lead with a story from the report saying the election was flawed. But both were correct.'

The BBC World Service correspondent was beginning to sound

like the president's press secretary. He confirmed what I had been told in the villages outside Astana that the opposition was mostly confined to the cities, and had scarcely bothered to campaign in the countryside. 'In the rural areas everyone is going to vote for Nazarbayev. He is the president, the father of the country, and the boss. In Central Asia you don't rock the boat. People see it as highly unpragmatic to vote for somebody who is not going to get on with the authorities, or who is untried in the business of government. I like the opposition guys but they have never been organized or very effective. They are well meaning and a lot of their criticism is well founded, but none of them has any experience in running a country.'

I ordered more beer, and asked about the Kazakh human rights record, usually reported in the West as 'dismal' or 'appalling'. Ian sighed and said that Kazakhstan did not have a terrible human rights record. There had been two people in jail who could be classed as political prisoners, but they had been released. The harassment of provincial journalists and newspapers was carried out by a residue of KGB and police who had not moved with the times. 'It's a hangover from the old days, and not directed from the centre or the president. In Uzbekistan, on the other hand, the human rights record is truly appalling – the Uzbeks lock everybody up, and prisoners sit in jail having their fingernails pulled out.'

It seemed to me, I said, that the further away from Kazakhstan a journalist was, the more critical he became (most of the reports on the election carried in the British press were filed from Moscow – 4,000 kilometres away). 'These moralizing articles about Central Asia always leave me with the feeling that an editor needed copy quickly and gave the job to a journalist who has never been here,' Ian said. 'The journalist then trawls through the Internet to see what dirt he can find, and the one that always pops up on a Google search is oil and corruption. But there is the matter of context. You do have to take account of where Kazakhstan has come from, and the rather obvious fact that it's not yet a perfectly evolved society.

'The West has a very simplistic view of everything in Central

Asia. It looks at the area as being run by a load of funny despots. And since Kazakhstan is the richest and biggest of them all, Nazarbayev must be a funny despot too. But I believe he genuinely has the interest of his country in his sights, and wants to build it up, and be remembered as a great leader. He has promoted the right economic policies and been sensible about the development of the country. Kazakhstan is doing well.'

At a later date I approached a highly informed Kazakh journalist known to be an outspoken but even-handed critic of the government to ask about a particularly murky area of politics, the deaths of two opposition figures. One had died in the period leading up to the 2005 election, another early in 2006. Neither death is intelligible to outsiders. The Kazakh journalist seemed relaxed and happy to talk to me, but only on condition that I did not use his name. 'Are you worried about repercussions?' I asked. 'That the authorities might take action against you?'

'The authorities do not concern me,' he said with a broad grin. 'I am worried you will misquote me.'

I asked about Zamanbek Nurkadilov, a member of the opposition found dead in his apartment in the lead-up to the election. Although he had been shot twice in the heart and once in the head, investigators came to the improbable conclusion that it was suicide. 'Clearly not suicide,' the journalist said. 'His family believe it was murder. But this man's life had gone wrong and was a mess. Drinking ... women. I do not know for sure, but believe he had trouble with people he owed money. A business deal with criminals that had gone wrong. Something like that. He was absolutely no political threat to the president – or to the government. Maybe there was some sort of clumsy attempt at a cover-up of the cause of his death because of the upcoming election, but political assassination? No!'

And what about Altynbek Sarsenbaev, co-chairman of the Naghyz Ak Zhol (True Bright Path) opposition party, who was found shot dead after the election, together with two aides, on the outskirts of Almaty? 'This is complicated and disturbing,' the journalist said. 'It was murder. No doubt. Maybe a beating that went wrong, but murder. Members of the security services were involved – and ten people were arrested and went on trial and were sentenced to life in prison. But I don't believe it stops there. There have been demonstrations by the opposition demanding a public inquiry.

'But no informed person in Kazakhstan, by the way, believes for a moment that Nazarbayev was involved in this. It was a PR disaster for him! He had just been re-elected with a landslide majority when this happened. He is eager to be taken seriously internationally, so this was terrible both for him and the country. He brought in the FBI from America to oversee the investigation to try to restore the confidence of the international community. But what is disturbing is the likelihood of some sort of dark power struggle going on within the élite for the succession. There are rich and powerful men – and some evil men – who want to take over when Nazarbayev goes.

'The real challenge for Nazarbayev and Kazakhstan over the remaining years of his presidency, before he stands down, is to make sure the checks and balances of democracy have evolved sufficiently so that the next incumbent will inherit a civil society, and be obliged to govern within the law. Or we could lose everything that we have gained.'

A radical reshuffle of the Cabinet at the beginning of 2007 demonstrated both Nazarbayev's absolute control of the country's political apparatus, and his intention to change its political landscape. In foreign policy the newly appointed Beijing-educated minister suggests a turn towards China, particularly in the economic sphere. Internally, the reshuffle indicates moves towards reform aimed at ensuring a quiet succession. The president has also expressed his support for amendments to the Constitution to further democratize the political system – namely majority parliamentary support as a pre-condition for approving prime ministerial candidates, budgetary oversight becoming parliament's responsibility, and the funding of political parties from the national budget.

There are also plans to overhaul the judicial system and introduce trial by jury. A new political structure is in the process of being created for a new leader, separate from the existing one connected to the president.

'At the moment the presidency has too much power,' the journalist said. 'Okay, Nazarbayev says the country first needs economic stability above all, and then more democracy. He is a gradualist. And that makes sense. But over the next five years certain powers must devolve from the presidency to other bodies. On the surface this big new Cabinet reshuffle can be seen as the traditional Kazakh method of testing officials in different posts. But beneath there's much more going on. A painless power transfer, and the transition to a properly functioning parliamentary republic acceptable to both the USA and the UK, would seem to be the president's goals. If he pulls that off, it would be among his greatest achievements. If not we could end up with a real dictator. Not a benign *bei* like Nazarbayev, not a traditional *khan* that Kazakhs know and understand, but a monster.'

•

Before the election, on the way back to Astana from Karaganda after my meeting with the Gulag survivor, I asked the driver if he would take me through Temirtau, a grim spot that contains one of the largest steelworks in the world. This created much grumbling. The town was hellish and there was nothing to see, the driver said, a place full of alcoholics and heroin addicts, with the highest HIV infection rate in the whole of Kazakhstan. It meant making a large detour on icy roads and would add hours to the journey. And he had no intention of driving at night. It was bad enough having to stay in Karaganda, but now he was anxious to get home to his wife and daughter (she of the demented laugh). My insistence further frosted a chilly relationship. It would cost, the driver said, and I agreed to pay. He lapsed into grumpy silence, put on his favourite CD of growling prison songs, and turned up the volume.

But he was right about Temirtau. The landscape actually looked as if the denizens of Hell had set up shop above ground and were hard at work tormenting damned souls. Mile after mile of hideous plant belched filthy smoke into a clear blue winter sky. Row after row of tumbledown wooden housing were well on the way to ruin, while more recently built blocks of apartments stood lonely and stark, and the centre of town was a deserted wasteland of dilapidated government offices. We drove to the spot where the sculptor Anatoly Belyk had recently placed a large work of two steelworkers feeding a furnace. I stopped to take pictures. It was a sign of the times that the workers portrayed in the sculpture were discernibly Kazakh; in the old days they would have had European Russian features.

I wanted to have a look at Temirtau because it was where the president had spent years from the late 1950s as a steelworker, possibly one of the most important times in his life when the young man's character was forged. The memories of the steelworks remained sharp, and he would even flex his arm muscles to show he had not lost the physical strength and stamina of the old days. 'A steelworks runs twenty-four hours, seven days a week,' he told me. 'It's a tough environment in every way. Temperatures of 2,000 degrees centigrade, pressure at six atmospheres – if you make a mistake, things explode and people around you die. You have to be sharp and concentrate every second. You cannot shift the responsibility on to the shoulders of your neighbour or you lose the respect of your team. It was not a bad training ground.'

This came out of a conversation held late one night after an exhausting three days in helicopters when I travelled with the president to the west of the country. The day had started for Nazarbayev at six in the morning when bodyguards woke his chief of staff for a game of tennis. It ended close to midnight after a rally for 10,000 supporters at a sports stadium in Kyzlorda. Even the press secretary looked tired and returned to his hotel. An aide approached me: 'The president has a little time to talk now at the governor's residence.'

The residence was a recently completed building in the grand style, situated directly beside the sports stadium. I was led through a dark hallway, and upstairs along echoing corridors. Nazarbayev sat in a chair alone in a large room almost empty of furniture. He had removed his coat and was drinking bottled water, like a boxer after a fight. I expected only a brief interview, but the talk went on for a couple of hours, roaming over his early life, beginning with reminiscences about his days as a young man at the steelworks.

Just as Nazarbayev was finishing his schooling, the whole of Kazakhstan was talking about the new city of Temirtau, where one of the biggest steel plants in the Soviet Union was under construction. An advertisement in the Almaty paper offered members of the Young Communist League an all-expenses-paid, year-long course at the Temirtau Technical School, where they would be trained to work in the plant. The money was good and the young Nazarbayev was eager to go. His father was less enthusiastic. Life as a steelworker was even harsher than that on a collective, while nearby Karaganda, then the centre of the country's Gulag, was notorious for violent criminal gangs that terrorized local residents.

The teenage Nazarbayev's first impressions of Temirtau were depressing. The place was little more than a village in the middle of a gigantic construction site. True to Soviet form the plant was monumental in size but haphazard in plan. There were cranes everywhere, and mountains of sand and building materials, but no roads, no housing, and few facilities for the construction workers, who were forced to live in tents.

Nazarbayev had scarcely settled in when he was offered the chance to go to a steel plant in the Ukraine to learn on the job, and he jumped at the opportunity. But the Ukraine was a long way from home, and a different world, and the country boy's early experience of a steelworks in operation was daunting. Used to fresh air and the freedom of the mountains, he found himself thrust into one of the Soviet Union's major plants. 'The plant made a terrible impression. The noise alone was unnerving. Sparks flew like snowflakes in a blizzard, and molten cast iron ran like a spring torrent. Few of us had been raised in a city and we had only a vague idea about the conditions in which Soviet industrial workers had to live and work. Life had been hard for us – but this was terrible!'

The young Kazakhs felt homesick and were eager to return to Kazakhstan, scouring newspapers for reports of progress on the Temirtau plant. Journalists did not spare superlatives in describing the magnificent city and mighty steelworks under construction. But disturbing rumours of unrest circulated.

Temirtau had been built at lightning speed, demanding long and exhausting hours from the construction workers in midsummer heat, when temperatures reached 35 degrees centigrade. Tents and hastily constructed barracks continued to be the only living quarters, the food was terrible, there was not much of it, and the drinking water was often contaminated. The authorities failed to supply sufficient protective clothing resulting in a high rate of injury. Even for men inured to hardship, life became intolerable, and the workers were pushed beyond breaking-point.

In 1959, thousands marched on the site's headquarters demanding improvements. Instead of talking to the ringleaders, the management barricaded themselves inside their offices. When the workers realized they were going to be ignored, the protest degenerated into a riot. An angry mob looted the town's liquor shops and went on a drunken rampage.

Inevitably, the authorities hit back. Troops moved into the town to restore order, and when the drunken workers refused to return to their huts and tents, the soldiers opened fire. The number of fatalities and wounded was suppressed – and remains impossible to verify – but it has been estimated that as many as fifty people were killed, and hundreds wounded. The ringleaders were arrested and punished, and a strict curfew was imposed on the town. 'It should be remembered,' Nazarbayev said, 'that this was the period of the so-called Khrushchev "thaw".'

A year after the revolt, the young Kazakh steelworkers returned from the Ukraine for the opening of the plant, a day marked by parades and speeches. Order had long since been imposed, life had returned to normal, and the future seemed promising. The violence had unnerved the authorities and luxuries had been brought in as a sop to the workers. The young Kazakhs were amazed to see how well the local shops were stocked in comparison to the Ukraine where there had been shortages of everything. There was red and black caviar, sturgeon and smoked fish, good-quality wine and brandy, and the clothes shops were full of imported goods, an unheard-of luxury.

But as soon as the speeches were over, and the military bands had stopped playing, the well-stocked shops emptied. Life for the ordinary worker became miserable once again. 'Our own living conditions were intolerable,' Nazarbayev remembered. 'After a short time in a damp and dirty basement we were moved to an unheated dormitory where we kept warm by sleeping in pairs on iron cots covered with mattresses. There was no place to hang clothes to dry. We left our canvas work clothes outside at night because it was easier to put them on when they were frozen than when they were wet. There were no recreational facilities – the only entertainment was to watch the numerous fights. Violent crime and murder were rife.

'We survived because we were young and strong, but there

was no justification for the hardships we suffered. There might have been in the 1930s when the Soviet Union's very survival depended on rapid industrialization, but this was the 1960s and still the Soviet system remained indifferent to the people. The country confused the means with the end and turned people into an extension of an all-devouring economic machine which demanded more and more of human beings while giving less and less in return.'

Work in the blast furnace, where metal was melted at a temperature of 2,000 degrees centigrade and the air was filled with gas and dust, was punishing and dangerous. There were few rest breaks and complaints were not allowed. A number of the young recruits cracked under the strain and had to quit. 'During a shift we had to drink half a bucket of water to replace what we had lost in sweat. After work, we needed half an hour in a cold shower to recover. The workers were permanently exhausted by the heat. Their muscles never had a chance to relax, and some had constant nosebleeds.'

The only compensating factor was that by Soviet standards the men were well paid. Within six months, Nazarbayev was earning 450 roubles a month – an unbelievable sum for a 20-year-old at the time, although every kopek was hard-earned. Half was sent back to his family, and on one occasion Nazarbayev's father travelled to Temirtau to see how his son earned all this money.

The father was horrified at the dangerous conditions the men accepted as normal. There was an accident on a night shift at the time of his visit involving a spill of molten ore, when the crew was obliged to remain on duty until it was cleaned up, working to the point of exhaustion. The father witnessed the long night's ordeal in silence, but before returning to the tranquillity of the mountains he asked his son, 'Why are you torturing yourself? I was an orphan at the age of three and have seen a lot in my life, but I never experienced such a hell. Give it up!'

•

Nursultan Nazarbayev is unique among world leaders in that as a child he awoke daily to pangs of hunger and fell asleep nightly to a chorus of howling wolves. He was born in a mountain collective in the Tien Shan on 6 July 1940. His parents were scarcely literate peasants descended from nomads of the Great Horde. His father worked as a shepherd but was badly burned trying to put out a fire in the camp when Nazarbayev was still a baby, and afterwards his left arm began to wither.

'The worst fear was of the wolves,' Nazarbayev told me. 'My mother used to turn pale every time she heard them howling. She was not afraid of the wolves themselves, because she knew my father could kill them even with only one good arm, but she worried that they might kill a sheep. And then what could they tell the collective farm bosses? No excuses were accepted. Any shepherd who did not protect his flock faced ten years in a forced-labour camp.'

The physical limitations imposed on the father by his withered arm, in addition to the severe privations of life on a collective, meant the family was perpetually hungry. As a boy, the father had gone to work for an affluent Russian kulak family – the Niki-forovs – in the village of Chemolgan, lower down in the foothills, forty kilometres from Almaty. 'My father quickly learned to speak Russian and to take care of a peasant homestead. He became indispensable – he knew how to make boots, plough the land, run a mill and come back from market with a profit. All the basic skills of a good peasant.' The Nikiforovs were a decent, hard-working family who treated their Kazakh employee well and paid him fairly. Their behaviour profoundly affected the future president's attitude towards Russians.

A mixture of ethnic groups lived in Chemolgan as a result of nineteenth-century Russian colonization. Kazakhs stayed on one side of the river, and settlers from Central Russia, the Don region and the Ukraine inhabited the other. There was enough land and water for everyone, and relations were good until one day the villagers heard a difficult word that they did not understand:

kolkhozy, collectivization, a concept utterly foreign to every nationality in the village.

The kindly Nikiforovs, condemned as kulaks, were among the first to be uprooted. Their property was confiscated and the family exiled north to Siberia. As a labourer, Nazarbayev's father avoided persecution. It was into this bleak world that Nazarbayev was born. As a child he saw exiled kulaks from other parts of the country pass through the village on their way to the mountains where they worked as forced labour on a road still known locally as the Convicts' Highway. 'My father took the family into the mountains and took up livestock herding. The events of these times marked him for the rest of his life.'

Nazarbayev's own childhood was a time of uninterrupted hardship, when staples such as sugar, tea and even bread were scarce: 'An endless winter night of hunger and cold'. The only respite came with the brief mountain summer, when his mother taught him to identify and collect edible roots and berries. The occasional evening of music and song was the only recreation known. His mother was renowned as a singer in the area, and his father played the *dombra*.

After the war there was some relaxation in the regulations controlling kulaks. Though the father had died in Siberia, the rest of the Nikiforov family returned to Chemolgan. And now there were new nationalities in the village, made up of the wave of deportees sent to Kazakhstan by Stalin during the war: Chechens, Volga Germans and Balkars. Russian was the bridging language between them all, and Nazarbayev learned to speak it with the other children.

'When I first went to school there were all these kids there from the North Caucasus who had been deported. They had been loaded on to trains in a single night without anything and scattered all over Kazakhstan. Mixing with all these ethnic groups was an everyday reality for us and brought with it a tolerance for different people. My father adopted a family of Balkars – father and mother and two kids. They slowly found their feet, and after a while the father got a job, and then they went their own way.'

As a boy, Nazarbayev rose before sunrise, harnessed the donkey and headed for the bakery in the nearby village. By the time he arrived a long line would already have formed. 'If I was lucky, I would finally get bread by noon. It was heavy black bread which dented when you squeezed it. I would queue up two or three times so I could bring home ten loaves. The bread could not be stored for long so it was sliced into small pieces and dried in the sun.' All the locals survived on such bread, accompanying it with *ayran*, a sour drink made from milk mixed with corn husks.

The collective provided the mother with a hectare of sugar beet to cultivate by hand. This demanded back-breaking work from spring through the scorching heat of summer until the first snowfall. In return for his mother's labour the family received a certificate for one and a half sacks of sugar. The father looked after the livestock but was also expected to plant several hectares of wheat on the mountain slopes. Again, almost the entire yield was claimed by the collective. 'When the wheat ripened, my father and I cut it by hand, working all through the night by moonlight. While we worked my mother would make sheaves which we took to the collective where they were put into threshers.'

Workers on the collective lived at subsistence level. The Nazarbayevs supplemented their diet with produce grown on a small allotment, but even this patch of land was eventually taken away. The family horse had to be given up because the collective refused to provide winter fodder. Cream from the milk of the single cow was also taken by the collective each day, leaving the family with a couple of litres of skimmed milk. The father had grown apples all his life, and taken them to market in Almaty by cart, but this became impossible when the government introduced a new tax on fruit trees. 'I couldn't believe my eyes when I saw my father cutting down his own apple trees.'

When he was ready to start school, Nazarbayev left the mountain camp to live with his paternal uncle, closer to town. The new routine was no less punishing. It meant rising at dawn and walking five kilometres through the snow to school. 'If the guard was kind he would let me in while he got the stove going. I could snatch some more sleep by lying next to it.' After a day's school-work, and the long trek home, there was hard physical work to be done at the uncle's house. 'I had to feed the cattle, clean the shed, fetch water and work in the garden. I hated it – hated it! And then I had to do my homework. After that I had an hour or so for reading. I learned to value and organize my time.'

Nazarbayev's parents had great respect for people who were educated, and insisted their son went on to further education. He left his uncle's house to attend a boarding school nearby where he attracted the attention of his teachers and was invited to join the Young Communist League. This was an honour, offering a path to power. 'My father did not approve, but he understood my decision because you could only achieve something in life then by being a member of the Communist Party.'

He was picked as a delegate to go to Moscow where he listened in awe to a speech by Nikita Khrushchev. When he returned to Almaty he told stories about his adventures in the capital while his elders listened, saying nothing. He spoke of Khrushchev's determination to close the gap between town and country, and the leader's rosy view of the future of agriculture. 'And I told my father I was ready to sacrifice my life for such a man.'

Carried away by the attention he was receiving, he mistook silence for agreement and failed to notice the mockery in his listeners' eyes. His father was barely able to conceal his contempt. When Nazarbayev repeated the Party line criticizing people for owning small plots of land, he was unable to contain himself. He called the young man into the garden, where he always withdrew to say anything that might be interpreted as critical of the regime.

'All the serious stuff was said in the garden,' Nazarbayev said. 'He said to me, "What the hell are you praising Khrushchev for? We hear too many of these speeches on the radio. Do you know he has cut the size of our plots? A farmer without a plot of land is like a shepherd without sheep. Do you know that we are not allowed to have more than ten apple trees, that we are only allowed one cow per family? How are we going to live like this? Has everyone in Moscow lost their memory? Don't take this personally, Sultan, but this is not good news you have brought back with you.'"

•

The father's peasant good sense curbed Nazarbayev's enthusiasm, but it was the Communist Party that saved him from a life spent as a steelworker. 'I joined in 1962 and even today make no excuses for that. Some of the best workers were Communists and I wanted to follow their example.' He met his wife during this period and their wedding was sponsored by the Young Communist League. 'As was customary in those days, we were presented with the keys to our own apartment. But when we went to the address we saw that construction work had barely begun. We had to live with a friend who had a tiny one-bedroom apartment that we shared with his wife, two children and their grandmother. We spent our wedding night in the same room as grandma.'

At first, Nazarbayev remained a full-time steelworker, but he soon became involved in Party organizational work and was noted by the hierarchy for his energy and leadership qualities. He was offered the post of First Secretary of the city's Young Communists, but the full-time job did not appeal, partly because it would have meant a dramatic drop in salary, and partly because he would have had to leave the plant and old friends. He turned the position down, earning himself a serious reprimand. 'The Communist Party was like an army in those days. It was simply not done to disagree even slightly with your superiors. We were all meant to be "soldiers of the Party", and soldiers had to obey orders. In the end I gave in and accepted the job.'

The new role was as demanding and exhausting in its way as manual work. 'Very little time was spent in the office shuffling papers. I spent day and night at the plant's various construction sites. The pace was dizzying. I could be at the blast furnace after an accident, writing schedules late into the night, submitting hundreds of different legal documents, organizing weekend overtime or overseeing the transport of concrete and metal. Every day I met dozens, sometimes hundreds of people. They came with all sorts of requests and problems – a foreman might be threatening to take his crew off a job because the supply of concrete was not regular, or a worker's wife might want us to persuade her alcoholic husband to stop drinking.'

Nazarbayev rose rapidly through the Party ranks, a journey that gave him an insight into the rot at the heart of the system. The steel plant was a microcosm of Soviet industry with all its faults, and important enough to attract a stream of senior officials from the Moscow ministries, especially before the annual Communist Party Congress when they reported on the achievements of their departments. 'Thousands of people would be taken off less urgent tasks to complete a project on time. I remember having to finish construction of a chemical plant, whatever the cost, so that an official could report its completion. He was able to make his report on time, but on the first day of the Congress one of the galleries collapsed.'

Poor planning, unrealistic quotas and rushed jobs meant the plant operated inefficiently all the time. 'The workers were under terrible stress. Because there were so many accidents they never had any weekends off, and their wages were allowed to fall cata-strophically. As a result, absenteeism was high, men were continu-ally late, and staff turnover reached 30 per cent. The management, meanwhile, was forever being reshuffled in the hope that this would improve performance.'

The higher Nazarbayev rose in the Party hierarchy, the greater the disillusion with the system, where every level revealed new absurdities. When he was promoted to the body responsible for the entire region's industry, he learned of the plight of Karagan-da's coal miners. 'Their living conditions were appalling. The mines were in constant danger of collapse, and the methane level was extremely high, explosions common. The miners were forever being chided for not reaching targets. The Party line at the time was "Less spending – more output!" Lack of investment prevented new mines being developed and the city began, literally, to be undermined – the ground sank, water pipes broke, buildings collapsed.'

Years of exhausting hard work, with no solution at hand, built a slow-burning anger. 'I saw all the flaws in the system. Every year the numbers were faked, and every year everybody worked flat out to show 101 per cent. You dared not show only 99 per cent. That would have meant everybody would be kicked out of their positions.

'Let me give an example of how it worked – Moscow gave you a target in a one-year plan of 50 million tonnes of coal, say. Five days before the end of the year you add up the numbers and find you have only 45 million tonnes. What do you do? Your boss tells you: "Do anything you want – but find five million tonnes." So you go to the mines all around Karaganda and count coal in trucks, coal in warehouses, coal on the ground. And that gives you another three million tonnes. You are still missing two million tonnes. So you fly to Moscow and beg the chairman of the State Planning Committee to change the original plan to 48 – and maybe this requires taking him to an expensive restaurant or giving him a gift. And the plan is adjusted.

'This was done by everyone all over the country all the time. We were just fooling ourselves. Everything was subject to the same mad logic. For instance, white bread in the shop cost 25 kopeks a kilo, but the real cost was six roubles. The bread was subsidized by the government. That's fine for bread, but this was done with everything – coal, steel, cotton, cars. So if all prices are artificial and all statistics false and everything is subsidized – how could this kind of state survive? It was very depressing.'

The Soviet system was trapped in an enormous vicious circle. Bureaucratic legerdemain made it appear that plans were fulfilled when the reality was the opposite. Projects known to be doomed to failure were approved for political reasons, and when they inevitably collapsed the plans were quietly revised. On top of everything the economy was measured in an absurd way. Even though it was planned, with no competition and arbitrary price fixing, performance was still measured in financial terms. The result was that the greater the cost of production, the more a plant could charge, and therefore the greater its turnover. In other words, the more inefficiently it worked, the better it seemed to be doing.

'The Party bosses may not have known the details of how all this was achieved, but they were well aware it was done. It was disgusting. So after I had worked in government for a few years at management level I realized how our economic system – a system that seemed eternal and immutable – was leading us into a dead end.'

The absurdities continued to pile up. In 1980, when Nazarbayev became secretary of the Central Committee of the Kazakh Communist Party, Moscow decided upon the construction of an enormous textile mill in the north of Kazakhstan that would provide women with thousands of jobs but which offered no employment for their husbands. At the same time he heard of plans to build a huge diesel engine factory several hundred kilometres away across the border in Russia. He flew to Moscow to persuade the authorities – in the form of a powerful Party functionary – to shift the factory to the same town as the textile plant.

'The man acted as Brezhnev's de facto deputy and welcomed me into his office and, for some reason, even kissed me.' Nazarbayev spent a long time pleading for the factory to be built in Kazakhstan, while the high-powered official seemed scarcely to be listening. His questions were off the subject and it was clear his thoughts were on other things, until eventually he interrupted: 'So what is your problem exactly?'

'I would like this diesel engine plant to be built in Kazakhstan.'

The functionary nodded and picked up the phone. He spoke briefly to the minister of the motor industry and then made a call to the relevant department head of the Central Committee. In ten minutes the location of a heavy diesel engine plant was moved hundreds of kilometres to a different republic. The resources involved were enormous and would affect tens of thousands of lives. 'This was how major economic decisions were taken in those days.'

The way in which bribery was institutionalized was revealed little by little to Party officials as they rose through the system, like the mysteries of an occult religion. Every year the chairman of the republic's State Planning Committee, its finance minister, and similar Party big shots in Kazakhstan, demanded bonuses for their departments to go to Moscow to defend the plans and budgets for the coming twelve months. It was the accepted practice on these occasions to provide lavish entertainment and hand over 'presents'. 'When I became prime minister of Kazakhstan,' Nazarbayev said, 'my predecessor told me in all seriousness how one national minister was fond of piglets and another liked to receive fresh tomatoes. You'll understand how such a distorting approach to plans and budgets could produce arbitrary results.'

Under the Soviet system it was essential to be on good terms with powerful Moscow officials. All the income from the factories of every region in each republic was returned to Moscow, divided up, and sent back to the republics. Kazakhstan, with its natural resources and heavy industry, was automatically the victim of such a system, for while billions of roubles flowed to Moscow, only a fraction found its way back. Anyone with a good personal relationship with the finance minister could expect a few extra million roubles in their budget, while a friend of the chairman of the State Supplies Committee might receive extra cement, metal or timber for their factories. The corrupted command system demanded that all the republics play the game, and no one considered the consequences of taking someone else's share.

'Whether you liked it or not, you had to follow the unwritten rules – you had to fawn on your superiors and offer hospitality. If not, your republic – its industry and factories – would be forced on to a starvation diet. The only way to get investment was to be clever and resourceful, and in our system this led to degradation, crime and corruption. The system virtually demanded it.'

Of all the republics, Kazakhstan was the greatest victim of this economic madness. The republic supplied the USSR with 90 per cent of its titanium and magnesium, 70 per cent of its zinc, 60 per cent of its lead and 30 per cent of its copper. It provided 90 per cent of its phosphorus, almost all its chrome, and large amounts of gold and silver. There were limitless deposits of coal, and huge oil and gas fields within the republic, which also had 10 million head of cattle, 40 million sheep and goats, and close to 40 million hectares of land under cultivation. And yet it remained one of the poorest and least developed republics in the Soviet Union.

The reason was simple: scarcely any of the raw materials were processed in the country. Gold and silver ore mined in Kazakhstan was sent out of the republic to be refined, and the same was true of copper and chrome. The natural resources that attracted the development of some of the Soviet Union's largest mining enterprises and heavy industry rewarded the country with little more than massive environmental problems. Kazakhstan provided millions of raw hides but had no tanneries. It produced ample milk and meat to satisfy the needs of its own population, but it had nowhere to process them. Instead, the republic had to import most of its consumer goods and suffered a shortage of everything.

The true rulers of Kazakhstan – and every Soviet republic – were the all-powerful central ministries in Moscow, none of which took into account the interests of the individual republics when they drew up their plans for the exploitation of raw materials. 'Moscow never sent us enough of anything,' Nazarbayev said. 'All the republic's resources were ploughed into heavy industry, while people's genuine needs were put on hold. For decades, the huge factories, the electrical power plants, the powerful blast furnaces and the enormous cranes were portrayed by Soviet propagandists as the source of hope for a better future. But finally that hope vanished.'

•

On the occasion of Kazakhstan's sixtieth anniversary as a republic, in 1980, the Soviet leader, Leonid Brezhnev, travelled to Almaty for the celebrations, accompanied by the entire Politburo. The geriatric Brezhnev had got to know Kazakhstan well when he worked on the Virgin Lands project as a protégé of Khrushchev. The fact that the project had proved a disaster did not hold back his plodding progress to the very top of the Party hierarchy. An increasingly decrepit leader, he had become the impotent figure-head of a moribund, absolutist bureaucracy running a totalitarian political system incapable of change, and a command economy that had becalmed the USSR in utter stagnation. During the Brezhnev years, fear had ossified into lethargy.

A reception for a thousand guests had been organized in Almaty to receive the USSR's most powerful man. Scarcely able to walk, Brezhnev was helped to his seat at the banquet by two large bodyguards amid light applause. The old man's eyes were dead, his manner absent. The veteran Communist Party leader of Kaza-khstan at the time, Dinmukhamed Kunayev, proposed a toast. As the assembled guests rose to respond, Brezhnev suddenly struggled to his feet and headed towards the exit. Everyone in his entourage was obliged to follow. Brezhnev was helped into his car and driven away with the official motorcade following in his wake. Nazarbayev, who was present, observed: 'It was clear he had simply forgotten where he was and why he had come.'

Even the advent of Mikhail Gorbachev as general secretary of the Soviet Communist Party in 1985 had little effect on life in Kazakhstan. 'Everything was much as it had been in the Brezhnev years,' Nazarbayev said, 'even down to the over-long, tedious and boring speeches at the annual Congress, and the unanimous rubber-stamp votes.' In our conversations, it became clear that Nazarbayev did not share the West's zeal for Gorbachev, whom he liked personally but saw as hypocritical and ineffective. The policies of glasnost and perestroika were deluded, and the declaration that the economy could be restructured within two or three years was a wildly optimistic miscalculation. 'It was unrealistic to believe that it was possible to turn the massive Soviet political and economic machine around in such a short period of time,' Nazarbayev said. 'Soviet history is full of examples of this Utopian approach to complex social, political and economic problems. It has always failed.'

Even so, early on Gorbachev had generated high hopes in Kazakhstan with his talk of revitalized political thinking and a streamlined bureaucracy. His popularity soared when he announced the removal of the Kazakh Party boss, Kunayev, who had dominated the republic for four decades. Kunayev had become synonymous with Kazakhstan but he was also linked to everything wrong with the place, for it was his corrupt political patronage that had resulted in the republic's economic growth falling to the lowest within the USSR.

The decision to remove Kunayev was welcomed – until people found out who was going to replace him. Gorbachev's choice was Gennady Kolbin, a Party boss from the Volga who had no link to Kazakhstan whatsoever. The man had never worked or lived in the republic and was unknown to its people. Worst of all, he was not Kazakh. Once again Moscow was demonstrating its usual indifference and insensitivity to the feelings and opinions of the inhabitants of a non-Russian republic. No one in the Politburo objected to the decision, or even discussed it, and at the end of 1986 Kolbin was elected unopposed.

The morning after the announcement of the new leader a large crowd of demonstrators, made up of workers and students, converged on the square outside the Central Committee building in Almaty. Glasnost and perestroika might not have delivered, but they had encouraged the expression of long-suppressed political frustrations. The demonstration was the natural reaction of people whose national identity had been denied for decades. At first the crowd behaved in an orderly manner, and many carried banners bearing a portrait of Lenin, but the message was clear

– the appointment of an outsider was humiliating and universally unpopular.

The new Party boss watched the crowd from an office overlooking the square. Kolbin was flanked by the Kazakh interior minister, the local head of the KGB, the public prosecutor and various cronies from Moscow. The advice of local leaders to appease the crowd, or risk provoking a riot, was ignored. Kolbin regarded the demonstration as an unacceptable and dangerous expression of Kazakh nationalism and one that could not be tolerated. He ordered the police to cordon off the square, while special units from the Interior Ministry moved into the area, and the Almaty army garrison was put on alert.

By the time local leaders were permitted to go out and address the crowd at three in the afternoon, a peaceful assembly of demonstrators had turned into an angry and aggressive mob. The officials were heckled and booed and had lumps of ice and rock thrown at them. Demonstrators climbed on to the podium and took over the microphone, while KGB agents gave the order to drown out the dissident speeches with loud music.

News of the disorder was relayed to Moscow where the demonstration evoked a real fear that it might spread to other republics. A group of top Moscow security officials flew to Almaty the same day, including members of the Politburo and the Central Committee, and senior officials of the KGB, the Ministry of the Interior and the Prosecutor's Office. Their analysis of the situation was unequivocal – the demonstration needed quick and total suppression.

Operation Snowstorm was launched against the crowd, and police and special units used truncheons and dogs to break up the demonstration. By nightfall, two people were dead, 200 had been injured and 8,500 had been arrested or detained. Many were beaten in custody. Others were expelled from the city in bitterly cold weather. (The head of the Soviet Army in the area, General Vladimir Lobov, was ordered to use his troops against the demonstrators but showed enormous courage by refusing to do so.)

The official Moscow line was predictable. Hooligans and

troublemakers had engaged in an illegal and disorderly manifestation of Kazakh nationalism. Gennady Kolbin clung to office for another three years, an increasingly unpopular and reviled figure. Inside Kazakhstan, he became a living symbol of the failure of perestroika, and was seen for what he was – a puppet in a political show directed and stage managed by Moscow. (On top of everything, he was an enthusiastic and sycophantic supporter of Gorbachev's 'sobriety zones'.)

The discontent grew so strong that even the Communist Party leadership in Moscow understood they would have to replace their man with somebody local, or risk the humiliation of seeing him forcibly removed. In June 1989, Nursultan Nazarbayev was appointed leader of the Kazakhstan Communist Party. 'I was determined to break the ring of stagnation which surrounded the republic.'

•

There had been no strategic plan for perestroika, which lurched along in a process of trial and error. The people of Kazakhstan, meanwhile, were worse off than they had been under Brezhnev: inflation was out of hand, the shops were empty, and the whole economy had regressed into a primitive barter system. As the country sank into chaos, a growing nostalgia developed for the good old days of stagnation.

'Gorbachev's fundamental error was his failure to listen to the republics' demands for economic independence,' Nazarbayev said. 'How could Kazakhstan be helped if 90 per cent of its industry was under the control of the Moscow ministries? The leadership in the Kremlin had no understanding of how fed up we were with their high-handedness, nor the bitterness we felt towards them for the rapacious plundering of our natural resources, the difficult conditions under which our people lived, and the ecological tragedies that had occurred. There was no desire for complete independence, but we did want greater freedom to control our own destiny.

If Gorbachev had set out at once to provide maximum independence for the republics *within* the Union, then we could have avoided much of the subsequent upheaval. At least the federal authorities would not have collapsed under the weight of the economic mess.

'For all Gorbachev's talk of restructuring, many of his top officials continued to behave in the old authoritarian way. Even the highly important plan for the USSR's changeover to a market economy was made without the involvement of the leaders of the various republics. It was all too hasty and feverish, like the desperate retreat of an army with no prepared fallback positions. With each year of perestroika, the number of mistakes increased exponentially, until by 1990 it seemed that the whole country was ablaze.'

In the West, Gorbachev was regarded as a reforming genius, the creator of a Soviet Union that could live peaceably with the rest of the world. But his own Communist Party inevitably resisted the dismantling of its monopoly of power, and he slowly lost control. He became hated by communists, nationalists and democrats alike. Communists condemned him as a traitor and blamed him for leading the Party to suicide, nationalists saw him as the West's poodle and blamed him for humiliating the Soviet Union before the world, while democrats and liberals dismissed him as two-faced, self-deluded and vain, a man who talked endlessly but who failed to deliver.

The coup against him in 1991 had been timed by his enemies to prevent the signing of a treaty that would have changed the way the Soviet Union was run. The treaty was intended to transfer power from Moscow to the various republics, and leaders like Nazarbayev saw it as the only way of saving the Soviet Union. The plotters saw things differently. To them the treaty was a death sentence for the all-powerful, centralized Moscow ministries, which constituted the hardliners' power base. The coup was a dramatic attempt to stop such a transfer of power.

Its failure heralded the death of the Soviet system. As the

political situation went into freefall, Gorbachev grew increasingly desperate. The balance of power had shifted to Yeltsin, who virtually dictated all the new appointments to replace the plotters. Kryuchkov, the head of the KGB, and Yazov, the former defence minister, were imprisoned. The interior minister shot himself. Others involved were dismissed from their posts. (Vladimir Lobov, the general who had disobeyed an order to use his troops against the Almaty demonstrators four years earlier, was made defence minister.)

When the Supreme Soviet – the USSR's standing parliament – met for the first time since the coup, Nazarbayev made it clear in a speech that in future Kazakhstan would no longer accept Russia as a big brother, but expected equal status. The parliamentary chairman remarked afterwards: 'That's it! If that's the position of Nazarbayev, who is always in favour of integration, then it's the end of the Soviet Union.'

In fact, although Nazarbayev wanted equality within the union, he was much more cautious than most of the leaders of the other republics who were already demanding full independence. He feared that the break-up of the Soviet Union would bring anarchy and chaos in its wake, and that economic meltdown would result in famine. No new political institutions were in place to take over from the old ones in any of the republics, and their entire production remained tilted towards Moscow.

But nationalist passions had been aroused throughout the Union, and people within each of the republics were demanding independence and voicing the desire to rid themselves of their colonial status. Russia herself became gripped by a virulent form of nationalism with sinister implications for the other republics. Suddenly, Communism looked as if it might be replaced by something worse. Immediately after the failure of the coup, an elated crowd in Moscow tore down the statue of Felix Dzerzhinsky, the hated founder of the KGB, as they chanted 'Rossiiya, Rossiiya, Rossiiya – Russia, Russia, Russia'.

The new Russian authorities increasingly behaved like their

Soviet forebears. Most alarming of all was the warning delivered by Yeltsin's spokesman that Russia had territorial claims against both the Ukraine and Kazakhstan, which it would raise if either tried to leave the Union. It was a threat, and a clumsy one, creating enormous alarm and resentment in both republics. Yeltsin immediately began to back-pedal, signing a document confirming that Russia had no designs on Kazakh territory. 'But the damage was done,' Nazarbayev said. 'In turbulent times it is far too easy to make trouble by stirring up nationalist emotions.'

◆

The most virulent and extreme Russian nationalist of them all was born and bred in Kazakhstan. Vladimir Zhirinovsky is the closest thing to a genuine, old-style fascist that the post-Soviet political system has produced. After the collapse of the Soviet Union, he alarmed the world by receiving a quarter of the presidential vote in Russia on a platform that would have led her into military conflict with every country along her new, shaky borders. And the reconquest of Kazakhstan was top of his wish list.

Zhirinovsky had been unhappy in the country of his birth. His mother, widowed when he was only a year old, was left to bring up six children in Almaty. Later, he would claim that, 'In all her seventy-three years she had not known a single day of joy. A few days before my mother died, she said, "Volodya, there is nothing to remember."'

His mother's hard life had turned her into a vicious racist, and her bitterness was expressed in an endless outpouring of resentment against ethnic Kazakhs. From the moment he was old enough to understand, the child was told that Russians did all the work in the country, while Kazakhs received all the benefits. In reality, it was the Kazakhs who were perpetually discriminated against. Even today people living on the ground and top floors of apartment buildings jokingly refer to them as 'Kazakh apartments', because they are the least desirable: the ground floor is the noisiest and most likely to be burgled, while the top floor is the least convenient. In almost every way under the Soviet system, Kazakhs were treated as second-class citizens in their own country. But blinded by poverty, and defeated by life, the mother was unable to see beyond her own misery.

'It was a joyless childhood,' Zhirinovsky remembered. 'I was the youngest, I was in everyone's way.' The family of seven shared a single room in a communal apartment, where he slept on top of a trunk. The childhood memories that he logged in bitter detail included envy of a little girl who had a ballpoint pen when he did not, and children who lived in apartments with hot water. 'In my apartment there were no children's books, no toys, no papers, no telephone ... I was always hungry.'

Many people throughout the Soviet Union lived in similar conditions of deprivation during this period, but Zhirinovsky chose to blame the Kazakhs for his family's plight. His impoverished childhood made him lonely, and left him with a sense of inferiority and an unreasoning desire for revenge on those who were more comfortable or happier. Although throughout his schooling ethnic Russians like himself were in the majority in the country, prejudice against non-Russian Kazakhs became the bedrock of his deformed psychology, which developed into a maelstrom of resentment and rage. In time, it grew to include all non-Russians in the old Soviet republics, and eventually it turned into hatred of the entire non-Russian world.

At high school, Zhirinovsky proved to be a gifted and hard-working student, clever enough to be accepted by the prestigious Institute of Oriental Languages in Moscow. The children of the *nomenklatura*, the Communist Party élite, now became the focus of his resentment. While this frivolous and privileged group drank and chased girls, Zhirinovsky pored over his books. Throughout his time at the Institute he remained friendless, and by the age of 24 had still not had a girlfriend. He was too concerned with social issues and studying politics, he wrote. His graduation was celebrated alone, 'with no one to share my joy ... Apparently that was my destiny – that I would never really experience any love or friendship.'

Self-pity and resentment, which drip from all his writing, turned into a poisonous cocktail of vengeance. Zhirinovsky's brand of politics was based on crude nationalist racism: 'I grew up in Central Asia. We considered it Russia, not Central Asia. At first only Russians lived there. Russians brought in civilization while the Kazakhs were living in mud huts without electricity, without anything, just raising animals, sheep, just like the primitive communities of tribes, where there were no states.'

Russian civilization had not brought the Zhirinovsky family hot water, ballpoint pens, children's books, toys or a telephone either, but this was now forgiven. 'If I had lived in good conditions, warm and well fed, maybe I wouldn't have become involved in politics.' Alas, want of warm water, a ballpoint pen and a little love created a monster. Politics was to be his revenge.

The political party that launched Zhirinovsky upon the world was wittily entitled the Liberal Democratic Party of Russia, a perverse misnomer if ever there was one – and its leader's diatribes ran in the party magazine, The Liberal. Zhirinovsky denies he is a fascist, although one wonders why he bothers. The unbridled and unashamed anti-Semitism of his political message – always a popular position in Russia – has played well with his target audience. Not surprisingly, given his racist invective and expansionist views, his opponents have often compared him to Hitler.

More damaging to those who admire him, and to his own self-image, is the suggestion of a Jewish background. Kazakh records show that in 1964 he changed his name from Edelshtein, his father's name. Jewish or not, Edelshtein certainly isn't a Russian name. Zhirinovsky has repeatedly denied that his father was Jewish, attempting to deflect questions with a joke: 'My mother was Russian, my father was a lawyer.'

Zhirinovsky's view of Kazakh independence was that it was nothing more than the illegal annexation of a legitimate part of Mother Russia by a bunch of uncivilized nomads who were eager to steal Russian oil and gold, and untold other natural resources. It was a position that appealed to the large constituency of Russians who feared the future and longed for the restoration of old certainties. Zhirinovsky offered the balm of nationalist demagoguery in the form of a fantasy of reconquest and expansion which would put the old Soviet Union back together again on an even greater scale: 'How I dream of our Russian soldiers washing their boots in the warm waters of the Indian Ocean. The pealing of bells of a Russian Orthodox church on the shores of the Indian Ocean or Mediterranean would proclaim to the peoples of these regions peace, prosperity and calm.'

Peace, prosperity and calm, however, were not the principal components of the programme. Zhirinovsky advocated a new Russia eager to confront a world in the grip of an American-Zionist conspiracy. Jews and foreigners wished Russia ill, he told television audiences, and the West was Russia's natural enemy. A demented blather of reactionary plans was unleashed upon the Russian electorate. The Baltic states would be punished for declaring independence by having radioactive waste buried along their borders, and the contaminated air blown across their lands with gigantic fans. Tanks would be sent in to take back Estonia, Latvia, Lithuania, the Ukraine and Moldova, and they would then push south to the Mediterranean. Russia would invade Europe to establish a common border with Germany. Poland would be divided between Germany and Russia, as it had been in Tsarist times. Germany would be encouraged to absorb Austria, along with the Czech Republic and Slovenia, as it had in Hitler's time. Plans were announced for the capture of Iran, Turkey and Afghanistan. Japan was warned that she could expect 'more Hiroshimas' if she did not drop her demands for the return of the Kuril Islands. As for the Americans – they would have to give up Alaska. 'I will terrorize them! ... New York will fry.'

Such crazy statements would usually condemn a politician to oblivion, but as the Soviet Union collapsed, Russia entered a political twilight zone. Millions lapped up these mad pronouncements – the more outrageous and wild they were, the more the public liked them. The simultaneous shocks of loss of empire and the collapse of Communism had left the population reeling. Both had happened so suddenly and unexpectedly that Russians felt lost. Zhirinovsky's words carried particular weight and comfort for the diaspora of 25 million Russians who would find themselves living in the newly independent republics – like Kazakhstan – unsure of their status and their future.

Zhirinovsky rapidly became a household name and powerful political figure. He was perpetually on television, a medium he intended to reform. 'We shall ban all commercials. There will be no sneakers, no chewing gum – and no beaches. We have eight months of winter – we need fur coats, not beaches and cool drinks. You will be able to watch good Russian films. Ninety per cent of all news on television channels will be about Russia in the good Russian language. You will be spoken to by Russian broadcasters with good, kind, blue eyes and fair hair.'

Zhirinovsky made jokes, posed naked in the shower for photographers, and clowned around for the media. He threw glasses of water over antagonists on TV, and punched members who opposed him in parliament – one of them a woman. He promised free vodka under his presidency, and said he would legalize polygamy so that no Russian woman need ever be lonely. Political enemies were threatened with jail or the lunatic asylum. He might have been dangerous and deluded, but he was never dull.

Over time, Zhirinovsky's popularity has waned. He retains a seat in the Duma as leader of the Liberal Democrats, but his following is greatly diminished as the novelty of the clown performer has grown stale. He is supposed to have a secret deal with Putin's government: in exchange for being left alone, he is wheeled out when occasion demands to pull in the brute nationalist vote.

Zhirinovsky continues to rant against the world and Kazakh independence. His pronouncements are as bizarre as ever but now frighten no one. He has asserted that the US Secretary of State, Condaleeza Rice, badly needs male company, he has offered political asylum to the disgraced American heavyweight boxer, Mike Tyson, and he has prepared a bill before parliament to ban Coca-Cola and Pepsi. Today it is safe to laugh, but for a time in the 1990s, a man who wanted Russian troops to invade half the world and who threatened the use of nuclear weapons came close to power.

•

There were other more rational, and more disappointing figures among the hyper-nationalists, who both opposed the idea of Kazakh independence and supported military intervention to prevent it. Sadly, among the most loathed in Kazakhstan is Alexander Solzhenitsyn.

I discovered how deeply passions ran when I mentioned his name to a couple of 'the boys' as we feasted on lamb one evening. Here was a man who had not only served eight years in the Kazakh Gulag but who had also lived in exile in the country for a further three. Naïvely, I imagined the Nobel Prize winning author and dissident might be revered as a national hero. The opposite proved to be the case. At first the boys denied that Solzhenitsyn had any connection to Kazakhstan whatsoever. 'No! He was never here!'

Solzhenitsyn's time in the Gulag and exile in Kazakhstan was a well-documented fact, I said, and gave details. 'Okay, so he was in a camp and in exile here – like a million other people,' one of the boys said. 'And once long ago he was brave and told everybody about Stalin. And then he fucked off back to Mother Russia and America. Good riddance!'

'He's no friend of Kazakhstan!' another of the boys declared.

'He certainly isn't! Screw him!'

The vehemence of the attack took me by surprise. I had imagined that this brave survivor of the Gulag, one of a handful of extraordinary men who had dared to defy a monstrous regime and whose books bore lonely witness to the horrors of Stalin's vast prison world, would have been proudly adopted as a native son.

It was disturbing to hear him so roundly abused, and all his work dismissed. I was an admirer of Solzhenitsyn, and while I knew he had become an old-fashioned and largely irrelevant figure in recent years, I couldn't understand the savagery of the rejection.

After serving his sentence in the Gulag, Solzhenitsyn had spent years living in exile in the south of Kazakhstan. On his release from the camp at Ekibastuz, he was sent to Kok-Terek, where he found lodgings in an old woman's adobe hut and slept on the earthen floor in his padded jacket. One morning he was woken by his landlady who seemed excited but fearful. 'You must get up, young man, and go to the square – listen to what the loudspeakers are saying.'

A large crowd had gathered in the main square and it seemed that a great tragedy had befallen everyone. Women wept openly and old Kazakh men held their hats in their hands and bowed their heads in grief. Only a few young tractor drivers standing to one side failed to remove their headgear. Solzhenitsyn listened to the radio announcement coming from the loudspeakers – Stalin was dead!

The local authorities now felt free to appoint Solzhenitsyn to teach mathematics, physics and astronomy at Berlik High School. The joy he felt as he entered the classroom for the first time and picked up the chalk, he wrote later, marked the first true day of freedom. His teacher's salary allowed him to move into a house of his own, a one-room, thatched hut with whitewashed walls. After school, he sat in the garden during the hot evenings, writing on the wooden suitcase that he used as a table. At first loneliness and isolation went unnoticed amid the intoxicating novelty of relative freedom and gainful employment. Then he began to lose weight and was often in pain, until an X-ray revealed that his cancer had returned. A tumour the size of a fist was growing from the back wall of the abdominal cavity. The condition needed immediate treatment, which could only be obtained in Tashkent, 1,600 kilometres to the east. The prognosis was grim, and Solzhenitsyn was given just a few weeks to live.

Permission to travel for treatment was granted for 1 January 1954, an inauspicious start to the New Year. The evening before his departure, Solzhenitsyn made his way to the local railway station in great pain, scarcely able to walk. At the hospital in Tashkent he was diagnosed with a rare form of cancer, prescribed a massive dose of radiation, and told his chances of survival were one in three.

Radiation sickness in the form of constant nausea followed, but despite his weakened condition, he pulled through. The pain slowly retreated, the tumour began to shrink, and the will to live returned along with his appetite. He was released from hospital in the spring, and headed back to his home in Kok-Terek. There, he looked in the mirror and took stock. His shoulders drooped, he was incapable of standing erect and he was painfully thin, with sunken eyes and protruding cheekbones – a sorry specimen for a 35-year-old, but alive.

Since the death of Stalin – and the subsequent fall of Beria, 'supreme patron and viceroy of the Gulag Archipelago' – the lives of exiles had become easier. The sentence of perpetual exile was now annulled, and Solzhenitsyn was free to go where he chose. After marking the final examinations of the school year, and packing his belongings, he caught the train to Moscow. It took two days and nights to cross the Kazakh steppe, and on the third day he crossed the Volga. He stuck his head out of the window and was overcome with emotion as the wind blew in his face, and he looked once again at the countryside of the central Russian heartland. Exile was over, the Gulag was behind him, and Solzhenitsyn wept with joy.

I tried to tell the young Kazakhs about Solzhenitsyn's time in their country, but they were interested in none of it. Another time, another reality, another world ... In the 1960s, when Solzhenitsyn's works were banned, people throughout the USSR – including Kazakhstan – laboriously typed them out or copied them by hand for clandestine distribution. His writing gave hope to an oppressed people, and his bravery and granite resolve in the face of inhuman pressure were magnificent. In the USSR he acquired an importance both as a writer and as a moral figure that is difficult to grasp in the West.

Solzhenitsyn was a perpetual thorn in the side of the government, but he was too important a figure to destroy, so finally he was sent into another kind of exile – twenty years in the comfort of rural Vermont, in the USA. Internationally renowned as the recipient of the Nobel Prize for literature, he became the conscience of Russia, and when his books were finally published openly in his homeland they sold in their millions.

After the collapse of the Soviet Union, Solzhenitsyn returned to Russia where the shaggy colossus cut an uncomfortable figure in a land where moral giants had become redundant. On what was supposed to be a triumphant train journey across the country, he lectured the ever-diminishing crowds that gathered to welcome him on patriotism, repentance and national revival. The writer also opposed Kazakh independence, and insulted national sensibilities by claiming the northern steppe to be Russian territory. He went on to suggest that Kazakhstan was a phoney, inflated country owing everything to Russia.

'It had been assembled from southern Siberia, and the southern Ural region,' he wrote just before independence, 'plus the sparsely populated central areas which had since that time been built up and transformed by the Russians, by inmates of forced labour camps and exiled peoples. Today the Kazakhs constitute noticeably less than half the population of the entire inflated territory of Kazakhstan. They are concentrated in their long-standing ancestral domains along a large arc of lands in the south, sweeping from the extreme east westward almost to the Caspian Sea; the population here is indeed predominantly Kazakh. And if it should prove to be their wish to separate within such boundaries, I say Godspeed.'

Kazakhstan was actually contained within the reasonable and logical boundaries originally delineated for the republic by the Soviet Union, but Solzhenitsyn still refused to accept the reality even after independence. In a speech to Russia's lower house of parliament, the Duma, he urged the government to take swift action or Kazakhstan would unite with Turkey and make the Russians living within its boundaries subjects of a new Turkish empire (a threat that had already been foreseen and was later defused by Nazarbayev). The speech went on and on, and while the members were men long pickled in boredom, even they found it hard to take. Many yawned openly, some fell asleep. But however dull the presentation, it was fighting talk – Solzhenitsyn was calling for Russia to keep Kazakhstan by military force.

◆

It was against this background of white-hot Russian nationalism, amid calls for military action, that Nazarbayev cautiously moved Kazakhstan towards independence. Inevitably, as the Soviet Union disintegrated, there was a reaction from the Russians to their sudden loss of power and prestige, but for Kazakhs it was a time when they counted their friends and marked their enemies.

Internal Russian politics was also hindered and complicated by the growing enmity between Gorbachev and Yeltsin. Although Yeltsin had saved the Soviet leader from the coup plotters, he had not been rewarded with the full Politburo membership that he coveted. As a result, he repeatedly humiliated Gorbachev in parliament and on television. As Gorbachev said, 'Yeltsin always wanted to hang noodles on my ears.'

'Personal chemistry – or rather the lack of it – was every bit as important as policies or questions of statehood,' Nazarbayev said. 'There was no love lost between Yeltsin and Gorbachev.' As Nazarbayev prepared to fly to Moscow to meet Gorbachev and the leaders of the republics to discuss the plan for a Union of Sovereign States, he received a call from Yeltsin. He was surprised to learn that the Russian president was in a hunting lodge on the Polish border near Minsk, in Belarus, together with the president of that republic and the president of the Ukraine. Yeltsin wanted to create a special political relationship with the Ukraine and Belarus, on the grounds that they were the surviving entities that had created the Soviet Union in 1922. Kazakhstan was being invited to join at the last minute for other reasons – it was one of the four republics with nuclear weapons.

It was seven in the evening when Nazarbayev spoke to Yeltsin, and the Russian's speech was slurred from drink. 'Come over and join us,' Yeltsin said. 'We have just created a Commonwealth of Independent States.'

'But we were meant to be discussing all these questions tomorrow in Moscow.'

'Come on, fly over,' Yeltsin insisted. 'We can talk about it. We're all sitting here, everything is ready – we just need your signature.'

'Hold on a minute! You want me to sign just like that? I have to study it first.'

'We didn't really read it ourselves. We just sat down and signed it.'

Nazarbayev asked for part of the document to be read to him over the phone so he could have an idea of its tone. He was horrified by what he heard: half-baked and hasty, the treaty removed all federal institutions at a stroke, but made no provision for maintaining ties between the republics, and was biased towards the Ukraine. The secret nature of it all did not appeal either, and Nazarbayev later discovered that even Yeltsin's vice-president had been kept in the dark, together with the other leaders of the republics – not to mention Gorbachev himself. 'The main aim appeared to be to ensure that the unfortunate Soviet leader was deprived of his powers, that he was left with absolutely nothing.'

Nazarbayev did not go to Belarus. Instead he met Gorbachev and Yeltsin in Moscow the following day. 'So you have agreed all this,' Gorbachev said to Yeltsin, consulting the text which had been presented to him. 'But what is going to happen about nuclear weapons?'

Yeltsin was silent.

'And what about the army? And the question of citizenship?'

Again, Yeltsin was silent. Gorbachev continued to raise one important point after another, all of which had been ignored in the agreement. Finally, Yeltsin lost his temper. 'What is this – some kind of interrogation?'

In the ensuing weeks the situation became very tense. The Central Asian republics sought their own federation, which would have created a Turkic-Muslim bloc that would automatically have included Kazakhstan. That in turn would have left a Slavic bloc consisting of Russia, the Ukraine and Belarus. The potential for confrontation was obvious. Worse still was the situation in which Kazakhstan would have been placed – a country with a Slav majority at the time, and nuclear weapons.

There has always been a minority in Turkey that dreams of a revitalized Ottoman Empire in the form of a Turkic bloc stretching from the Great Wall of China to the Adriatic, and the collapse of the Soviet Union made the dream a possibility. The idea alarmed Nazarbayev, who is fond of pointing out that the spread of the Turkic peoples actually went from east to west. ('Modern Kazakhs are descended from the Huns. They moved west and conquered the known world, until they became overstretched and their empire collapsed. Modern Turks are actually people who left the territory of what is present-day Kazakhstan, went west, and settled in the country where they live now.') The affinity and warm feeling between Turk and Kazakh are real enough, but Kazakhstan's genuine independence was more important. The concept of a pan-Turkish political union, later put forward by the Turkish president, was politely but firmly dismissed. 'Mr President, we just left the Russian empire,' Nazarbayev said. 'We don't want to enter another empire now.'

The Central Asian leaders eventually agreed to join the Commonwealth of Independent States on condition that they were all considered founder members. The leaders of all the republics – with the exception of the three Baltic states that wished to be entirely free of old ties – met in Almaty on 21 December 1991 to sign the treaty. 'The feeling of relief all round was enormous,'

Nazarbayev said. 'The main thing was that we had done everything to prevent the Slav and Turkic people of the former Soviet Union from being set against one another. We had also taken one of the most momentous decisions of the twentieth century to create fifteen fully fledged independent states. The Soviet Union was dead.' For the first time in its history Kazakhstan was an independent nation, and this time it was the Soviet Union that had disappeared.

•

Kazakhstan might have been independent, but it was also very much alone. At first, its newfound freedom seemed a poisoned chalice. The country had been left with all the old creaking Soviet institutions but with no plans or money to replace them. To avoid economic and social collapse, radical reform was needed from top to bottom, and needed quickly. The new country declared itself a presidential democracy on the French model, with a constitution defining it as a 'democratic, secular and unitary state'. The old Soviet-era Congress of People's Deputies – an unwieldy part-time body that only met in full session twice a year – was replaced with a bicameral parliament with a directly elected lower house, a Senate and a strong presidency.

Legislation was also needed to allow a market economy in which private property could be owned and state industries could be privatized. Similarly, an open banking system, civil law and a tax code had to be created from scratch. Most importantly, the old Soviet principle of the supremacy of politics over law had to be reversed, and for the first time in Kazakhstan there were free elections. Around 700 candidates from various political parties stood for 135 seats, and 75 per cent of registered voters went to the polls. The resulting chamber pretty much reflected the ethnic make-up of the country – 58 per cent of the seats went to Kazakhs and most of the rest to Russians, with other minorities such as Ukrainians, Germans and Koreans also represented.

Some international observers criticized the way in which the election was run. 'I am not ashamed to say there was something in their objections,' Nazarbayev admitted candidly. 'Kazakhstan's political culture had been deeply marked by decades of Communist Party discipline and totalitarianism from which we had only just emerged. It was naïve to expect that we would achieve overnight the level of democracy of the United States, France or Britain.

'Being an Englishman, you may have difficulty understanding where our nation stands today. Your country has a history of democracy developing over a thousand years and we have never had that. We were caught between the two great empires of China and Russia. Kazakhs have always been under pressure from the Russian advance and had no time to think about identity. The main objective of Kazakhs over the years has been to survive. The important thing in an evolving democracy is not that it is perfect, but that it is always moving in the right direction.'

The transitional period was difficult. A balance needed to be achieved between an evolving electoral process on the one hand and economic growth and political stability on the other. Too heavy a hand in either direction would attract criticism. To go too fast risked chaos, to go too slow risked a disenchanted electorate. At first, the elected parliament proved to be a brake on reform, opposing laws to create private property, and baulking at necessary but unpopular price increases. Only a handful of laws were passed, as the economy seemed to implode. Presidential powers were strengthened to push reform through, creating the suspicion that the country could end up with an elected dictator.

'I have heard the cries that there could be a dictatorship in Kazakhstan,' Nazarbayev said. 'True democracy is fostered by economic growth and stability. The danger of a real dictatorship comes in the wake of chaos and anarchy. Then people call for a firm hand.

'There has been talk of a Western model of democracy or an Asian one. I do not believe in such a distinction – democracy is democracy. You either have it or you don't. Its basic elements are universal. The real distinction is between a democracy that has evolved over many years and one in the embryonic stage. It's far too early to compare the current political situation in Kazakhstan with that in Britain. You have had centuries in which to refine concepts of individual liberty. We have only had a few years.'

The last time I saw the president for a talk he was riding high, seemingly invincible in his power and popularity. It was not always so, as he cheerfully pointed out. 'There was a very difficult time for me personally after independence when I was very unpopular. And this went on for a period of years. I would go to meetings and the silence would be icy. Sometimes there was open hostility. The Communists were in opposition and saw me as a traitor to the cause, selling the country out to the West. Nine opposition parties were against me. I tried to explain what I was doing, and that it needed time, but people were understandably impatient.'

As more and more privately-owned magazines and newspapers came into being, almost all were critical. 'And one of the harshest of these critics,' the president said with a smile, 'is the gentleman sitting opposite.' Reminded of his previous role as savage columnist, the press secretary looked sheepish and grinned uncomfortably. It was a surprise to learn that the president's most energetic proselytizer had once been one of his most vociferous and unremitting critics. Later, when we were alone, I said, 'And all the time I thought you were a True Believer.'

'Every day after independence I wrote sharp articles attacking Nazarbayev,' the press secretary admitted. 'Every day! Nazarbayev became very unpopular because he was carrying out tough economic reforms most of us didn't understand. You have to remember, capitalism was a bad word here. For seventy years we had been told capitalism was monstrous and we believed it.

'Everybody in the country knew Kazakhstan was rich. We had oil, we had gas, we had every metal known to man. So after independence the question became – "Why are we so poor when we're so rich?" We knew that before the Soviets took everything, but now we were independent, and so we thought the reason was bad management – the government ... and the man at the head of the government, the president.'

Life in Kazakhstan remained grim for years after independence, as the country went through the painful transformation from one economic system to another. Under the Soviets everyone had at least the basics for life – suddenly there was nothing. 'Nothing in the shops and no money,' the press secretary said. 'No money to pay teachers, no money for students. Old people didn't receive their pensions for a year at a time.

'Every day as I walked to my newspaper office I saw the rouble fall 5 or 10 per cent. Inflation was so bad that industrial production just shut down. And as paper money became worthless, people bought everything around to hoard – sugar, salt, canned goods. And that meant there were even greater shortages. The whole country was reduced once again to a barter system – "I'll give you a sheep for gasoline". Agriculture collapsed. There was zero construction – not a crane was working in the whole of Kazakhstan.'

Nationwide privatization started in 1992 – with the sale of a row of shops in Almaty – but there were few immediate benefits for the general population. Although the new currency, the *tenge*, was introduced in 1993, four years later there were still Kazakhs in the provinces who had not seen what the new money looked like. 'We thought the government was selling national assets to foreigners for nothing,' the press secretary said. 'We didn't understand that our production could be sold nowhere but in Kazakhstan because of the quality. And that the equipment in the factories was so old and outdated that it was the equivalent of something used in Germany and the UK in the Second World War.'

Billions of dollars of investment were needed to get the oil out of the ground, build new pipelines and modernize outdated factories and industries. But to the Kazakhs it seemed that foreigners were buying their industries at bargain prices while they received nothing. 'For instance, I wrote an article about the sale of a factory worth $10 million to an American company for a million,' the press secretary said. 'It seemed ridiculous. I did not understand that the purchaser would have to invest a further 5 million at least, and then wait three or four years before it could become competitive. And even then the enterprise was a risk. I thought that anyone who bought a factory cheap should start paying taxes in the first month.'

I asked the press secretary when he saw the light to become the evangelical convert before me. 'It didn't happen that way. There was no sudden flash. But in 1996 I started changing my mind. Business was entering a second stage of development, things began to take shape, and you could see what had been going on. By 1997 the privatization programme was beginning to bear fruit and in 1999 there was a budget surplus. In 2000 there was a major breakthrough in the minds of Kazakhs, both about what had happened and towards Nazarbayev. To most people the future looks pretty good.'

Kazakh independence is secure. The long border with Russia has been peacefully ratified, and the country's relations with its powerful neighbour are excellent. Kazakhstan is oil rich, booming and the clear power of the region, a phoenix risen from the ashes. The Russian nationalists, whose earlier fury and hostility were rightfully seen in Kazakhstan as symptoms of a new form of Tsarist or Soviet colonialism, are no longer a threat.

'The Russians wanted their old empire back,' one of my young Kazakh friends told me the last time I saw him. 'But we were never going to let them get it. They wanted our oil and gas, and our minerals and our coal and our wheat like before. The Soviets were used to stealing everything and taking it back to Russia, now they have to pay for it like everybody else.

'The old slave days are over.'

EPILOGUE

At the beginning of my Kazakh travels I harboured a vague idea to track down the Arkansas romantic who had unwittingly fired my imagination about the country. It would be good to know how it had all worked out in Almaty with the Russian widow, Ludmilla. Or had it been Astana, or even Karaganda, and was the widow actually called Tatiana? Or Anastasia? None of the Kazakh place-names had any meaning for me at the time of my brief encounter on the plane to Moscow, and I had only ever heard the sweetheart's name mentioned once. But I *was* certain my travelling companion had told me he was from Little Rock. How many men could there be in Kazakhstan from Little Rock with Internet brides?

I posted messages on the Kazakh Expat website. One or two of these must have been ambiguous, suggesting I was looking for love, for I received a reply in fractured English that I *think* was an offer of marriage. And an outraged feminist lambasted me as a 'rich foreigner' preying on the less fortunate, suggesting unkindly that I was probably fat and ugly, and certainly pathetic – why didn't I burden myself on someone from my own country? After that I was more careful about the way I worded my inquiries.

There were two replies from Americans who had met Kazakh women through the Internet and later married. Both had taken their brides home to America. One man wrote to say he was very happy in his choice, and offered to enter an email correspondence on the subject; another invited me to visit him and his wife in Chicago. But there was no news from the Arkansas romantic. My man, I began to believe, was probably long gone, and back in the bosom of Uncle Sam.

•

The last time I was in Kazakhstan I met Umbetov in Almaty for a Sunday lunch, and we went to one of his favourite restaurants, an up-market establishment serving traditional food, frequented by the town's well-heeled. As we tramped through the snow from the hotel I tried out a theory on my friend. It struck me, I said, that the natives in winter did not seem as friendly as in summer. I had worked up quite a good hypothesis on the effects of weather on the human personality, and jotted down a number of highly original aperçus on the subject in my notebook. But Umbetov failed to respond to the brilliance of the insight. 'Maybe,' he said. 'Maybe it's other stuff.'

'What other stuff?'

'Don't be offended,' he said. 'But maybe it's the hat.'

'I don't understand,' I said, self-consciously touching my natty rabbit-fur headgear. The hat in question had been bought in Moscow just after the coup in 1991 and was both souvenir and prized possession. An old Russian spy had taken me to a special Party shop not open to your average Ivan where I had made the privileged purchase. At the same time I had bought an unfashionable but practical three-quarter-length quilted car coat and a pair of heavy army boots. The outfit had since weathered several Russian winters and was doing its bit against the Kazakh elements. The hat was a lifesaver. Warm as toast, it had flaps that folded down to cover the ears in particularly harsh weather. True, with the flaps lowered and tied together under my chin with a ribbon, I looked a little like Elmer Fudd, but this was hardly a sight powerful enough to depress a nation. 'I've seen people in extraordinary fur hats,' I said defensively. 'I saw a guy come into the hotel in Astana with a fur hat the size of a bush.'

'Yes, people wear fur hats ... but not like yours. Not any more.'

'I had no idea the style of men's fur hats in Kazakhstan was so vulnerable to the whimsy of fashion,' I said stiffly.

'Chris, you look Soviet! You look like a mid-level bureaucrat from the Brezhnev days.'

It was not winter that had wiped the smile from the Kazakhs' faces and dulled their usually bright eyes, but the vision of a resurrected, old-style Communist Party functionary. My ensemble of cheap fur hat, dated Siberian army boots and dreary overcoat was the dull uniform of the past. It represented everything people were trying to forget and move away from – grey men from a grey world reviving grey memories.

The world had moved on. Inside the restaurant privileged Party functionaries had been replaced by successful entrepreneurs. Just how far Kazakhstan had moved on became clear as we settled at a table and I asked, 'What's new in Astana?'

'The president's building a giant yurt the size of a city to provide winter fun for everyone.'

I looked at my friend to see whether he was pulling my leg. But he had the evangelical light that came into his eyes whenever he became excited about things Kazakh. 'Just how big is this yurt?' I asked.

'Very, *very* big! It is called Khan Shatyry – tent of the descendants of Genghis Khan. It is transparent and will have palm trees, sandy beaches, a river with boats, gardens! There will be a golf course, shops, a concert hall. It will be paradise! So when a blizzard is blowing, and it is minus

30 degrees centigrade outside, people will not have to stay home watching TV, they can go to this yurt and sit on a beach sipping iced Coca-Cola. Work has already begun on the foundations.'

'Amazing,' I said. 'A fulfilment of the poem: "In Xanadu did Kubla Khan / A stately pleasure dome decree." '

Anywhere else but in modern Kazakhstan – or possibly Las Vegas – a giant yurt containing an artificial ocean would sound unbelievable. Yet, fantastic as it seems, I found out later that the yurt – another project of the architect Norman Foster – will be pretty much as Umbetov described. Larger in area than the Millennium Dome, and three times higher than Nelson's Column, its skin is formed by Teflon-coated, translucent plastic pillows that allow for three different climatic zones. Inside there will be terraced gardens, a river flanked by palms, and beaches of sand washed by an artificial sea powered by wave machines. There will be a dolphinarium and an underground shopping mall, while the central arena is to be used to put on concerts.

I proposed a toast: 'To the pleasure dome!'

We were drinking Putinka, a pepper vodka named after the Russian president Vladimir Putin. In the course of conversation I asked, 'What do you think of Putin?'

'I like his pepper vodka.'

Our lunch went on a bit. We arrived at the restaurant around one o'clock and did not leave until after six. The traditional Kazakh food was delicious – manty dumplings, plov and slow-cooked lamb, all washed down with Putin's pepper vodka. Halfway through our marathon feed Umbetov grew a little tetchy, a mood induced either by the vodka or prolonged exposure to my company. As I finished telling him about my attempts to find the Arkansas romantic he lost patience. 'You are funny,' he said, and it was clear he meant peculiar not amusing. 'You decide to write a book about a country you had never visited and knew nothing about because a man on a plane told you it's where apples came from. And now you do know something you are wasting time looking for this silly American.'

Put like that it did sound odd. I tried to explain that finding the man from Arkansas, and comparing his experiences in the country with my own, would be an interesting way to end the book. Umbetov remained unpersuaded. I began to tell him more about what I intended to write, and although he listened politely, he grew increasingly agitated.

'I don't understand you!' he said at last. 'You have the chance to go skiing, to visit remote beautiful mountains, national parks ... we have better scenery than New Zealand! But you go to look at apple orchards ...'

'Wild apple orchards!'

'And then you go to ecological disasters! You go to Aral Sea which breaks our hearts. You go to nuclear test ground! You go to Gulag! Your book will make people think Kazakhstan is a big radioactive prison camp with apples and Internet brides!'

'There will be other stuff in the book too.'

' Why don't you write about delicious food?'

'Okay, I will.'

'Why don't you write about Altai mountains ... about beautiful Mount Belukha, its highest mountain, where Russia, Mongolia, China and Kazakhstan meet. This is where we believe the shamanic culture of Siberia and Central Asia came from – in the heartland of these mountains. A culture that goes back to the Ice Age. These mountains were a dwelling place for old gods – a site of Shambhala.'

'Naturally, there are going to be a lot of mountains in the book, and a hell of a lot of steppe.'

'All this sad stuff. We've had enough unhappiness here. Tell people the good things.'

I tried to explain that in the end it wasn't a country's scenery or folk customs that counted, but a people's experience. I wanted to put across a sense of Kazakh courage and heart. I had been deeply moved again and again by the stories I had heard, and while I had seen truly beautiful sights, the memory of even the most magnificent scenery dissolves, while certain experiences and encounters would remain with me for ever. 'Unless people understand where

Kazakhstan has come from,' I said, 'they won't be able to appreciate what it has become.'

Umbetov thought for a moment. 'I like this,' he said, regaining his usual cheerful equilibrium. He raised his glass to me. 'To your book. I know it will not be as bad as you say.'

Later, as we floundered in the snow outside the restaurant waiting for taxis, Umbetov grew sentimental. 'Christopher, you are a friend of Kazakhstan.' He embraced me warmly, pepper vodka tears in his eyes. 'I know you like my country.'

It was true. Kazakhstan, one of the largest and least known nations on earth, had found a place in my heart. I had become proprietary about the place and its hospitable people, and had greatly enjoyed my haphazard travels. A country that had once been little more than a name, had become real for me, with its sad history and unlikely motley of people. Few nations can have emerged so confident and optimistic from such an unhappy past as Kazakhstan, jangling its oil dollars and looking to the future.

I never did get a lead on the Arkansas romantic and maybe it was just as well. I didn't want to risk bursting the fantasy life I had imagined for the middle-aged lovers on the run from the unhappiness of their individual lives. I seemed to remember being told in the conversation on the plane that Ludmilla – or whoever – was reluctant to leave Kazakhstan for family reasons. I cherished the notion that my man had not returned to the USA, but had chosen to stay on in leafy Almaty. It was not a bad place to make a new life. I imagined him eating shashlyk with his wife at one of the open-air restaurants in Panfilov Park on a Sunday, and learning enough Russian to go shopping in the Green Market. A fanciful notion, perhaps, but I had a lot to thank him for.

I retain a wealth of images and memories ... a golden eagle perched upon my arm in falling snow ... beggars sitting on the wall in front of the Orthodox cathedral snatching pigeons for their dinner ... feasting in a yurt beside the turquoise Aral Sea to the sound of a *dombra* ... snow blowing through the Green Market and powdering the fruit ... the unspoilt grandeur of the red-earth

Charyn Gorge ... helicopters skimming across the endless steppe ... a president dancing in the street with an old Kazakh woman ... fermented mare's milk drunk on a stud farm in lush meadowlands in the shadow of mountains ... veterans of the Great Patriotic War in shabby jackets thick with medals seated in a line under a variety of Kazakh hats ... the delicious pickled tomatoes of the wife of a Gulag survivor ... too much vodka with men half my age ... the smell of wormwood crushed underfoot in springtime ...

On a recent visit to America, an immigration official noted the profession in my passport and asked what I was writing about. A book on Kazakhstan, I said. The officer asked me to repeat the name *three* times, shaking his head sceptically, as if the country didn't exist. He pushed a piece of paper at me on which to write the name. I printed it in large capitals and he slowly read it out loud: 'KAZ – AKH – STAN.'

'Four times the size of Texas,' I began ... and was about to mention all the oil and minerals, horsemen hunting with golden eagles, the endless sea of grass ... but stopped. As the official stamped my passport, I couldn't resist: 'Apples are from Kazakhstan.'